NEIL WARNOCK
THE
GAFFER

THE GAFFER

THE TRIALS AND TRIBULATIONS OF A FOOTBALL MANAGER

NEIL WARNOCK
WITH GLENN MOORE

headline

First published in the UK in 2013 by
HEADLINE PUBLISHING GROUP

2

Cataloguing in Publication Data is available from the British Library

Hardback ISBN 978 0 7553 6277 6

Typeset in Bliss by Avon DataSet Ltd, Bidford-on-Avon, Warwickshire

Printed and bound in Great Britain by Clays Ltd, St Ives plc

Headline's policy is to use papers that are natural, renewable and recyclable
products and made from wood grown in sustainable forests. The logging and
manufacturing processes are expected to conform to the environmental
regulations of the country of origin.

HEADLINE PUBLISHING GROUP
An Hachette UK Company
338 Euston Road
London NW1 3BH

www.headline.co.uk
www.hachette.co.uk

To Sharon: Now that I'm home we can start having the times we've talked about and share more magic moments together. As I say to you every day, I really do love you loads darling.

To James, Natalie, Amy and William, you are simply the best. You have had to put up with all the rubbish that comes with the job but we've had some great times. Thanks for being down-to-earth through all the highs and lows. I know you have had to grow up learning to turn the other cheek but I couldn't be more proud of how you have all turned out.

To my Dad, who worked so hard, and my Mum, who went through so much.

To my brother John and sister Carole, who have always been there for me.

Acknowledgements

Management can be a lonely job and I couldn't have done it for so long without the men who have been alongside me in the dug-out for the last three decades. I first played against Paul Evans when we were teenagers, I scored a hat-trick for Chesterfield and Paul was in goal for Sheffield Wednesday. I never let him forget that, especially when he gets a bad back. I tell him I caused it with him having to bend down so much to pick the ball out of the back of the net. He kept goal for me at Burton, and helped me start my management career at Scarborough and Notts County. Paul's still my best mate and I always take note of his opinion, which is all the more valuable now he is not in the professional game. Thanks pal.

Thanks too, to Mick Jones, my assistant manager for most of the last 20 years, Kevin Blackwell, who was with me 16 years as player and coach, David Kelly, Keith Curle, Stuart McCall and Ronnie Jepson. Different personalities all, but football people, good blokes, and great company.

I've had a lot of chairmen, including some good ones: Ben Robinson at Burton was amazing in his backing and loyalty while Simon Jordan had everything. He was knowledgeable and support-ive. Thanks also to Amit Bhatia for taking me to QPR where I had a wonderful experience turning the club around and worked with Gianni Paladini, who always made me smile and still does.

It has been a love-hate relationship with the newspapers over the years but there are some good guys including Rex Page, Mel Booth and James Shield in local media, and the late Brian Woolnough, John Sadler and Oliver Holt in the nationals. In particular I'd like to thank the various sports editors at The Independent where I've really enjoyed writing a column charting the ups and downs of the last eight years. Thanks especially to Glenn Moore, who has collaborated with me on those columns and on this book. He captures my voice brilliantly and we've had some good laughs together.

Jonathan Taylor, at Headline, has been hugely supportive of this project, and not just because he is a QPR fan, as has my literary agent David Luxton. Thanks also to Humphrey Price and Holly Harris for their input and Phil Shaw, author of several volumes of *The Book of Football Quotations*, for his assistance.

Last, but certainly not least, thanks to the players. You can't do anything in management without the right players. There has been too many to mention, but I have been lucky enough to have some good ones.

Contents

Introduction

I would never tell a plumber, a lawyer or a journalist how to do his job, but they all know better than me every Saturday.

Joe Royle

IT'S SATURDAY NIGHT, I'M DRIVING HOME FROM A GAME, and the radio is on. A phone-in starts. On they come, the armchair experts: 'he's taken the club as far as he can go', 'he picked the wrong team', 'he puts his subs on too late', 'he puts his subs on too early', 'he's tactically naïve', 'he just hasn't a clue'.

The calls might be about me, but it is just as likely they are about Arsène Wenger, or Roberto Mancini, Harry Redknapp or Andre Villas-Boas, even Sir Alex Ferguson. As a manager once said, 'there are two jobs everyone thinks they can do, prime minister and football manager.' It doesn't matter how many trophies and promotions you have won, they know better.

But they don't. Not because they are daft, most football fans can see when a team is struggling and some can work out why, but because they will never have the whole story. Maybe a defender was left out because he has a personal problem, maybe a substitution had to be made as a midfielder was carrying an injury, maybe the manager is buying average strikers because he has not been given enough money to buy any better. There are a lot of things going on at football clubs most of which, for all sorts of reasons, the fans don't hear about. As far as possible this book goes behind the dug-out and describes what it is really like to be a football manager in the modern game.

I began managing in 1980, at Gainsborough Trinity in Lincolnshire. Mrs Thatcher had been in 10 Downing Street just over a year, mobile phones belonged to science fiction, there were fences up at football grounds, and the record transfer fee was £1.5m, for Wolves' Andy Gray.

Football and society has changed immensely since then, and so has the manager's job. Take transfers. The days when I could buy a player with two phone calls, one to the opposition manager, another to my chairman, are long gone. Transfers are now complicated, long-drawn out affairs involving agents, lawyers, shareholders, doctors, chief executives, directors of football – you name it, they all need to be spoken to. Except on transfer deadline day when everyone is in a panic and we buy in haste then repent at leisure.

There have been similar changes in other aspects of the game, from the treatment of injuries to scouting for players, from pre-season training to dealing with the media. The biggest development has probably been the shift in the manager-player relationship. We are now dealing with millionaires, which calls for a different set of management skills.

Over these pages I've written about over thirty years of experiences, framed by three crazy years with Crystal Palace, QPR and Leeds; each one set against the destabilising backdrop of a takeover. There have been times I wanted to scream, times I felt like crying, but also times when I laughed. There were also many times I was grateful for those three decades in management; I'm not sure many managers with less experience could have put up with what I did, or achieved what I did with the difficulties I faced on a daily basis.

While I was wondering whether to write this book it was put to me that Charlie, my first grandson, would one day ask: 'Grand-dad, what does a football manager do?' This book would be my answer.

I hope it provides Charlie, his little sister Evie, and all my other readers, with an insight into the life of a football manager, and that everyone enjoys reading it as much as I have enjoyed writing it.

Prologue

Football is like a beast. It can overtake your whole life so you forget who you are and who your family are.

Ian Holloway

THE EAGLES, MY EAGLES, WERE LITERALLY FLYING WHEN IT happened. It was 26 January 2010, Crystal Palace were 25,000 feet over Yorkshire on the way to play Newcastle United and full of optimism. We had taken off from Gatwick in the hunt for promotion to the Premier League. By the time we landed we were in a relegation scrap. A company I'd barely heard of, doing something I didn't understand, had brought the Eagles crashing to earth as thoughtlessly as a farmer shooting pigeons. But I've always believed that in life things happen for a reason and that day launched the most extraordinary years of my career. After 42 years in football, from Northern Premier League to Barclays Premier League, I thought I'd seen it all; I was wrong.

That, though, was for the future. As I sat on that flight north I felt confident. We all knew money was tight at the club – we were only flying as I'd persuaded a wealthy supporter to pay for it, but we had been on a good run and fancied our chances of getting something from our biggest game of the season so far. We had a good mix of youngsters and old hands and, after winning six previous promotions, I could recognise the signs of a team on the up. Then we came down to earth in more ways than one.

We all know you are not supposed to turn on a mobile phone until the plane has come to a stop, but nobody takes any notice, which is why, as we taxied towards Newcastle airport the plane was suddenly full of little beeps as text messages alerted me and my players and staff to the terrible news. While we had been in the air the club had been put into administration.

At first I thought someone was joking, but then players started to ask questions:

'What's happening, gaffer?'

'What's "going into administration" mean, gaffer?'

'Are we going to get paid, gaffer?'

'Do we lose points, gaffer?'

I had to pretend I was in the know, but the reality was I didn't know much more than they did. I knew pressure was being put on Simon Jordan, my friend and chairman, to repay a loan he'd taken out but the timing didn't make sense. We were in a transfer window. Once we got a decent fee for Victor Moses, our brilliant young winger who obviously was going to play at a higher level, we'd be OK.

We stood by the carousel at the airport, waiting for our bags. People chatted in little groups, everyone a bit dazed. I rang Simon to find out what was happening. It turned out the hedge fund Agilo, who had made the loan to Simon, had for reasons known only to themselves put us into administration. I'd never even heard of a hedge fund a few months earlier and still don't really know what they do. Five million pounds was a piddling sum by football standards, but it was the death knell for Simon's chairmanship, the club's promotion prospects and, ironically, any prospect of Agilo getting their money back.

I was shattered. I told Simon if he was leaving I wanted to resign. He asked me not to, telling me Palace needed my help to get though the situation. I agreed to stay though it had not been the same since Simon had put the club up for sale about 18 months earlier. He had a new daughter and he had realised there was more to life than football. With the economy plummeting it had become a bottomless pit for him, and the John Bostock decision – of which more later – had left him disillusioned. But even then no one could have worked harder for the club. He tried everything. The hedge fund was daft. They'd have got more money if they had waited, without a gun to our heads we would have sold better in the transfer window, and we could even have gone up. They pulled the rug from under Simon's feet and it served them right when they didn't get the money.

All this was going round my head on the way to the hotel. When we got there I gathered the players together and explained the situation. The most crushing aspect for all of us was that we had lost ten points and a season that promised so much was now a survival scrap. I tried to rally them. I said they had done brilliantly to get in play-off contention and it would be a shame if they didn't continue to perform like that – starting at St James' Park.

It didn't take long for me to discover what being in administration meant. Word must have spread fast because when we arrived at the hotel the driver pulled me aside.

'Sorry mate, but I can't take you to the ground tonight.'

'What do you mean?'

'My boss has been on the phone. He's heard Palace are in administration and he's worried he's not going to get paid. We've had this sort of thing before.'

'Well how else are we supposed to get there? In a fleet of taxis? Walk?'

'Sorry mate, not my problem. The boss won't let me drive you unless he's guaranteed payment up front. I can't take you back to the airport either.'

I thought about it. It was ridiculous. We couldn't turn up at St James' Park squeezed into taxis – assuming we could find any. It was like a Sunday League outfit. I couldn't blame the bus company I suppose. There was only one thing for it.

'What if I take responsibility for it? I'll guarantee payment on my own credit card. It's mine, not a club one.'

'I'll check with my boss, but that should be OK.'

It wasn't all doom and gloom. When we got off the bus at St James' Park one of the fans gathered around the entrance brought a smile to my face when he shouted, 'You should be managing here.'

'Being in the away changing room is the nearest I'll ever get to managing Newcastle United,' I replied with a laugh.

By then the administrator, a man with an enthusiasm for personal publicity called Brendan Guilfoyle, had been in touch and told me I couldn't play Moses in case he was injured. I'd already told Vic I was leaving him out because I wanted to play Danny Butterfield, our right-back, at right-wing to try and restrict Luis Enrique, Newcastle's left-back and one of their best attacking players. But I didn't mention that to Guilfoyle. I didn't want to spoil his moment. However, I could have done with Vic in the squad as Claude Davis and Alassane N'Diaye were injured in training the day before so I only had three fit players to put on the bench.

I was counting the fit bodies when the assistant referee came into the dressing room to check the players' studs before kick-off.

'Any more?' he shouted after seeing most of them.

'Stop taking the Mickey, linesman,' I said, 'these are all the players we have.'

I didn't let the players know about the bus and the administrator and come the match they did me and the club proud. We had a terrible start, conceding a daft own goal, then suffered another injury when Johannes Ertl pulled up. I turned to Matt Lawrence on the bench, only to find he did not have his socks, shinpads or boots on. So Ertl had to struggle on for several minutes. The team could easily have folded in the circumstances but, roared on by magnificent backing from our fans, who were sat up in the gods, we had a go and nearly levelled before conceding a late second.

In the press conference afterwards one journalist asked what would happen if we sold six players. 'I doubt the League will let us play with eight men,' I replied. Everyone laughed. There weren't to be many more laughs from then on.

Chapter One

Life in Administration

I said to the lads, 'This is what we get paid to do'. Then I remembered, we were not being paid.

Michael Appleton after Portsmouth
went into administration

I WAS GETTING READY FOR TRAINING ONE MORNING A FEW days later when Nigel Cox, the Palace physiotherapist, came into my room.

'Gaffer, we've had a call from the hospital about Charlie Holness.'

Charlie was a young defender, about 18, who needed surgery for an injury.

'They won't do it, gaffer, because we're in administration. They need a letter saying the costs of theatre and the surgeon will be paid. He's been prepped, they are waiting to wheel him into theatre, but they want assurances the bill will be met.'

I couldn't believe it. This sort of thing doesn't happen at professional clubs. The poor kid is lying there, terrified, about to have an op. The club are supposed to be looking after him.

'Have you rung the administrators?'

'I can't get hold of anybody, gaffer.'

'Well, we can't leave him there.' I had to get my credit card out again and guarantee payment while we sorted it out.

Administration is a terrible thing for a football club. When I left Palace I said I had felt as if I was being 'slowly poisoned'. Looking back it was not just me, it was the whole club. Administration is worse, of course, for the people who lose their jobs. There is a lot of money in modern football, but most of the people in the game don't see much of it. I'm talking about the unseen many, the laundrywomen, the kitman, the gateman, the tea lady, all those people who make up the community of a football club, who are there long after the flavour-of-the-month superstar, or the manager, has gone. It is those people, despite their low salaries, who are most at risk of being laid off when a club goes into administration. At Palace some of the office staff were laid off immediately.

But it is not much fun for those who are left behind either, especially the manager. The administrator has two aims, to cut costs and find a new owner. The manager has one aim, to win matches. You'd have thought these were compatible as it must be easier to attract an owner with a decent team, one that can win matches, but the administrator doesn't care about the football side, only about the money. Since players can't be fired he has to sell them and, inevitably, he can only find buyers for the good players, and those buyers know he is desperate to sell so they don't want to pay the market rate.

I met Guilfoyle for the first time the day after the Newcastle match. 'There'll be changes,' he said. 'We don't want you to go, but I can't guarantee you your job.'

I thought, 'That's not very secure is it?' I said I could work with him as long as he was honest with me and didn't sell players for silly fees. I knew Victor would go, but we'd always planned to sell him. I was concerned about the other players. If we sold too many we'd be facing relegation – and who would want to buy us in League One?

There were six days left to the end of the transfer window and I was determined to hang onto as many players as possible. First out was Victor. I'd recommended him to Brian Marwood and Mark Hughes at Manchester City, that's how good I thought he was going to be. I'd also spoken to Roberto Martinez, at Wigan, and to QPR and West Bromwich Albion. Newcastle and Nottingham Forest were other possibilities but it was Wigan who were keenest. We had talked £3m plus £1m depending on how many games he played for them. After we'd gone into administration, Roberto got Moses for about £2m. In the summer of 2012 they sold him to Chelsea, for £9m. That's a nice profit, though Crystal Palace did get a cut.

The next bargains being hawked around were Neil Danns, a useful box-to-box midfielder who'd scored both goals in a 2–0 win over Peterborough in our first home game since administration, Darren Ambrose, a skilful midfield man with an eye for making and taking goals, and Nathaniel Clyne, a gem of a full-back who had come through our youth scheme. Premier League Wolves wanted Clyne, and I knew why. We were engaged in a fourth round FA Cup tie with them and before going into administration we drew 2–2 at Molineux. Claude Davis was sent off after a minute, then Clint Hill shouted over to the bench, 'I'm struggling, gaffer.' We were up against it at the back but Clynie was brilliant. Mick McCarthy had signed a winger from Belgium on loan, Mujangi Bia, who Mick said was 'like lightning'. Bia came on as a sub and soon afterwards pushed the ball past Clyne and went to run past him. Clynie just moved up a gear. I looked across at Mick McCarthy and we both smiled.

When we went into administration Wolves made their move, agreeing a £700,000 fee. I didn't blame Mick McCarthy for trying to get him on the cheap, but I told the administrator that was a third of what Nathaniel is worth. Trouble was, he wasn't bothered as long as the money came in; that was his job, to get in cash to pay the club's creditors. The ability of the club to compete on the pitch in the long-term was my concern; the short-term future of the business was his. We were never going to agree. I wanted to get the best deals for my players I could, and sometimes that meant them staying put and playing games for us. On deadline day morning he informed me that Clyne could speak to Wolves; and that if Clyne wasn't going to take their offer up, he would have to look again at selling Danns to Southampton for the lowly sum of £300k.

Arriving at the club I was told Clyne was with Dave Moss, head of the youth system, and Phil Alexander, the club's chief executive and who Simon had begun to mistrust. I was told Dave, who wasn't the most popular man with me and my senior coaching staff, was trying to talk Clyne into going to Wolves on the advice of the administrator, apparently telling him it was in his best interests to go and all that rubbish. The administrator had told Moss if he didn't go we all wouldn't get paid. That's a lot of pressure on a young man.

When Clyne came out I got him in my office. 'Nathaniel, have you been told you've got to go?'

'Yeah, to pay the wages.'

'Trust me, son,' I said, 'you haven't got to go. I don't think it is the right move for you because I don't think Wolves will play you, they want you as back-up. You need another 50 to 100 games under your belt at this level.'

Most of the agents who 'look after' my players would have thought only of their commission, and persuaded Clyne to go.

Fortunately Nathaniel was managed by a good friend of his family, who put the player's future ahead of his own payday. They didn't take much convincing that he was better off staying at Palace, and paying the wage bill was nothing to do with him.

'Look at Kyle Naughton,' I said. Kyle had been with me at Sheffield United. He had gone to Tottenham for £6m in the summer and was now on loan to Middlesbrough after barely getting a kick at Spurs. 'Look at your old youth-team colleague, John Bostock,' I added. Bostock had left us for the high life at Spurs and ended up loaned and on the bench at Brentford. 'Just stay put and you'll get the games, you need another couple of years playing, then you'll go to the Premier League,' I concluded. (That is just what he did, moving to Southampton, newly promoted to the Premier League, in the summer of 2012; Palace got two more years out of him and compensation far in excess of the fee Wolves would have paid.)

Then the administrators rang me up and said they had accepted £350,000 from Southampton for Danns, he had to go, and I had to tell him. I rang Danns' agent to tell him of the bid but said, 'He hasn't got to go – and I don't want him to.' Danns then told the administrator he didn't want to go.

The administrator's response was to tell me, 'If he doesn't go I'll sell every player I can. I'll start by selling Darren Ambrose.' That didn't worry me, I knew Ambrose wouldn't go if I didn't want him to. In the end neither Danns nor Ambrose went before the window shut, preventing Guilfoyle selling anyone else – the only time in my management career I've been glad of the transfer window system. Both celebrated by scoring in our next league match, a vital 2–0 win over Scunthorpe. Ambrose went on to score some vital goals for the club, including that screamer in the money-spinning Carling Cup win at Old Trafford, while Danns was sold a year later for £650,000 to Leicester. It is nice to be able to reveal to the Palace faithful, who always treated me so well, the extent I had to go to to keep that team intact. If I hadn't I am convinced we would have been relegated.

The postscript to all this was to discover that though I'd been told we had no money to pay anyone for anything, which meant freelance staff like Bev the caterer, and the masseuse, were not getting paid, the administrator had found the money to pay the agent on the Moses deal. I kicked up a fuss and Bev and the masseuse were paid, but our Prozone performance analysis tool was cut off because we hadn't paid the bill. I also had to find sponsors to cover our rail fares and avoid bus trips to places like Scunthorpe, Doncaster and Barnsley.

What made things even more frustrating was that the team were more than earning their keep. We pulled off a fantastic win over Wolves in the FA Cup replay, which brought in well over half-a-million pounds as it earned us a televised fifth round tie with Aston Villa, which also went to a replay.

I like to think that night against Wolves was my 'thank you' present to Palace fans for their fantastic support. I bet even the most faithful wondered if I'd lost my marbles when they saw I'd picked Danny Butterfield in attack. Danny had played well at right wing at Newcastle even if he had missed a sitter. With Moses gone I kept him there against Peterborough and he missed another sitter. It was beginning to become obvious why he'd scored seven goals in 250-odd games. But I had a hunch. 'Have you ever played up front?' I said to him on the morning of the game.

'No, gaffer.'

'Well you are tonight and I think you'll score.' Mick Jones, my assistant manager and 'Curly', my first team coach Keith Curle, both thought I was nuts. As anyone who saw it will remember,

Danny wrote his name into Palace folklore with the club's quickest hat-trick in history, six minutes and 48 seconds. I just managed to resist the temptation to point out to the administrator that, if Clyne had gone to Wolves, Danny would have had to play at right-back. In the end we made as much money from the FA Cup as we would have got from selling Clyne.

If that was a great night I received a real 'morale booster' on the morning of our tie against Villa from Guilfoyle. He texted to say he had a potential buyer and as a result my job was now 'insecure'. This, the League Managers' Association lawyers told me, was all but giving me notice and meant if I wanted to I could walk out. In fact I even had a letter of resignation drafted detailing the ways my contract had been broken.

But I wasn't prepared to do that and leave Palace, the players and fans, in the lurch. So I immediately told Simon about the text. He obviously had a word and told Guilfoyle that if he didn't hang onto me Palace would be in even bigger trouble because 24 hours later — by which time we'd forced the money-spinning replay against Villa — the administrator's tone had changed. He texted to say what a good job I was doing in difficult circumstances. It was obvious he didn't have a clue about managing a football club.

It was inevitable that the administrator and I would fall out. The most important person in a football club is the manager and the most important relationship is that between him and the chairman (or owner, or whoever it is making the big decisions). At every club I have had success at I've enjoyed a one-on-one relationship with the chairman. The ones I've left in general have either let me down or lied to me, although I've had some good ones too. The writing has been on the wall as soon as the relationship starts to break down. After that it is usually just a matter of whether I quit before I'm fired, though sometimes we both know it's over and that horrible phrase, 'by mutual agreement', is accurate.

A lot of people thought Simon and I would fall out within weeks. One of us is outspoken, demanding and doesn't suffer fools gladly, and the other is, well, just the same. In fact, the first time we dealt with each other was because of a row. I was manager at Sheffield United and I rang the Palace manager and suggested a swap deal, Marcus Bent for Clinton Morrison. They said 'no' and as far as I was concerned that was that. The next thing I know the London *Evening Standard* carries a story that Palace have rejected swapping Morrison for Bent and I've got an angry striker banging on my office door. So at my next press conference I had a go at Palace, saying I was not interested in Morrison at all and blaming the manager and chairman (Simon) for leaking stories to the press. We played Palace a few weeks later, Simon came over to take issue with me and we finished up getting on like a house on fire.

My main concern about working for Simon was that it could ruin our friendship but we got on brilliantly. Simon was very good at one of the big roles of a chairman – motivating the manager. Management can be a lonely job. You are constantly taking decisions, many of which upset people and some of which take a while to bear fruit. While at QPR at one stressful point I found myself talking to the deer in Richmond Park which probably wasn't a good sign looking back – even if it was a magnificent stag. You do need someone of significance to talk to, someone who, while prepared to question you, will also back you. Simon and I spoke every day, often several times a day. He never told me who to pick, but he was informed, interested, and supportive.

Newcastle was not the first time he had talked me out of resigning. In September 2009 we lost 4–0 at home to Scunthorpe

United. Scunthorpe were a better club than their unglamourous image suggests, and certainly a lot better than they were when I played for them in the early Seventies, but it was still a terrible result. That afternoon was one of the worst of my career – and there's some competition for that. We'd not only been thrashed, we'd deserved to be thrashed. Six games into the season we had won one match and were hovering above the relegation zone.

A lot of chairmen would have been having second thoughts but Simon, who was under huge financial pressure himself trying to balance Palace's books, spent nearly two hours sitting with me in our tiny kit room, persuading me it was a one-off, a blip, that I was the right fit for the club and he was confident things would turn around.

I woke up the following morning with that old buzz back. My renewed enthusiasm must have rubbed off on the players as we took 11 points from the next 15 including victories against two clubs, West Brom and Blackpool, who would end the season being promoted. That's what a good chairman can do.

I always tell aspiring managers who ask me for advice that the key thing is to make sure the chairman is singing off the same hymn sheet. I was very lucky that early in my career I had Ben Robinson at Burton Albion. I'd played for Burton so I knew Ben was everything you could wish for in a chairman. He didn't disappoint. He was a football man but he let his managers manage. It is no wonder Nigel Clough spent a decade at Burton before finally being lured away by the prospect of following in his dad's footsteps at Derby.

Since then I've worked with umpteen chairmen, good, bad and indifferent. I had four in two years at Scarborough. I often joke that I was the first manager who gave chairman a vote of confidence. In fact one died, one went to prison, another was Geoffrey

Richmond who later over-reached himself at Bradford City. I found Geoffrey impossible to work with at Scarborough but we were both inexperienced at the time. We became friends later and I recognised that, as at Bradford, he was only doing what he thought was best for the club.

It is surprising how many chairmen think they are the reason the club is getting success, that any manager could do it. It doesn't work like that but when a manager is successful he tends to get the media attention, and some chairmen get jealous. They want all the kudos themselves. That's what did for my relationship at Plymouth Argyle with Dan McCauley. He had put his money into the club and felt he deserved more credit for any success, but when you have a manager like me the media want to talk to the manager all the time. You are not being disrespectful to the chairman, and you put all the good things about the club out. In the end we communicated by fax and when he fired me it was through a third party. In later years we became friends again and I think he realised if he'd supported me more we'd have had a great time. That was one of my biggest disappointments because I loved Plymouth Argyle and I liked Dan and his wife Anne and really thought I could do with them what I had done with Notts County.

Now at Palace I was working for an administrator who, I felt, liked his name in the papers and the experience was doing my head in. I'd heard it was tough being a manager at a club in administration, but now I realised just how tough. It wasn't just things like not having ProZone and fighting to avoid losing players, it was the sense that winning football matches was no longer the club's priority, and the manager was no longer in control.

Football clubs are top-down hierarchies and the manager sets the tone. If you can get the whole club behind you it doesn't half help. At QPR they brought in a bonus scheme which meant if the club stayed up everyone got a reward, right down to the car park attendant. That gave everyone a stake in the club's results and meant they each did everything they could to influence things positively. A manager takes care of the players' needs because it's their performances that dictate your future, but I also take an interest in everyone else. I talk to the groundsman, to the washer-woman, the people selling tickets, the community staff. Some people never notice those people but they are part of the fabric of a club. It is all about making people feel involved and wanted. I've always done it. When I began, with a Sunday League club, Todwick, I bought the players tracksuits with my own money because I wanted them to look the part.

It was working with those lads in the Sunday League that persuaded me to have a go as a manager. I'd never been that good as a player. I made more than 300 league appearances over 11 seasons so I wasn't rubbish, but the fact I played for eight clubs in that time, none higher than the Third Division, will give you an idea of my standard. Managers wanted to buy me, but rarely wanted to keep me.

Ron Ashman signed me at Scunthorpe on deadline day, they were next to bottom of the old Third Division. Ron said he wanted to sign me as there was only one way we could go, up. I proved him wrong, we finished bottom and got relegated.

The constant free transfers meant I always had an eye on the future. I trained as a chiropodist, doing a correspondence course while at Scunthorpe; I opened a practice when I went into non-League which I kept going even while I was taking Scarborough into the Football League. I still get my tools out occasionally – at QPR I did a bit of work on the feet of Tommy Smith and Joey Barton, one of them had an ingrowing toenail I treated. I also had a go at selling insurance, flogging frozen food wholesale and running a greengrocers while I was still playing. The good thing about all those clubs and managers was that when I did start managing I had learned a lot, often how *not* to do things which is just as important as how to do them.

But my first management job wasn't even Sunday League. When I was playing for Hartlepool and living in digs at Seaton Carew there was a group of scruffy urchins who used to play on the green where I lived. They knew who I was and one night they knocked on my door. 'Will you coach us?' they asked.

How could I say no? I'll never forget how before one game we had worked a set-piece, a corner, and we scored from it – I ran down the touchline celebrating. I was like Brian Glover in *Kes*.

That buzz, the feeling you get from working on something with your players, and seeing it come off, has never left me. So when my playing days were winding down I started looking for a job in management. I hadn't played for England, like Bryan Robson or John Barnes, so I wasn't going to be offered a top job because of who I am. I had to start from the bottom. I began at Gainsborough Trinity in the Northern Premier League. Martin O'Neill began at a similar level a few years later and I'm sure, like me, the experience he gained then has been invaluable.

It's all very well being handed a plum job but if you don't know what you're doing it can be horrible. Look at what happened with Martin Johnson in rugby. He was an icon as a player, but then he was given the responsibility of managing the England team without any coaching or management experience at any level. He was a great leader as a player, but it is completely different as a manger and it wasn't fair on him. People say he could have said no, but when your country calls how many people would turn it down?

It's no coincidence most top managers are in their sixties or older. You can never underestimate the value of experience. Harry Redknapp and I often have a good laugh over the hype that can surround young managers. The League Managers' Association do a good training course for young managers but one thing they can't teach is man-management, the main ingredient in the management recipe; you can role-play all you like but you only really get that from experience. So Harry and I would say to each other about the latest young gun, 'Wait 'til they have a few problems. Let's see if those qualifications will help them cope then.'

Funnily enough I played in Harry's last league game in England, in September 1976. He'd been playing in America, in Seattle, and came back in their off-season looking for a few games somewhere to pay the bills. Harry had played in the old First Division at West Ham for years but it wasn't like these days when a few years in the top flight would set you up for life. He joined Brentford and made his debut against Aldershot during my spell there. Midway through the first half he cracked his ribs, had to be substituted, and decided to call it a day. I'll have to remind him next time I see him.

From Gainsborough I went to Burton, then to Scarborough, which is when I got into the league, taking them up. I'll never forget our first match. The famous Wolverhampton Wanderers came to Seamer Road; they had been a great club when I was a boy and we really thought we were in the big time. Then their fans started smashing the ground up and when I went over to try and calm things down, with Wolves manager Graham Turner, a Coke can whizzed past my ear. I picked it up and realised it was full of sand. If it had been a foot closer it would have probably killed me. So we left it to the police.

We drew that game, and we drew the return at Molineux too. But fortunes change in football, and not always for the better. While Wolves recovered their top flight status and turned Molineux into a fabulous modern ground, Scarborough were wound up in 2007 having finished in the relegation zone of Conference North. A couple of years later Seamer Road, which some of you will remember as the McCain Stadium after the oven-chip maker sponsored it, but I remember for so many fantastic times, was demolished. I think they are going to put housing on it. The stands ended up at Featherstone Rovers rugby league club and a reformed Scarborough Athletic are playing in Bridlington and trying to climb their way up the leagues. Boro's debt was £2.5m, chickenfeed in the modern game – there were players with me at QPR being paid that every year.

Notts County was next and two promotions later I was in the top flight. It was all glamour. The chairman decided to scrap overnight stays before matches which left us eating our pre-match meal on the coach out of the sort of plastic trays you get on a plane. I suppose it helped keep the players' feet on the ground, and so did a mid-season break I organised to Scarborough. Most clubs would go abroad, or at least to a four-star hotel, but I decided to stop at a couple of guesthouses I knew. I showed our two young stars, Mark Draper and Tommy Johnson, to their room. 'Lads we've special accommodation for England under-21 internationals,' I said, 'take a look at this.'

'It's got bunk beds in it, gaffer.'

'I know. What a treat. None of the other lads are in bunks. Don't tell them, they'll be jealous. Now who's taking the top one?' In fairness they took it well.

When Notts County sacked me, a year after I'd turned down Chelsea to stay at Meadow Lane, I went to Torquay United.

They were bottom of Division Four and heading towards the Conference. People thought I was mad and even now it seems a strange decision, like me taking over at Barnet or Hereford, who were fighting relegation from League Two, when I left QPR, but it's never been about the money for me, or the status. It's about the challenge. Some of the lads there were on £100-a-week but they gave everything.

When we won at Carlisle in the penultimate game of the season to secure our safety I was so happy I stayed on the coach all the way back to Devon instead of going back home to Nottingham. We had a Chinese at Lancaster to celebrate, it tasted like caviar and lobster.

I moved on to Huddersfield Town, Plymouth Argyle, Oldham Athletic, Bury and my hometown club Sheffield United before Simon lured me to Selhurst Park in October 2007. At all these clubs one thing was constant. Once I felt the man in charge was no longer giving me his full backing it was time to go.

That became the case at Palace once it was clear that Guilfoyle and I didn't see eye-to-eye and the new owners were unlikely to have a role for Simon. He left feeling he had been dealt with unfairly. I had learned a long time ago you can't take a club forward when you are watching your back all the time.

Chapter Two

A New Dug-out

Fulham Football Club seek a Manager/Genius.

Newspaper advert

EVERY JOB INTERVIEW IS DIFFERENT, BUT NOT MANY START with a butler opening the door. Nor do many applicants bring their children because they can't find a babysitter. But in March 2010 there was myself, Sharon and William being shown into a drawing room (or parlour, depending on your background), at the house of Amit Bhatia, co-owner of QPR.

After a few minutes William stood up. He turned and looked at the wall behind me. 'Dad, is that a Picasso?''

'Don't be silly, son, sit down.'

We carried on talking. After about five minutes I got up to stretch my legs. I looked at the painting William had seen. 'Oh,' I said to Sharon. 'Actually, he's right, it is a Picasso!'

The route to an audience with one of London's most charming art-collectors began with a phone call. Football's a small industry and after you've been in the game a while you get to know most people in it. Someone I'd know for years, and liked, was Gianni Paladini, a dapper, gregarious Italian with a loquacious tongue who was always on the phone. Gianni always seemed to have a different job title at QPR but whatever was on his office door he had basically run the day-to-day football business at Loftus Road for years, so when he rang one day my first thought was that he wanted one of our players. Rangers, despite a big squad and bigger wage bill, were only one point above us. He didn't. He wanted me.

I wasn't happy at Palace, but I wasn't sure that going to Rangers was a good idea. Everyone knew Flavio Briatore called the shots at Loftus Road and he was a manager's nightmare, as anyone who has seen the film *Four Year Plan* will understand. It wasn't just that he sacked managers every few months; the word on the grapevine was that he interfered in team selection and transfers as well. After a bad experience late in my playing career at York, when Charlie Wright dropped me because two of the directors didn't like me, I'd decided when I went into management that no one was going to influence my team selection. That resolve was tested in my very first job, at Gainsborough, but I stuck by my guns. Working under Flavio would be jumping from the frying pan into the fire. It could only end in tears and I'd told Gianni that when he'd asked me to be manager on a couple of previous occasions.

But Gianni assured me that not only was Flavio's recent decision to take a step back genuine, Flavio and Bernie Ecclestone were planning on selling up. I wouldn't have to deal with them, the club was going to be run by Gianni and two men I didn't know, Amit Bhatia, son-in-law of Lakshmi Mittal, QPR's billionaire co-owner, and Ishan Saksena, who had just been named the new chairman. So we arranged to meet.

This is how it works in the managerial job market. Occasionally you will see an advertisement in the newspaper for a football manager, but it is only there for show and attracts the nutters and jokers who want to tell their mates in the pub they've applied to be manager of their team. Then you get the chairmen who like to think they and their club are important and tell the press they've had dozens of applications including 'some surprising names'. The reality is football jobs are usually filled by word of mouth.

People ring you and tell you there's a job coming up, so-and-so's 'on thin ice', or 'another bad result or two there and he'll be out'. Within weeks of leaving QPR I started having calls like that about a decent Championship club who were thinking of making a change. Then the team started winning and they decided to stick with the manager they had. Most clubs don't sack you now without having someone lined up. They don't want to look a fool, though some still panic, act after one bad result, then end up chasing around. What annoyed me when I left QPR wasn't so much that Tony Fernandes had lined up Mark Hughes but that I'd been told he'd been persuaded to bring him in by Kia Joorabchian – who I thought was helping me buy one of the players he represents, then-Chelsea defender Alex. It turned out he also represented Hughes. How naive of me.

I got my first job myself. I'd heard Gainsborough Trinity were looking for a manager so I went to their next match, collared the chairman outside the ground, and asked him if his club was as ambitious as I was. That got me an interview. I did something similar with Sheffield United. They were managerless and I was looking to leave Bury where things weren't working out, mainly because the fans hated me. I rang Kevin McCabe, who pulled all the strings at Bramall Lane, and who'd I'd known for 15 years, and talked myself into an interview where I talked myself into the job. By contrast at Crystal Palace Simon had to talk me into taking the job. I've never worked in London and didn't particularly want to, but I'm so glad he persuaded me to try it.

I'm good at interviews, as you might expect, but not infallible. I had an unsuccessful one in a hotel near Preston for Burnley once, passing another manager as I drove out. Years ago Norwich sent what seemed like a 400-page dossier to fill in ahead of the interview to give the board an idea of what I might do. When I arrived the first question was, 'Do you think Norwich City fans would appreciate a Neil Warnock team?' I looked everyone round the table in the eye, stalling, and then I said, 'You mean a winning one. I think they'd all like a winning one.' They appeared unconvinced and I thought to myself, 'I won't be getting this one.' They went for Bruce Rioch, who I think had been promised the job already anyway.

These days agents are often involved, sometimes acting for more than one manager. They want their ten per cent, but they get you a better deal because they are more ruthless. I could have done with one when I turned down Chelsea (an agent set that up, and that was back in 1991). Chelsea would have trebled my £60,000 salary and while Notts County gave me an increase not only did it not match that, I agreed if we got relegated I'd go back to £60,000. I shouldn't have done that, especially as I knew the players weren't good enough so there was a fair chance we'd go down. I let my heart rule my head.

I didn't learn. At QPR I trusted Amit to give me a rise if we went up, but he left so I ended up in the Premier League on the same deal I had in the Championship. Nor had I bothered checking the clauses with regard to the staying-up bonus. I assumed if we were doing OK I wouldn't be sacked. It turned out I wasn't entitled to a bonus when QPR stayed in the Premier League, despite the fact that we were not in a relegation position when I left, as the contract said I needed to have been top half. When I asked my legal man why he hadn't spotted that he checked his notes and said he had mentioned it to me, but I'd said: 'Don't worry about that, Amit will look after me.' I hadn't considered Amit might not be in charge.

So when I got the sack I got nothing for staying up because of my trust in people. Yet despite all the money spent on numerous players after my departure, without any one of the three away wins under me QPR would have gone down. (It was to be a whole calendar year later – after Mark Hughes too had been sacked – before QPR won away from home again.)

As well as a trustworthy chairman, and either some decent players or the cash to change them, you want to go to a club with a chance of winning something. Scarborough was a bit of a gamble as they were 50–1 outsiders to go up from the Conference. Bury was a mistake as they had had successive promotions and were never going to sustain a First Division (now Championship) club on their resources, and as manager I would get the blame when football gravity took hold. That is when I wasn't clearing dog poo off the public park we trained at.

In that respect QPR looked ideal. There was a promise of cash and after several lean years supporters would be grateful for a sniff of success. In fact, after six managers and several caretakers in four years, they'd be happy just to have enough stability to persuade fans at other clubs to stop laughing at them.

I met Gianni and Ishan in a casino club in London, the Ambassador. A lot of football people go in there. We got on well so they asked Guilfoyle for permission to speak to me. Which is how Sharon, William and myself came to be admiring a Picasso on the wall of Amit's amazing house. Then we saw another painting on the floor in some wrapping paper. It was a Van Gogh. They say most interviews are settled on first impressions. Mine was that there was clearly a bit more money around at QPR than at Palace. The first impression that mattered, however, came when Amit walked in. We just clicked. I trusted him totally from day one and I knew he wouldn't let me down. We talked about their plans for QPR, how we could work together, and what needed to be done.

I agreed to move, but insisted Palace received proper compensation. The LMA lawyers said I had a case for constructive dismissal because Palace had been taking payments out of my wages for my pension, but not putting it into the pot, which was illegal, but I didn't want to walk out on Palace. I may not have had much time for the administrator, but the fans had been wonderful to me and I felt I owed them that. It made things a bit easier with Simon too. He had said he didn't want me to go, but to make sure I got adequate compensation if I did.

So the haggling started. It went on for a week until I eventually said to the administrator, 'If this is not done by noon I'm staying put'. He was desperate for the money and almost as keen to get shot of me. Within a couple of hours the phone went. QPR were first, telling me I was theirs. Then Guilfoyle rang telling me they had agreed a fee. He got around £500,000 which was pretty good for a Championship manager who they wanted rid off. I recommended Gareth Southgate to Guilfoyle to manage the club to the end of the season but he said he had someone else lined up. It turned out to be Paul Hart, who I was replacing at Loftus Road and who the administrator had known from Leeds.

Just before the deal was settled I received another call, from a Premier League club. They asked me if I would manage them. I told them I'd already agreed to go to QPR.

'Have you signed a contract?'

'No, but I've shaken on the deal'

'But you've not signed a contract. You don't have to go.'

'That's not the way I do things. I've given them my word.'

Had the club come in earlier I might have gone there, but Palace had been in administration for five weeks so they had had plenty of time to get in touch.

While they were Premier League I didn't have any regrets about sticking with QPR. Amit told me he and his father-in-law were going to buy out Briatore and Ecclestone within weeks and be majority shareholders; unfortunately it didn't work out like that but at the time I had that excitement, that buzz, back again. Even my first visit to the training ground, which was a bit of a dump, didn't put me off though it was a bit disconcerting when Sharon reported that she had asked a member of staff, 'Who was the last manager?' and that the woman paused for a minute before then admitting she couldn't remember. Sharon said to me: 'They change managers so much here they can't remember the names.'

It reminded me of a story John McGrath, who was a tough-tackling centre-half for Southampton in the days when you could make a tough tackle, used to tell about his management days. When he went to Port Vale he was shown around by an old guy who'd been there donkeys' years – every club used to have someone like that. John followed this wizened old guy down all these dark and dingy corridors round one corner and another until they came across a door. On it was a blackboard, and in chalk he put 'Manager: John McGrath'. We all laughed but John paused, and said, 'That's not the punchline. The funny bit was seeing a wet sponge in a holder attached to the door.' Funnily enough at Leeds there was no nameplate on my door, it didn't even say 'Manager'.

Guilfoyle was obstructive to the end, banning me from returning to Palace to say goodbye to the players and staff. Did he think I was going to smuggle a couple of defenders and a striker out in my bag? It was disappointing and petty, but it didn't surprise me. I was also unable to say a proper goodbye to the fans, at least until QPR went to Selhurst a month later. I got a great reception from them even though both clubs were scrapping for points to stave off relegation. The press speculated that I'd be booed but I knew they'd be brilliant with me. They always were. I think they knew I was swimming against the tide.

I started at QPR with a press conference. Sample question: 'You're the fourth or fifth manager in a year, how are you going to go about the job?'

'I think I'll be renting my house, not buying one.'

Then I went to the training ground and met the players.

New managers usually inherit a squad of players who are low on confidence and possess a negative outlook. After all, except in those rare cases where the previous man has left for a better job, in which case the squad tend to be nervous about change, the club have hired a new manager because things were going badly. So my first job is to lift the players, put a smile on their faces. Then I have to assess the squad for character, ability and balance.

I told the Rangers players I expected them to work hard, but I also expected them to enjoy the work. I told them I wanted to see smiling faces. I love it when players want to come to training, to exchange banter with their team-mates and get out there on the park and show how good they are. It's the dressing room atmosphere I'll miss when I pack it in.

I always start the first training session, after the warm-up, with a match: two big goals 40 yards apart, ten-a-side, shinpads on. If anyone doesn't head a ball when it's there to be headed I give a foul. If anyone doesn't make a tackle it's a foul. The aim is to let everyone know they have to give everything from day one. I judge their characters from what they are like in those types of games. These days you couldn't do this at Premier League level, they would just walk off, but the clubs I've worked at I've been able to do it and it's a great way to find out what my new dressing room is like. One problem I noticed immediately when I looked at the squad list was that there were far too many loan players. Loan players won't die for the cause as they're contracted to someone else.

There were two players who'd been with me before: the skipper, Mikele Leigertwood, and Marcus Bent. Both had played for me at Sheffield United. I expect their team-mates had been tapping them for information about me. Most of the rest of the squad I'd seen in matches but I'd also studied DVDs of recent QPR games. There was talent there, not enough to go up, but enough to stay up. They just needed some organisation and belief.

There was also one player who stood out in that first training match, a Moroccan lad on loan from Tottenham. The QPR staff I inherited told me, 'You can't play him, he'll get you the sack. He doesn't give a toss about the team, he just pleases himself.' It was Adel Taarabt.

I had to admit Taarabt was the sort of player who, when I was younger, I would have bombed out straight away. He was a nice lad but he wasn't very reliable and he wasn't 'an English pro': he didn't fight and run back, but he had ability, he could find a pass out of nothing. I'd never seen anything like him, or some of the things he did in training. I realised if you looked at the things he couldn't do you wouldn't touch him with a barge pole, but if you looked at what he could do . . . well, he could score and make goals which is the hardest thing in the game. So as I watched him I had this hunch, 'I can do something with you.'

I called him over after the game. He told me he'd not been playing much; the previous manager had left him out. In fact he had not started since January. I wanted him to know I had faith in him. 'I've been told if I play you, you will get me the sack.'

'No, gaffer.'

'Well, I'm picking you for every game from now until the end of the season, whether you're rubbish, or if you have a nightmare, you'll play every game. Is that OK with you? Do you understand?'

'Yes, boss,' he said, probably adding under his breath, 'I can't believe this.'

Adel was one of four changes I made for our first game, which was a peach: West Bromwich Albion, second in the table, looking good for automatic promotion and with one defeat in their last nine. At least it was at home.

Before the game I read out the team and named the substitutes. Then I put the team-sheet up on the wall. Bent had a long, hard look at it and I wondered if he was upset as he had only been named as a sub. He came over and I thought, 'Oh no, I can do without a row about team selection before my first match'.

'Gaffer,' he said, 'you've picked five loan players in the team. I'm a loan player too.'

In the Championship you can only pick five loanees in the squad. Bent was too smart and honest for his own good. I had to replace him with someone else so he missed out on the chance of some appearance money, and to show what he could do. But he saved us a fine, and probably a points deduction too.

The game couldn't have gone much better. We won 3–1 and played really well. After about 15 minutes the right-back, Matt Connolly, came jogging past as we started an attack. Given the team had been losing, and we were defending an early lead, he obviously didn't want to push forward too much. I screamed at him, 'Get on there, push on, get round the back'. He only went and scored and all the bench looked at me like I was a magician.

We won our next game as well and although we then went seven matches without a win we only lost twice so confidence held up. Even so, when we went to Selhurst Park on April 10, with five games to go, we needed a result. Palace were only two points behind us with Sheffield Wednesday, in the relegation zone, only a point further back.

It was an emotional day for me. At Selhurst Park the tunnel is in the corner of the ground so the staff have to walk alongside the main stand to get to the dug-out. It can be a long walk if the crowd don't like you. It was while making that walk Eric Cantona was abused by a fan after being sent off playing for Manchester United and infamously jumped into the crowd to attack the bloke. I was touched to get a fantastic reception from the Palace fans. They needed the points even more than we did but the fans put that aside for the moment. Come kick-off they got behind their team but we scored early, added another in the second half, and won relatively comfortably. I didn't celebrate the way I normally do at the goals. I just couldn't. I actually felt sick in the stomach throughout the game and didn't enjoy it one bit. I still felt ill at the final whistle even though I was delighted as the result meant we were probably staying up, especially as Wednesday had also lost.

We won two more games, which meant we were mid-table and safe by the final match of the season. That was at home to Newcastle United whose victory took them past 100 points. As we looked at the Newcastle team celebrating on our pitch I said to Mick Jones and Curly, 'That'll be us next year'. I was speaking more in hope than belief. I knew I had a lot of work to do to turn the squad into one capable of challenging for promotion.

The season wasn't quite over though. I went into my office, turned on the TV and waited for the rest of the Championship scores to flash up. There it was: 'Sheffield Wednesday 2, Crystal Palace 2'. I was relieved and delighted for Palace. I didn't feel guilty at leaving, but we'd put our soul into the club, I had a lot of friends there, and loved the fans. It would have been a sad end to the season if they had gone down. And who scored the goal that kept Palace up? Darren Ambrose, who the administrator wanted me to flog three months earlier. I think he had justified my refusal to sell him.

Chapter Three

Building A Winning Team

I haven't seen the lad, but he comes highly recommended by my greengrocer.

Brian Clough on signing Nigel Jemson

I SAID TO AMIT AFTER A COUPLE OF WEEKS, 'ONCE WE'RE over this relegation scrap we'll do well next year – there are players here I can build a team around.' Then I realised I meant one player, Alejandro Faurlin. Ali was a gem of a player. The best I've ever had under my command, but he wasn't going to win promotion on his own. Like Yul Brynner in *The Magnificent Seven* I needed to recruit a band of brothers to take the Championship by storm.

I knew most of them would have to be found outside Loftus Road. I had 14 games at QPR at the back-end of that first season during which I used 23 players. It's hard to believe now that Aston Villa won the title with just 14 players in 1981. So many players had been signed by QPR's various managers this didn't even include all the players, indeed, two of the best were out on loan,

Fitz Hall at Newcastle and Heider Helguson at Watford. Helguson's contract was up at the end of the season and he'd be 33 before the next one started so when I called him in on his day off I think he thought he would be getting his cards.

'Heider, did you enjoy it at Watford?'

'It was OK, gaffer.'

'Do you want to come back and play here?'

'If you want me, gaffer, I'd love to.'

'I want you, Heider. I tried to sign you twice when I was at Sheffield United. You are going to be my centre-forward next season and you are going to get me promoted because there isn't a better centre-forward in the Championship.'

'Thanks, gaffer. That's great to hear.'

He went away ten feet tall. Heider scored 13 goals in our Championship year. Flavio then told me to get rid of him as he was 34, but I refused and he scored another seven in the top flight before Christmas.

Most of the loanees I sent back to their parent clubs which meant poor Marcus Bent went back to Birmingham without ever kicking a ball for me, but one loanee I wanted to sign permanently. Adel Taarabt hadn't scored that many goals for me, and he'd rarely played the full 90 minutes, but I'd seen enough to think he could be very influential in the right system. It would mean setting up the whole team for his benefit, but I hoped it would benefit everybody in the long run because he had such talent. I'd never done this before but because of the type of player he was there really was no alternative. Either he played and you adapted the team to him, or you left him out.

In my younger days I would have left him out because he doesn't do what footballers call the dirty side of the game. I don't mean kicking people, I mean marking them, tracking back, all the stuff that often goes unseen by fans but which makes the difference between teams winning and losing. I watched Milan at Old Trafford a few years ago. They had three up front including Ronaldinho and none of them tried a leg when they lost the ball. United won 4–0. I pointed this out to the team at training the following day. It doesn't matter how good your front players are, if none of them work when you lose the ball the team will struggle. But opening up defences to make and score goals also makes the difference between winning and losing, and players who can do that are a lot harder to find than ones who will run around. Adel has that ability. He's not a team player, at the last minute he'll try and put it through somebody's legs instead of passing it, he does frustrate you, but he can win games. You couldn't have three Taarabts, but I thought we could afford to carry one. To do so though I knew I'd have to get the senior players onside because players like that can damage morale.

At the end of the season I said to Amit, 'I want to buy him as I can put a system around him people won't be ready for.' Amit was OK, he loved watching Adel. Now I had to persuade the player – and his agents. I went to speak to Taarabt in Morocco. I was there three or four days in a lovely hotel he told me to stay at as he would also be staying there. I asked for him when I arrived.

'Sorry, he's not at the hotel,' said reception.

'What, is he out?'

'No,' they said, 'he's not registered here.'

I had three great days in Morocco, but never spoke to him once. I did ring his agent and told him how annoyed I was. Then I found out Adel was frightened to ring me because he'd told me where to stay and now he was terrified because he hadn't turned up. So I told him it was OK, but he would have to come and see me.

His agents were desperate for him to go abroad. I don't know why. I told him and the agents his career needed me at that stage. He needed to play games and playing for QPR would not only give the club a better chance of getting into the Premier League, but also Adel; I couldn't see a Premier League club signing him, just like I couldn't see a Premier League club appointing me.

'We'll have to do it together,' I said. 'You'll have to trust me. There'll be things we won't agree on because of the way you are, but you'll have to treat me with respect and I'll do the same with you.'

He agreed to come and Gianni thrashed out a fee with Daniel Levy at Tottenham.

I needed a top class goalkeeper so I went for Julian Speroni who'd played for me at Palace. But first the administrator wanted too much money, then after we'd agreed a fee Julian wanted to wait. He thought Fulham were coming in for him to replace Mark Schwarzer who looked as if he was going to Arsenal. The problem was he was going back home to Argentina for a holiday and I wanted it sorted before he went. I had him in my house and I said, 'If you go without signing I'll move for someone else.' He went, so I bought Paddy Kenny. An agent had told me he had a £750,000 buy-out clause. You can't keep that quiet as agents want people to know so they can move him and get another fee.

There was a major snag though. The deal was all done, just ready to be rubber-stamped, when QPR said they could not sign him as he had been done for taking drugs. It was bad for the club's image. They couldn't be seen condoning that sort of thing.

I was distraught. I went to Amit and explained that he was not a drug-taker, he had taken something for a cold that happened to have a banned substance in it. It had simply been a daft mistake. He agreed and said to leave it with him. Five minutes later he came back and said, 'We'll do it.' What a good decision that turned out to be.

Both goalkeepers were people I knew because they had played for me. The same with Shaun Derry and Clint Hill, who came across from Palace. I wanted both because you do need talkers and leaders at the back and in midfield. Players need reminding all the time, they need organising, and I can't do it all from the touchline. I knew I could trust those two to do it. The QPR fans weren't impressed that my first two signings were free transfers from Crystal Palace. They must have thought, 'Does he know what he is doing?'

I still needed a few more players. When I need a player I work out first what type of player I need for that position then try and identify a player who fits the bill. We might need pace at right back, or one who is good at covering his central defenders. We might need a big lad at centre-half, or someone who reads a game well. Obviously you'd like someone who does all of it, but they are usually playing for Manchester United or Chelsea. We might want a goalkeeper who comes for things as well as being a shot-stopper, a midfielder who can hold things together defensively and one who has the legs to get from box to box. I like wingers who can take men on and someone that can hold the ball up and bring people into play up front. The icing on the cake is usually the one around that player. In our case Helguson would hold the ball up and Taarabt would be the icing on the cake.

You normally know pretty quickly if a player is the right one. When I was at Huddersfield I went with Mick Jones to watch a window cleaner called Darren Bullock who was playing for Nuneaton Borough against Birmingham Police in a cup replay. I had heard about him. He was said to be good and physically strong. We got there a bit late, but after only five minutes I said to Mick, 'Let's go.'

'Ve've only just got here. What do you mean?'
'ow already.'

'. new I wanted to sign him. He was aggressive, he wanted to win it, he didn't worry about anybody else, he could pass a ball, shoot, head it, and he was fearless. He had every attribute you could wish for. He was a bit of a lad which may have been why no one had taken a chance on him before, but that didn't worry me. We paid £30,000 in the end and he got us promoted at Huddersfield. A great signing. I even took him on loan for Sheffield United for a month and he won us a local derby against Sheffield Wednesday playing against Carlton Palmer. It was worth it for that.

Sometimes you get lucky. At Notts County I went to watch Barnet play Macclesfield, I was looking at the striker Dave Regis, a big, tall, quick lad. Within 15 minutes not only did I know I wanted Regis, I also loved this lad called Paul Harding, a midfielder. He did everything. He'd come out of non-League and was living in a caravan when I found him, but he was a great team player and a nice lad. He lived for the present and was one you'd want beside you in a scrap. Paul Gascoigne elbowed him in the 1991 FA Cup quarter final at Tottenham because Harding hadn't given him a kick. The ref saw it and didn't do anything. He should have sent him off. Gascoigne got the winner, and went on to do his knee in the final. A lot of things could have been very different if the ref had done his job.

I do like a lovable rogue like Harding. You tend to get them cheap, as their previous manager couldn't handle them. As well as Bullock and Harding there's been Paul Devlin, plus Michael Brown and Paddy Kenny, both of whom I had playing for me again at Leeds. The first one I had was a lad called Gary Clayton who began playing for me in my non-League days, a lovely lad who I later signed for Huddersfield and Plymouth because he was great in the dressing room and always made me smile. Another I'll never forget is Ronnie Mauge who scored the winner in the play-off final to win promotion when I was at Plymouth. Ronnie could really handle himself. On the pitch he didn't take any prisoners, but off it he nearly ended up as one after a scrape with the law. I was a character witness and told the judge we were prepared to let Ronnie live in my home if he would grant him bail. We were 20 miles out of town and the deal was Ronnie could not set foot in Plymouth at night-time. He was good as gold at home, Sharon loved him and we did have some laughs. And after a while doing my domestic chores I think the penny dropped and he began to sort his life out. He now helps a local team in Suffolk and some-times rings for advice and also informs me of one or two good players I need to sign. He's not a bad judge. Another wonderful lad.

Managers, especially as we get more experienced, are always convincing ourselves we can change rogues, we will be the one who presses the right buttons, who will get them to wise up. You always think that, but with some players eventually you have to hold your hand up and say, 'I can't do anything with you, it's impossible to work with you.'

One example that didn't go right was Ashley Sestanovich. He'd been on the books at Millwall and Manchester City without making it, had a spell in Belgium, and was making waves in non-League. He was six feet plus and he went past people like they didn't exist. I just fancied him. He looked so much like Thierry Henry he had been a body double for him in an advertisement and I had an idea that at our level he might have a similar impact if he put his mind to it. We'd heard tales that he mixed with the wrong sort and Mick said he wasn't 100 per cent sure but he'd go along with my decision. So we signed him.

I sent him on loan to Scarborough to get some league experience, but a couple of times when he went home to London I got phone calls from police and press asking if I was aware he was in trouble down there. I called him into my office.

'Ashley. I've been getting calls from people in London, people who should know, telling me you're been linked with some bad things. Your car has been spotted somewhere it shouldn't have been. What's going on?'

'No idea, gaffer. I lent the car to a friend overnight. I don't know what you are on about. I've just had a quiet weekend.'

I didn't believe him. So I said to him, 'Son, you have so much pace and ability, you have everything going for you, you could either end up playing top level, or end up in prison.'

I remember the words so clearly. Unfortunately, it turned out to be the latter.

He went on loan to Grimsby but they sent him back after a few problems and we let him go. The following year, by which time he was back in non-League, he got eight years in prison after being found guilty of being involved in a payroll robbery in which a man was killed.

When I first started in management a long-distance scouting trip meant crossing the Pennines. As I moved into league football it meant getting acquainted with every service station on the motorway network. There was a time when I could have told you what the coffee tasted like at Knutsford, how hot the pies were at Membury and whether the toilets were clean at Woodall. We did all the scouting ourselves until we went up the leagues with Notts County. Then it became too much and Mick organised a scouting network. We had scouts all over the country, plus others to look at opponents, and one just looking at up-and-coming youngsters in the lower divisions.

Now, often as not, finding new players means getting on a plane because although there are a lot more matches on TV now, so you see more players, the market is so much bigger because of the foreign aspect. Agents send you all these DVDs and tell you their player is the best thing since sliced bread. Some you can trust; you know if they suggest a player he does have a chance, while others are just embarrassing. You end up on a wild goose chase to watch someone who should be playing Sunday league. But you don't know that until you go and have a look yourself. Which is why I can now tell you what the coffee tastes like at Heathrow, how hot the pies are at Gatwick, and whether the toilets are clean at Stansted.

There have been some interesting trips over the years, some memorable for the wrong reasons. When Sheffield United got into the Premier League we had to look further afield for players. I'd heard about this Jamaican playing in Sweden, Luton Shelton. So I went to watch him playing for Helsingborgs. As we drove towards the stadium it began tipping down. I got drenched just getting out of the car and running into the ground. When I saw the pitch it was as if a giant tap had been turned on. The ball was barely moving and it was an absolute waste of time. Henrik Larsson was playing but even he couldn't do a thing. I don't know why they didn't just call it off.

Another time with QPR I went to see Rodolph Austin, a Jamaican midfielder playing in Norway who I later signed for Leeds. Mick and I flew out there, got to the ground, and found it was a plastic pitch – the agent had never said a word, we couldn't possibly judge him on that. 'What a waste of time,' I said to Mick. We didn't see him make a tackle until he came over on trial. We liked what we saw then, but we couldn't afford him, as they wanted £2m. There was a happy ending though as I got him for a steal at Leeds – £300,000.

Then there was a trip Mick Jones and I made to Poland. We flew to Warsaw and met an agent in a little Fiat who took us up towards the Russian border to watch this left-back. We went in the boardroom and they offered us coffee. I've never had coffee like it, it was so thick. There was a plant nearby, so when no one was looking I tipped the coffee into the plant. The next minute someone saw my empty cup and they came and replenished it. Mick was killing himself laughing. We half expected the plant to keel over.

When the game kicked off it was obvious to us his team-mates weren't passing to him. They were avoiding doing so at all costs. He only had about eight touches in the first half. It was as if they'd heard we were there and had decided he wasn't going to get a move. We said at half-time, 'We can't judge him on this, let's hope he sees more of the ball in the second half.' Two minutes after the restart he made a tackle and got sent off. It wasn't a completely wasted journey. On our way back we stopped and had one of the best, longest sausages I've ever seen, a giant hot dog, at the side of the road. It cost about a million Polish zlotys.

That, though, was a breeze compared to a trip to Turkey to watch Ozalan Alpay who used to play for Aston Villa. He was at Cologne by then. It was a good stage to watch him on, a World Cup play-off against Switzerland which the Turks had to win to make the finals. The match was at the Fenerbahce stadium, which is actually over the water in Asia. We found our tickets were in with the fans and we got caught up in the scrum to get in. It was such a huge crowd; you couldn't move independently, you just had to go with the flow. I had my hands in my pockets, on my phone and my wallet, but there was a big surge, I took my hands out for a second to steady myself and had my phone lifted. I knew who'd done it, this guy in front with a big overcoat. I had a Turkish guy with me and he collared the bloke but the thief opened his coat to show he had nothing. He must have passed it on to an accomplice straight away.

Inside was frightening. It was an amazing atmosphere but very hostile. I've been to some intimidating places in England but they pale into insignificance by comparison. There were blokes next to where I'd sat with flares in their hands. I'd never experienced anything like it. It got tenser and tenser and I was soon waving a red-and-white flag above my head to blend in.

There were some tackles flying but Switzerland did ever so well and went through on away goals after a 4–2 defeat. When the final whistle blew it all went off, bedlam, players running and punching, flying kicks. Alpay was right in among it throwing punches. He ran quicker then chasing people than he had any time in the match. It was unbelievable. Fifa banned him for six matches after that. I didn't buy him, though we met up after the game in the hotel and he proved a really nice guy.

I also got pick-pocketed in Vietnam when I went to look at a Chinese player for Sheffield United. The club were trying to make money from a Chinese link-up, even buying a club, Chengdu Blades, and thought having Chinese players would help. The theft was a clever scam with a wizened old lady bumping into me. A couple of minutes later I felt for my wallet and realized it had gone.

There have been some better trips. With QPR I went to the UAE to look at a few South Korean players. Owner Tony Fernandes thought buying one would be a way into the Asian market. The only problem was the young midfielder I went to see was playing centre-half. Tony later went and bought Ji-Sung Park from Manchester United. While out there we went to the Grand Prix in Abu Dhabi, which was a great experience. Tony had a team racing so I was able to go onto the grid, meet drivers like Lewis Hamilton and Mark Webber, enjoy Eddie Jordan playing guitar at the after-show party and watch the race. I also bumped into Roberto Mancini and Patrick Vieira there, but I doubt if they had needed the excuse of looking at a player first.

Ideally you spot a player yourself, and sometimes you just get lucky and find one under your nose. With Heider and Adel in the team I knew I needed a striker with boundless energy who could go wide and come inside, plus chip in a few goals. Then I remembered a lad called Jamie Mackie who I'd seen the previous year when we took Palace to play Plymouth Argyle in a pre-season friendly. He had taken Nathaniel Clyne to the cleaners and I hadn't seen anyone do that before. He'd come out of non-League and he was so honest he wouldn't even go down in the box when he was fouled. The crowd loved him for his commitment and his enthusiasm was so infectious he made a great sub, but that's unfair on him because he's also worth picking from the start. I signed him, and by the end of October he was a Scottish international.

Of course you don't get all of them right. At Sheffield United I bought a centre-half, Danny Cullip, with a view to him being my leader on the pitch, my captain. I thought he was a good talker. I realised within a week he talked a better game than he played. Nothing on the pitch was his fault, and if I suggested it was he'd argue back at me. Now I can admit to being wrong, things happen in games sometimes that you miss and the player explains why he did something you've criticised. I don't mind that as long as they respect you as boss. You can't have players questioning your authority. If you have a problem like that with a player the only answer is to get shot of them quickly. I shipped him out on loan after three months to Watford and at the end of the season I struck the jackpot flogging him to Gary Megson at Nottingham Forest. They were made for each other.

I've not got the best track record with strikers to be honest. I was offered Bobby Zamora when he was about 19. He was available for loan from Bristol Rovers but I didn't think he worked hard enough. He went to Brighton and banged in some goals. They sold him for £1.5m to Spurs a couple of years later and he ended up playing for England. A few years later I spent a million pounds plus on each of Ade Akinbayi and Geoff Horsfield to provide that final push to get Sheffield United into the Premier League. They were decent players, but once I put them in the team it became clear they weren't right for us. Fortunately by then I had the experience and strength to take the hard decision and leave them both out. A few of the directors must have grumbled and I doubt I could have done that when I was younger, but it worked as we went up.

It is about creating a balance of players and then getting them to work hard for you, themselves and each other. The biggest compliment you can get, to my mind, is to have other managers not wanting to play against your team. You might not have too many stars in your side but if they say afterwards, 'I don't want to play them again, that's the hardest game we'll have this season,' you're doing all right.

Chapter Four

Team-Bonding

Motivation + Ambition + Team + Spirit = Success.

Jose Mourinho

IT WAS PITCH BLACK, SO DARK YOU COULDN'T SEE YOUR hand in front of your face. It was cold and I was hungry, but all I had to keep myself warm was a polythene sheet; I'd already eaten the chocolate bar we'd been given for food. I was somewhere on the North Yorkshire Moors and beginning to feel nervous. Then a hand gripped my shoulder. They probably heard my scream in Scarborough.

Legend has it pre-season training consists of lots of running – and in the early Seventies it usually did, I lost count of the amount of golf courses I've jogged round and hills I've climbed. I wasn't bad at it, but it didn't suit me at all. When are you going to do that in a match? It was all one-paced. At Hartlepool it was more enlightened, up to a point. Len Ashurst did a lot of work in grids with balls, and he hired an ex-commando called Tony Toms. Instead of long-distance work Tony had us all doing sprints. It was never more than 400 metres and it was over hurdles to keep your mind working as you tired and also to help your agility. I felt so fresh when we started the games I've kept that as the bedrock of my pre-seasons.

But some things I've not copied. Such as that overnight trip to the Moors for a team-bonding session. After we were dropped off we marched for a while then Tony called a halt. One by one he led us away from the group for 30–50 paces then sat us all down, on our own, in the dark. I waited for what seemed like ages, and then I felt that hand on my shoulder. I nearly filled my pants. It was Tony. I hadn't heard a footstep. Not even a breath. Once he'd scared the wits out of all us we played a game. The winner got extra food, the loser went in the river – he was ahead of his time Tony, it's the sort of thing they do now on *I'm a Celebrity . . . Get Me Out of Here!* But there weren't any celebrities at Hartlepool. I was so pleased when I realised it wasn't going to be me going in the river. Finally, when dawn broke, we were told to find our way home. I used my initiative; I reversed the charges from a call-box and got picked up.

Tony followed Len to Gillingham and Sheffield Wednesday and stayed on there after Jack Charlton took over before going with Jack to Newcastle United. He also had a spell at Kent County Cricket Club. Just think, there must be a whole generation of sportsmen who were scared out of their wits on a moor somewhere. I don't think the players' agents would let you get away with it now.

My pre-season is more benign. It helps that players don't let themselves go any more during the summer. We give them programmes to keep to and they know themselves if they come back out of condition they will struggle to get in the team. It happened to Adel when QPR got promoted. We had to get him in as many 11-a-side games in training as we could as then he would do the running he needed to do to get fit. Personally I still find fitness is best judged by the naked eye. We have all these fitness experts now. I have guys who say 'They've done enough now, gaffer,' but I just tell 'em, 'I'll tell you when they've done enough, not the computer.' There's still a feeling you get.

But even though players are fitter those first two weeks of pre-season remain important. Clubs like to buy players late as it saves on the wages but managers like to get their squad settled so the players can sharpen their fitness and gel as a group. My squad was coming together by the time we started pre-season at QPR. I'd signed Bradley Orr, who'd always played well against us, from Bristol City, and Leon Clarke from Sheffield Wednesday. As if to prove I can't pick strikers it didn't really work out with Clarke who failed to score once for us, but maybe it wasn't me who was at fault, as Paolo Di Canio found out the following season at Swindon. I tried really hard to make Leon a player for us but it never worked out. It was good to see Leon enjoying himself at Coventry a couple of seasons later and being nominated for League One Player of the Year.

I go to Cornwall pre-season. I used to go to Scarborough; having been manager there I knew it well. I did that with Notts County and Huddersfield. We'd train on the beach and up Oliver's Mount. Then when I went to Plymouth I fixed up matches with local clubs pre-season and found some places to train I liked, so I kept going there with Oldham, Bury and then Sheffield United. By then I'd found the Trethorne Golf and Country Club. They had some accommodation blocks. We hired the lot. They were quite basic, no televisions or anything like that, at least until Marcus Bent gave the kitman £300 to go into town and buy him a telly. They've improved the facilities now and cater for quite a few football teams and other groups.

The other bonus is that it's only 15 miles from home, so I get to see more of the family. After the first game I always take all of them, including the new signings, to my local pub, The Springer Spaniel, to get to know each other. We have a buffet and a drink, nothing excessive. We also have a barbecue at our house. I cook, though I remember the great Derek Dooley putting his apron on and cooking one year. Derek was a wonderful man loved by both sides of Sheffield, he and his lovely wife Sylvia were adored by everyone who met them. I let the lads play golf, as much as they want as the results don't matter in the warm-up matches. I'm just looking at developing fitness and team understanding.

The QPR lads had a great time down there and we played friendlies against Bodmin, Tavistock and Torquay. Then we went to Italy, Gianni fixed it up and I took the family. The atmosphere was very relaxed. As at a few clubs new signings have to sing a song. As a twist, and maybe to save time since there were so many, they decided to do it together. So one afternoon there they were, Clint, Dezza and the rest, dressed up as JLS and standing on a balcony and singing, 'Everybody in love, go on put your hands up'. The players, and the hotel staff, were all there cheering them on. On another day I gave William €20 to soak Akos Buzsaky with a water pistol while he was sunbathing. It's all quite childish in a way, but it helps create that bond a team needs if players are going to work for each other during a long season.

At Gainsborough I would take the players to the pub after training. We'd put posters up, go to a different pub each week and play pool and darts against the locals wearing the smart blue V-neck sweaters I'd bought them all. The players lived all over the shop, they had no link to the community and the town had no real commitment to the team. I thought it would bring the players and the community together and help the team bond. It did, and we used to get a great response.

During the season I'll often take players off on a break. Crystal Palace used to have a sponsors day at Lingfield which was a good day out. I've taken other squads to racecourses, or fishing at a lake. We used to go go-karting, but that can get a bit dangerous and with players worth so much now it is not such a clever option.

Sam Allardyce likes to go to Dubai; I took a few teams to Scarborough, which could be fun, especially in winter. One year with Sheffield United I had three games for the lads to play, in each case the loser would have to go for a swim in the North Sea. First I gave all the players a piece of paper and told them to write down the name of someone they thought should have to go for a swim. Danny Cadamarteri topped the poll. I don't think he was particularly unpopular, it's just the boys knew he would hate it. Then, on the beach, we played 'stones'. I made a circle in the sand and each player threw a stone. Every round those who got their stones in the circle could drop out. The last man left went swimming. Paul Gerrard, who was on loan from Everton, lost. I thought, 'He's a Premier League player, he's only here for a few weeks, he won't do it. Then what do I do?' I decided to wait and see how things panned out and we moved onto skimming stones. The players all grabbed a stone and we had another game of elimination. It came down to a play-off. Michael Tonge had to beat a four-er. He had no chance; you could see the dread in his eyes as he waited for the right wave while we all clapped in unison. He lost. Then it was time for a dip, to my relief and admiration Gerrard had no qualms, he sprinted straight in along with Danny and a reluctant Tongey. What was that slogan the local marketing people had? 'Scarborough – it's so bracing'. It certainly was that day. Brrrr.

Players do need a break. I couldn't understand the fuss that was made when some of the England rugby players let their hair down in the World Cup. If the footballers were allowed a similar release we might have won another World Cup by now. At Notts County, in the hotel on a Friday night before an away game, I used to take the players' minds off the game by having them drink glasses of sherry and raw egg. I'd start with asking one player to nominate someone, and work from there. You soon found out who were friends with who.

I love going in the dressing room, taking the Mickey out of the lads, building that team spirit. I really learned the importance of that when I was playing for Len Ashurst at Hartlepool. We had nothing there; he made something out of us. At one stage we looked certs to get kicked out of the league but we survived because he built a team spirit which got us all working for each other. I learned more off him in 12 months than all the other managers I had.

You need good characters, people who put the team first. I played with a centre-forward once, Bob Gauden at Burton, who scored a hat-trick; we lost 4–3 and he was absolutely bubbling. I wasn't impressed but that's goalscorers for you. Generally in my career my teams have won, and done so against the odds, because they had that camaraderie, that spirit. But it doesn't take a lot of rotten apples to ruin a club and you have to keep on top of things.

It wasn't all fun and games in Cornwall and Italy. We spent a lot of time working on our team shape, bedding everyone in and making sure they knew what I expected of them. I was still aiming to play Adel in what was essentially a free role so I called together the senior players, Helguson, Derry, Kenny and Hill. 'You may not like this,' I said, 'but trust me. I've never had a player like this in my career so I'm changing my philosophy. Adel's going to have a free role. I know he doesn't work hard enough, but he does things other players can't so everyone else is going to have to do his work for him. You lads are the leaders in the team, the rest will follow you, so as long as you are prepared to go along with this Adel will take us up.'

'Yes, gaffer,' they said with varying degrees of enthusiasm.

Then I told them Adel was going to be captain. People like Derry don't need an armband to behave like a captain but, as I told the lads, 'If this makes Adel work back a bit more, give us a bit more here and there, it could be the factor in us going up.' They all agreed. Of course, it's easy to say that when they are chilled out in Italy, a bit harder when they're chasing the ball at Oakwell or Turf Moor and Adel's not pulling his weight. I thought, 'We'll see how it goes.'

As a manager you tend to want to play a system, then get your players in. But you can't do it that way. You have to look at your players, identify the good ones, and then find a system that suits them. I've been pigeonholed a bit as an up-and-up-'em long-ball merchant, and there are times my teams have played that way, but I've played most ways over the years. At Notts County we had two great centre-halves, Dean Yates and Craig Short, and Don O'Riordan who could play behind. Or at home he could play in front of those two like an anchor defender. So we used all three. At Scarborough we had three great centre-halves. I looked at about 40 players over pre-season, signed 18, and three of the best were centre halves so it made sense to play them. Then we had Neil Thompson and Cec Podd bombing on as wing-backs.

We had a lot of good players at Sheffield United, but they weren't playing as a team when I got there. In that situation your first aim is to be solid and disciplined, and make sure you stay up. Then you worry about the next season. At Palace we had a big lad up front, Alan Lee, Neil Danns making runs from midfield, Shaun Derry and Nick Carle behind him. The following year I brought in Darren Ambrose who I knew could score goals from midfield and I gave him more or less a free role down one side so he could come inside. But we had no pace and no money. One day at our Beckenham training ground I called across Gary Issott who's done a great job as youth team coach there.

'Have you got anybody worth giving a run in the first team,' I said, 'someone quick?'

'Not really, gaffer. We've Victor Moses, who's got great ability but who's still learning how to be a pro, and Sean Scannell who'll run all day and work hard, but he's not really ready for the first team either.'

I called them over.

'I'm thinking of playing you two next week, are you good enough for us?'

'Yes, boss.'

It was about the only time I heard either of them speak, they were both quiet lads. 'Right,' I said, 'you're training with us now.'

We had nothing to lose, it would give the fans a lift and they gave us pace. I proceeded to give 14 players their debuts from the academy including Moses, Scannell, Nathaniel Clyne and John Bostock.

Pace is vital. The game is now more athletic, players are quicker and bigger. Arsène Wenger was an early advocate of this. It was as if he was looking for a type, telling the scouts: 'Six foot, quick, both feet, can tackle. Give us some names.' In the past you got by if you were 5'6'' but could tackle or were quick. You have to be a very good player to do that now. I know Barcelona's players are short, but they are also very good and besides, La Liga's less physical than the Premier League.

When you first go to a club you tend to start with the defence. If you can stop goals going in you have a chance. I've always had a big thing about centre-halves being defenders. I tell them: 'Head it and kick, that's your job. I don't want you to be Beckenbauer. Stop crosses, they cost you goals, they always have done.'

At QPR I was trying to make a point to Anton Ferdinand soon after he signed about not taking chances when playing the ball out. It wasn't sinking in so I went on the pitch and to emphasise I side-footed the ball, then whacked it 30 yards into the top tier of the stand. The lads laughed. 'That's where I want it to go,' I said. 'Do you understand? I don't want you turning, dribbling, trying to pass back. If you're not sure, kick it in the stand; they'll not score from there. If you get caught in possession we're on the hop. We can get organised to defend a throw-in.' In our second match against Wolves he was near the dug-out when he whacked it into the stand. He looked across at me and smiled.

Early in November I came into training after Gaël Clichy had given away a goal in the Champions League trying to play the ball out of defence with Arsenal when it wasn't on. I gathered the players together.

'Anyone see the winner against Arsenal last night?' Clint, Gorkss and a couple of others said they had. 'Did you think of me?' I asked.

'Yes, gaffer. When we saw Clichy, gaffer.'

In my column with *The Independent* I thanked Gael for doing my job for me.

At set-pieces I am very much in the man-marking camp. There has been a lot of debate about this in England since foreign managers such as Rafael Benitez and Roberto Mancini brought in zonal marking, but I think that allows strikers to get more of a jump on the defender by having a run at the ball while he's stood still marking space. The other reason I favour it is that each individual has a responsibility. If your man scores you'll get blamed, and my players know they really will get blamed. That should make the defender more determined to ensure whatever happens their man doesn't score.

Very occasionally I'll ask a player to man-mark in open play. Against a good winger like Jobi McAnuff I'll say to the full-back: 'We go 10 v 10, you take him, if he goes to the loo you go with him.' One day the left-back was booked early on for fouling him. So I swapped full-backs. Then the other one got booked for fouling him.

Curly said to me: 'What do we do now, gaffer?'

'Cross your fingers and say a prayer.'

What can you do? At Notts County we played Manchester United at home. I played five at the back and man-marked everyone: 11 v 11, even the centre-backs. Chris Short was on Ryan Giggs. After about 25 minutes I remember Giggs looking at the bench and saying something like, 'Can you get this bloke off me, he's like a rash?' Chris just followed him everywhere. We were winning 1–0 but just for a change Man U got a late equaliser. From a disputed penalty.

It was at County I got tarred with a long-ball reputation. We came up the divisions fast and the team weren't good enough to play it around against good teams. Brian Clough used to walk his Labrador past our training ground. His Nottingham Forest had these salubrious acres, like Wembley; we had a postage stamp about 40 yards square. There we'd be, up to our knees in mud, pads on, kicking lumps from each other. Then we'd see him walk by and stop. He'd shake his head with this look of disdain and walk on. But as I used to say to Brian, 'Look at my back four, they can't pass water. How am I supposed to get us knocking the ball around like your team?'

I used to love watching Cloughie's Forest team play, just as I love watching Arsenal and Barcelona now. Those Arsenal fans who criticise Arsène Wenger just don't realise what a good thing they are enjoying. They are the only English team I've seen who can play like the great Brazilian sides. I was lucky enough to see Pelé in the flesh, playing for Santos in a friendly at Hillsborough. I was 13, Pelé would have been about 21. To someone brought up on English football of the time it was like watching a different game. The way they passed it around was fantastic, and whenever Pelé touched the ball time seemed to stand still. He scored from a penalty which I still see clearly because he walked up to it, dummied, watched the goalkeeper dive one way, then rolled it into the other side of the net. No one had seen that before. Then Sheffield Wednesday got a penalty and Colin Dobson, their winger, tried to follow suit. But the keeper didn't buy the dummy. He just waited and picked up Dobson's shot.

I'd loved to have played like that, but you need the players. Playing long-ball at County wasn't a choice, it was a necessity. I know Crewe knock it about now but in the lower divisions twenty years ago you couldn't pass it around for fun. We tried playing a lot of football to start with at Plymouth and were bottom and winless after five games. We'd spent money too. I changed it and we never looked back.

Obviously I've had better players at more recent clubs, and the game is more conducive to passing now, but I still want the fans to go home thinking they've seen some action: shots, crosses, saves and so on. I'd be hopeless managing England, not that I'd ever get the chance. All that passing 20 times to get to the halfway line, it bores me daft. I really think we should play our natural game, play at a good tempo – you do have to gamble sometimes. Remember when Manchester United were 2–0 down at West Ham a couple of seasons ago and Sir Alex Ferguson moved Ryan Giggs to left-back, gave it a right go and won 4–2? No other manager would have done that, but that's one reason he is so successful. A lot of people think if you are winning a game you should put a defender on or a midfielder and kill the game. Why? Why not keep doing what earned you the lead to start with rather than invite pressure?

In recent years I've changed my opinion on going down to ten men. We had a man sent off at Palace against Reading, we went without a man up front, played two wide and let their centre-halves have it. We lost to a late goal – a disputed one, mind. Two years later, at QPR, we had Hogan Ephraim sent off at Reading. This time I decided to go three up front and we won through a late Wayne Routledge goal. I think that is a better way of playing now. I go 4–2–3. It's hard for the two midfielders but the wide lads come in to help.

But you can over-complicate things. When Barcelona came to Loftus Road to train ahead of a Champions League match at Arsenal I went along to watch. They didn't work on free-kicks, they didn't work on shape, and they didn't work on marking. They just knocked the ball around in circles, having fun. I guess when you have players like that perhaps you can just let them go out and play. I'd love to find out. What was obvious to everyone was their team spirit. When you see how hard Lionel Messi works that is no surprise. Everyone else in the team will think, 'He's the best player in the world, and he's putting in a shift for the team, I'd better do the same.' Hard work and talent, that's the recipe for success.

Mind you, if I could have smuggled one or two of those players off the pitch and into a QPR shirt for our next match, I'd have done it. I'm sure they'd have enjoyed playing against Ipswich with us.

Chapter Five

Matchday

I love football and all the build-up to a game, but I absolutely hate matchdays. I wake up with a knot in the stomach and it never goes away until the final whistle.

Sam Allardyce

HOWEVER LONG YOU HAVE BEEN IN THE GAME THE FIRST match of the season is a nervous one. You've done all you can on the training pitch; you think you are ready, but you don't really know until that first competitive match. Opening day results can be misleading but momentum is very important in football and you can't beat a good start. We got a fabulous one beating Barnsley 4–0. Mackie scored on his debut, which was good for him, Heider scored, Adel scored. Even Fitz Hall scored. I played five new signings, seven if you count Adel and Heider, and the new system worked well.

It was a great start, but I was nervous the following match too. I always am, I've been playing and managing in professional football for more than 40 years but I still get so nervous on match-day I cannot eat properly. It wasn't a problem when I played; with some clubs, if we were heading to the north east, we would stop at Scotch Corner about three hours before kick-off and have a fillet steak with loads of buttered toast. That was typical then. A club dietician would have a fit if he saw a player eating that on matchday now. In theory I can eat what I want as manager, but not in practice. I usually have a cup of tea after I've got up and let the dogs out. Then at ten I have breakfast and I eat as much as I can. I usually have a cheese, ham and red onion omelette with four slices of brown toast, and I eat and eat because I can't eat anything else until about six o'clock. If there's toast over I'll have marmalade.

Then I'll shave with the same razor as last week – if we've not lost – and follow the same routine in how I wash, shave, put my contact lenses in. Then I read the papers – I take five or six on a Saturday. About half-eleven I'll start getting ready. By 12 I'll be getting some nerves in my tummy. I'll drive in the same way as the last time we didn't lose, stop at the same lights, make sure I have the same things in my pockets. If I had a sweet or something similar last time we didn't lose I have one again.

I normally aim to get to the ground about an hour-and-a-half before kick-off if we're away. Some grounds you don't want to get to any earlier as they are such a dump. If it's at home I'll arrive two hours before, especially when I was in London when you had to factor in traffic jams. Once there I always try and sign everybody's autograph when I get off the bus, or out of the car at home games. As a kid I waited one night at Sheffield United for a player until about seven. It was chucking it down and I was wet through. The player came out and I asked him for his autograph and he said, as he rushed past, 'Sorry, I'm too late.' I thought, 'If I ever get famous I am never going to refuse an autograph.' People will write in now having read this and say I have refused them, but I always try to sign as long as people are not rude.

We'll go to the dressing room where the players will start their individual routines, put on their strappings, have massages and so on. They will have their music on which is when I usually shoot off; it seems to get louder and less tuneful every season and it does my head in. I always say to them: 'I'm sure this record will be remembered in 50 years' time.' At Leeds I got so fed up I made them listen to my music: Motown. I'm sure they played better after listening to Marvin Gaye and Jr. Walker & the All Stars.

If I have family with me I'll take them upstairs and have a chat and a coffee. There was a lot of comment about the England players having caffeine tablets before matches after that World Cup qualifier was rained off in Poland. Because they hadn't played they hadn't got the caffeine out of their system and needed sleeping pills to get to sleep that night. I've never given my players caffeine tablets, but I usually have a couple of cups of coffee in the 90 minutes before kick-off in the belief it will sharpen me up.

Then I go down and see the lads. I have a laugh and a joke, there'll be bits and bobs I have picked up in the papers that morning, anything to help relax them. If we are away from home I'll have gone into the dressing room with them. These can vary; as a player in the lower divisions in the sixties and seventies I was used to some very basic facilities, real Sunday league stuff. One of the smallest was Millwall's at the old Den, but the dressing room was the least of your worries. Walking down the tunnel, with the fans baying for your blood, was the most intimidating walk I've ever experienced.

Many of the grounds have nice facilities now, especially the new ones, but there are still some which are like going back in time. Peterborough's has old-fashioned charm, but the showers at

Burnley could do with a makeover. Bloomfield Road used to be even worse but they have a new stand now, which has made a big difference. Inevitably away dressing rooms are rarely as good as the home ones though QPR was an exception. Ours was a disgrace, the visitors had five-star luxury. Apparently the guy who did it thought a nice away dressing room might help us attract players – I soon swapped them over.

Next Mick Jones and I will talk about the game. I'll go back in the dressing room again, then take the team-sheet into the ref's room and have a bit of banter with the officials. Some managers let their assistants or captains do that but I think it is important to show respect and go in to speak to the officials myself before a game. I'll have a look at the opposition team-sheet, give a copy to Mick and tell the lads their team.

Unless there's an injury doubt that might change things I'll have told our lads our team on the Friday. I don't see any point in keeping them on tenterhooks waiting to see if they're in the team. Usually I'll have spoken to the ones who have been left out, and might have expected to play, in advance. My first manager, Jimmy McGuigan at Chesterfield, used to simply pin a team-sheet up and we'd all gather round to see who was in the team. That's no way to find out. The exception was my last few weeks at QPR. It was quite obvious to me most of the new signings that season only thought about themselves, they didn't care about me or the staff. So I kept my distance and just told them the team.

Just once I've named a team a week in advance, in my final season at Crystal Palace. We were due to play West Brom, who were the Championship leaders and had just won 5–0 at Middlesbrough, who had been second. I told the players how we were going to play, and how we were going to beat them. I could see all their little young faces thinking, 'We lost 4–0 to Scunthorpe at home last week, what's he on about?' We worked and worked on a system. We had Sean Scannell up front, quick and small with Victor Moses and Darren Ambrose playing off him. We also had this big midfield player, Alassane N'Diaye. We had no height so he had to go for every goal-kick and free-kick. We beat them one-nil and N'Diaye scored the winner. I saw Jeremy Peace, Albion's chairman, afterwards and he said, 'I knew something would happen with you being here. I smelt it.' I do love upsetting the odds.

About 45 minutes before kick-off the players go out for their warm-up and I change into my tracksuit. When Sheffield United were promoted into the Premier League I decided to wear a suit on the touchline and went out and bought a couple of good ones. I had this feeling that referees would be more favourably disposed towards me if I looked smart. There's since been some university research suggesting players pay more attention to managers in suits on a matchday. Well, it didn't work for me. We got what I thought was a diabolical decision given against us in the opening game, when Rob Styles gave a penalty against us. He said it was 'for intent' after Chris Morgan attempted to tackle Steven Gerrard but never actually touched him. Keith Hackett, the referee's chief, later told me there is no such thing as 'intent' but it was too late. Then we lost the next two. To top it all they must have been the warmest three days of the year and I'd have been hot under the collar even if the refs had been perfect. I then figured if a tracksuit was good enough for Brian Clough and Martin O'Neill it would be good enough for me.

When the team is out, I like to be on my own for a minute to collect my thoughts, so I also kick all the staff out. I put my set-pieces up – how we defend theirs, how we execute ours – on a flip chart, along with some general bits of information about the opposition that I didn't tell them the previous day. The IT man will have already pinned up some information about set-pieces around the room.

This is my time to reflect before the game, though a couple of seasons ago it was interrupted when my phone went. I answered and a guy said: 'Mr Warnock? It's Specsavers here. Your contact lenses have arrived. Will you be picking them up?' He obviously didn't know who I was, or what I was likely to be doing at 20 to three on a Saturday afternoon.

The players will come in about quarter to kick-off and I'll tell them to have five minutes before we sit down. You can't usually tell how they will play from the way they are in the dressing room so I always ask my coach, Ronnie Jepson now at Leeds, Keith Curle at Palace and QPR, how they were in the warm-up. If they say, 'A bit quiet, gaffer,' I'll do a bit more in my team-talk.

The team-talk is vital. I know some managers say the preparation on the training ground during the week is the most important thing, but so are team talks. I'll send out the subs to warm up, and anyone else I don't need there, so it is just the eleven that are playing. I want them to concentrate, to focus. There'll be about four or five minutes now before the bell goes to send us out. I'll make sure everyone is sat down. I'll reinforce some points about the opposition, remind them how we want to put the other team under pressure, and try to gee them up. I always have three or four minutes and I'll finish with something like 'Come on. Let's go.'

There'll be a few lads with superstitions. One wants to be last out, one wants to be first after the goalie, one wants to put his shirt on as he goes out, another wants to do his hair at the last moment. At Leeds, Michael Brown always liked to be last, but Dioufy was slow getting out. Brownie was sometimes waiting for him so long I'd be saying 'Come on, they'll have kicked off.' After they go out, the staff will follow, and before we go to the dug-out I'll say hello to the other manager.

The first thing I'll do is clear the dug-out area of any litter, water bottles, paper, tape, that sort of thing. I hate any litter in my area, I tell the staff all the time during the game, 'Get rid of that bottle', 'Clear that away'. Dug-outs vary a lot. The worst one must have been at Oldham. It was half-way up the stand. I used to have to run 25 steps to get to the touchline. Leeds is horrible, I can never sit there. It is so low down I'm never able to get out, and you can't see what is going on. That means I stand up all game. Unfortunately you are exposed to the elements and can get absolutely soaked.

The dug-outs need to be about 30 yards apart, then you can operate without risking an unnecessary confrontation with the other managers, and get messages on without being overheard. At QPR they are right on top of each other, which is not great. Ideally you have a little bit of protection from fans too, but at some grounds they are right behind you.

At the Emirates the technical areas are a long way apart. When I went there with Sheffield United for my thousandth game as a manager I stood with Arsène Wenger in the centre-circle and turned towards them. I said, 'Look at the dug-outs, Arsène, they are miles apart, you'll never hear me.'

He pondered, looked down at me from his great height, smiled wryly and said, 'You will find a way.'

There's a bit of thought gone into the positioning at some clubs. Quite a few have swapped dug-outs so the home one is able to influence the linesman on that side (referee's assistants always run the right-wing while the referee runs a diagonal from right-back to left-wing).

I've never been one to write things down on pieces of paper like some managers do. All mine is in my head. During games people think I'm always shouting at the ref but most of the time I'm shouting at the nearest player to get a message on to someone else. Maybe we need to swap markers around, or if a midfield player is going into a dangerous area you need to tell the team how to cope with him. The opposition might be playing differently to what you expected, or they might change something, so we would be thinking how we can negate that. Away from home, whenever you stand up the crowd start screaming at you. Portsmouth's the noisiest, every time you dare stand up you get dog's abuse. Neither you nor the players can hear a word unless they are right on the touchline next to you. It must be brilliant to have that crowd on your side.

You also shout at players to give them a gee-up, or a wake-up. Most need it every now and then. Then when we've scored a goal I always try and get the lads to concentrate because then you are vulnerable. I stress to them the need to try to get the ball back immediately when we have scored a goal, and the need to attack the opposition quickly if we've conceded one.

Wingers are always in the frontline for a manager's rollicking as they are closest, but I think most have been pleased to have me as a manager because I was a winger and I understand the position. Wingers always get the blame from fans and managers, 'They don't tackle, they don't head it, they don't do enough,' but you rely on everyone else as a winger. You need teammates to give you the ball in the right area, so I see a lot more plusses than minuses in wingers. I always say it is easier to be a defender than a forward, as you have to be negative; a forward has to create things, which is far more difficult.

At full-time I always have a word with them, whatever the result. If they have lost a game they will be quiet, so I walk around in the shower area for two or three minutes while they get their drinks. I'll have a chat in there to my coaches about the game, then I'll come back to the main dressing room and have a say. If we've lost I'll probably give one or two rollickings as to why I thought we lost – individuals who didn't do what they were told, who we asked to do something and ignored it. Occasionally I'll flip my lid and let it all go. Smoke comes out of your ears when you are frustrated at losing a game you thought you could have won because of individual errors. My defence know what to expect, every week you see someone on *Match of the Day* trying to shield the ball to go out who ends up conceding a goal. Come Monday morning all my defenders are thinking, 'Thank God that weren't me,' because they know I want it kicked into row Z.

But I'll also sit them down, when they have got a result that outweighs what people expected and tell them how proud I am of them, and why they got that result – why an individual or a group has got us a win when no one has given us a chance. I'll tell them to 'Enjoy these moments because this is what you want, this is what you play for. For games and results like that, for feeling like you do tonight.'

The lads will then go out for a warm-down and I'll have a bath. Someone will bring me a cup of tea and I'll think about the game, about what the fans will be saying as they go home. At Sheffield I would cast my mind back to when I went to Bramall Lane with my dad. We'd walk round the corner, past the Territorial Army camp, up the hill, and I'd say to him, 'It was brilliant today, Dad, wasn't it?'

It was devastating for me to leave Sheffield United the way I did, relegated with the last kick of the season, especially with the Carlos Tevez affair being so crucial. For those unfamiliar with the case, Tevez was playing for West Ham at the time and during the season it emerged that his signing not only broke regulations, but West Ham covered it up when the Premier League first investigated. They should have had points deducted – standard practice when a player is ineligible to play because his registration is invalid – but instead they were fined £5.5m and allowed to continue playing him. Tevez was West Ham's best player and of course it had to be him who scored the only goal at Old Trafford on the last day of the season. If West Ham had lost that day they would have gone down instead of us.

I know my evidence helped Sheffield United receive £25m compensation from West Ham, but I never received a penny of it myself – even though it cost me my job and my staying-up bonus. Funny game, football. But I've always been a big believer in fate and it may be the best thing that ever happened to me. Moving to London and managing Palace and QPR gave me a new lease of life. I went back to Yorkshire, with Leeds, re-invigorated.

Then I'll go and talk to the press. I'm usually quite happy working with media men, even the snakes, but those press conferences can be difficult. It wasn't much fun after QPR lost 6–0 at Fulham, or when Leeds shipped seven at home to Nottingham Forest. Even when QPR battered Manchester City but lost 3–2, and the press were saying, 'You played well today, great performance,' deep down I was hurting because I knew we could have beaten those billionaire players but for a couple of defensive errors. Instead we got nothing because praise doesn't get you up the table.

Usually after the game, win or lose, you nip into the other manager's office. You do the press then make five minutes to pop your head in. There's nobody in our league I don't try and see. It's courtesy. You talk about other results, who you and they are playing next, a bit about the game. If you've won, though you're happy, you try not to show it as you realise what the other guy is going through so you don't rub it in. Likewise if you've lost they try and be constructive, maybe mention the things they thought we did well, they are obviously happy and you want to get off but you always stay a few minutes. A few times you are with the press so long they've had to shoot off to get the bus, or sometimes the plane, but they'll tell Mick to give me their regards.

All the British and Irish managers take part, right up to Sir Alex, but the foreign managers don't do it as much. It doesn't seem part of their culture to socialise with the opposition the same way we do, even when they have been here for years. I think I've been in once to Arsène's office at the Emirates, with QPR – we had a picture taken with Amy and Will. Jose Mourinho was quite amicable, but he didn't invite us in for a drink. With Andre Villas-Boas I didn't really expect him to have a glass of wine at our place after my QPR beat his Chelsea team, and they finished with nine in the match made infamous by the John Terry-Anton Ferdinand affair. You accept in some games they won't be coming in. My Leeds team also beat Spurs in the FA Cup so I suppose AVB will be glad when I retire.

Staff are normally invited in, so Mick and whoever is my coach at the time will go in while I do the press. Sometimes the physio will be invited in as well if the opposing physio is in there. Then I'll join them. I'll have a glass of wine or something, there'll usually be a few bottles of beer there. Sometimes there'll be sandwiches or slices of pizza. A lot of places the families are there too, the wives and children. Offices are bigger than they used to be so that's often possible now – when I went to Leeds I walked into the biggest office I've ever had.

If we're away it's then time to get on the bus for the drive home. We often go by train but always come back by bus, except for the rare occasions we've flown and can get a flight back. If we're at home I might then go to the boardroom, it depends on the club. Early in my career I always went to the boardroom after doing the press and team and had five minutes with the chairman. With Derek Pavis at Notts County we used to finish with the kids running around in a room next door. At Crystal Palace I'd always go up and speak to Simon Jordan. He was an intelligent man football-wise, Simon, he would always come up with some constructive suggestions and he would spot things. Sometimes he would come down to see me, because by the time I'd done team, press and the opposition manager it was quarter to six. It was the same at Sheffield; directors would sometimes come down to my office. I've never been one to insist they keep out – it was probably more sociable below stairs than in the boardroom.

By then I'll have seen the family if they are there, and I'll have had something to eat. Having not eaten since breakfast I'm usually ravenous. Then I'll go home. Sharon normally drives if she's there as about half-six the tiredness, that feeling you get when the adrenalin wears off, hits me. By half-seven, ideally, I'll be home and relaxing in my pyjamas. Sometimes I've not been living so close to home and I may have to drive myself. Then I can normally stave off the tiredness until nine. Soon after I got to Leeds I decided to use a driver. It's a long way from Leeds to Cornwall, five hours minimum, and I realised doing it myself would kill me. There is a flight from Exeter to Leeds/Bradford in the morning but the first time I did it the flight was cancelled at short notice and I had to hire a car, a Golf, and drive up in the pouring rain. We had to put training back to 4pm. Then come October 1st they cancelled the flight until March.

Match of the Day is a Saturday night staple. It's a good package. It gives me the opportunity to look at all the controversial incidents and listen to the managers' response and make my own judgement. It has certainly come in handy doing my column for the *Independent* as it enables me to analyse things without watching ten hours of video. I've been on *Match of the Day 2* a number of times, and I have enjoyed it. I worked with Alan Hansen and found him very intelligent and articulate – and a big favourite with the women, though I am not sure why! My favourite pundit though is on Sky: Gary Neville. I think Gary is outstanding and he's brought a fresh voice. It would be easier for him to sit on the fence but not only is he articulate he doesn't pull any punches and his analysis has been excellent.

I don't mind if the programme finishes quite late, as I can't sleep immediately after a game, my mind is going at 100mph. The result doesn't make as much difference as you'd think, win, lose or draw you are still running through the game in your head. I used to take a sleeping tablet, but I began to have problems sleeping without them, which was a bit of a worry. I cut down to half a tablet and gradually managed to wean myself off them. I don't know how insomniacs cope. It must be very easy to get hooked on them.

Chapter Six

Lucky Shorts

You want to try sitting in the dug-out when it is your arse in the bacon slicer.

Mick McCarthy after being told he looked tense
during a game

I'M NOT A GREAT FAN OF INTERNATIONAL FOOTBALL. I can't get excited about all that sideways passing. It doesn't suit England either. We should play with some tempo, and a smile on our faces. The players always seem terrified of making a mistake, especially at Wembley.

I'm even less a fan of international breaks. The only good thing about them is they provide managers with a lull in which to recharge and maybe get away with the family. I've managed to get as far afield as New York and Morocco during international breaks, though normally we opt for a few days in Cornwall. However, this means the season is longer than it need be and fixtures are squeezed in more tightly, so it is of no great benefit for managers in the long-term.

Then there is how it affects your international players. First there is the risk of injury. I once watched Taarbs play an international and every time he went down I worried he was injured. That's the worst thing about international weeks and I do feel for managers when that happens to one of their players, but even if they do not get injured they often return so exhausted by the travelling it damages your preparation for the next game. Heidar Helguson at QPR went to Cyprus to play a friendly for Iceland. He was flown straight back to Iceland after the game, then had to come back to London the following day. By then he was stiff and aching. Yet some Icelandic officials had stayed overnight in Cyprus then flown to England to watch their U21s play. Why didn't they do that for Heider? When Rob Snodgrass was at Leeds United he went to Slovenia with Scotland to play half-an-hour in front of a massive crowd of 4,200. He then flew back to Glasgow getting back at 4am Thursday morning. After a few hours sleep he had to drive to Leeds. Why can't Scotland stay overnight in Slovenia to preserve the players' sleep patterns, and then fly back? Are they that hard up? In my experience, when you do something like Rob did you feel absolutely shattered for 48 hours. It's is not exactly good preparation for a game. When international teams don't look after your players you are bound to feel angry.

At least that was a fair match. Kaspars Gorkss went off to Turkey in February 2011, in the middle of our promotion campaign, to play for Latvia against Bolivia in a double-header with a match between Bulgaria and Estonia. Yes, that's right, the host team, Turkey, were not even playing. Seven goals were scored in the two games, all of them penalties including one that was retaken after being missed. Suspicious? Fifa thought so. They had an investigation and banned the referees involved for life – the players were not implicated. Meanwhile Kaspars came back so tired he was unable to finish our weekend match against Nottingham Forest.

Some of the games just seem pointless, and there was never a better example than the opening week of the 2010–11 season. How did I build on that 4–0 start against Barnsley? By waving goodbye to three of my key players. Adel jetted off to Africa to play for Morocco in an eagerly awaited match against those superstars from Equatorial Guinea. Heider flew to Iceland to play in a real clash of the giants with Liechtenstein, finishing in a gripping 1–1 draw. And Kaspars boosted his confidence in a Latvian defence that conceded four in a friendly against the Czech Republic. Meanwhile, back in Blighty, I had to field a weakened team in the Carling Cup first round against Port Vale, and lost 3–1 in front of 6,619 disgruntled Hoops fans.

Fortunately my trio of adventurers returned unscathed from their jaunts to play at Bramall Lane where a fantastic 3–0 win had the edge taken off it by the Blades sacking manager Kevin Blackwell, who had been my assistant when I was at Sheffield United, immediately after the match. It was just two games into the season and the first had been a very good draw at Cardiff. I did wonder whether Kevin McCabe, the chairman, would have been so hasty if the defeat hadn't been against a club I managed.

I was also disappointed at the way some United fans barracked Paddy Kenny, after the years of good service he had given the club. Paddy said all he needed to by keeping a clean sheet. In fairness to those fans they didn't know the full story. Sheffield United were upset that having, they said, supported Paddy through his nine-month drug ban he activated a clause in his contract allowing him to leave for £750,000. What they did not say was that while he was banned he had to take a big pay cut on the understanding that if he proved his fitness after the ban was up he would be given a new deal. As the ban, until the final few weeks, extended to the training ground, Paddy had to train alone for eight months, hiring a personal trainer and working out six days a week. He was so fit when he came back he went straight into the first team, yet Sheffield didn't produce a new contract until QPR made a bid for him.

Paddy was banned for taking an over-the-counter medicine he'd bought because he had a cold. It turned out to include a prohibited substance. The scientist who tested him said he would have to take 50-odd tablets just before kick-off to get a performance-enhancing effect, which would only last a few minutes anyway, but rules are rules. I guess when you see what happened in cycling with Lance Armstrong you have to be vigilant even if Paddy's ban did seem over-the-top. I did wonder how it was that Paddy got a nine-month ban after unknowingly taking a banned substance, but a couple of years later Manchester City's Kolo Touré only got six months for failing a test after he apparently took his wife's slimming pills.

The issue is a nightmare for managers. The list of banned drugs is huge; there are thousands of things you cannot take, more than any individual could possibly keep track of, even an expert. A lot of them are in everyday things that you or I would take without even thinking about it, even Lemsip used to be on the banned list – I don't think it is now, but I certainly wouldn't let any of my players take it without checking. I tell my players over and again. Don't guess – ask. If you have a cold, or an infection, or anything you might need to tale a pill for, check it is OK with the club doctor first.

We have to tell the drug-testing organisation where our players are going to be every day of the week, as my secretary reminds me whenever I change the players' day off. We also have to notify them if an individual has a day off for a personal issue or medical appointment or something, so they can be found at the drop of a hat on any particular day. The testers come maybe five times a year at training and matches combined, testing two or three players each time. They draw lots to decide who to test. I sometimes say, if someone's been really poor in the previous match, 'Can you test him?' They don't take any notice. What annoys me is when we've played an away game that's several hours drive back, especially at night, and everyone has to wait on the coach while the lads doing a drug test try and produce a sample. After a match players can take ages to pass water, they are inevitably dehydrated. I've asked why the testers can't supply a car to take those players home, then at least the coach can go and the other lads can get to their beds. It is not as if we can arrange a car in advance as the tests are random and a surprise.

I can understand a need for testing but I don't think football has a problem with drugs, whether recreational or performance-enhancing. There might be a few silly players who take something when they are out in a club but I think cheating is very rare. I admit in my early management career I gave a player who said he felt a bit off-colour (he was a noted hypochondriac) a pill with the instructions, 'Don't ask any questions – but take this and you'll be fine.' He played magnificently, he thought I'd given him something special. It was an aspirin. That's probably banned now.

The win at Sheffield gave us a record of played two, won two, scored seven, and conceded none. It couldn't last, but it did. We won the first three games without conceding a goal; we then ended August by snatching a draw at Derby despite being 2–0 down after 88 minutes. That showed the spirit of the side. I added Tommy Smith and Rob Hulse as the transfer window closed to give us a bit more depth up front, then watched as we won the next four games without conceding a goal, and Mackie banging them in from all angles.

When a team is doing well it lifts the whole atmosphere around a club, from the secretaries to the directors. The mood in the dressing room was so buoyant my biggest problem was preventing the players from over-doing it. Everyone wanted to come into training and they lingered over lunch together. I really enjoyed seeing all the different personalities knit together.

Not that there wasn't the occasional hiccup. We got a cracking win at Ipswich but the press made a fuss about Adel kicking a water bottle when I substituted him. 'It looked as if he was aiming at you,' they suggested with glee. 'If he had, he'd have hit me,' I replied, 'because he's been spot on in his shooting this season.'

I wasn't going to make a big deal of it. Players shouldn't be happy at being substituted. I took Adel off in most games, partly because he was a key player and I needed to protect him. We had a small squad and we certainly didn't have another Adel. He also lacked a bit of stamina and conditioning because he didn't train as hard as he could, so he was going to be prone to injuries if he played the full 90 minutes.

The drama wasn't over though. We picked up some of the lads at Waltham Abbey on the way to Ipswich, as it is more convenient for them. When we dropped them back after the game the driver took the wrong turning back on to the M25. We suddenly realised we were heading back east instead of going west. Unfortunately you can't turn round at the next junction, with the M11, so we ended up driving down the M11 and then through central London to our training ground near Heathrow. Luckily for the driver we were in a good mood after winning 3–0 so the banter was light-hearted. I felt bloody tired though, when I got home towards 2am. Not that I sleep much after a game.

We then had a run of draws, six in seven, which was frustrating as they don't do you much good in the era of three-points-for-a-win and it meant we slipped behind Cardiff City into second. I could have done without that because Flavio was reported telling the press in Italy he would make Marcello Lippi QPR manager if we got into the Premier League. Lippi's last job was winning the World Cup with Italy.

Sharon said she quite liked the idea of me winning promotion then being paid up, but I didn't so I asked Flavio what was going on. He claimed he spoke to a journalist who was talking generally about Italian managers working in England – Fabio Capello, Carlo Ancelotti and Roberto Mancini. Then Flavio said it had always been his dream to take QPR into the Premier League and have Marcello Lippi as his manager. He assured me he did not mean it to happen now. I told Flavio 'It doesn't bother me,' but inevitably the press asked me about it. They said, 'Do you think Marcello Lippi would enjoy managing QPR?' I said: 'I'm sure he will enjoy managing QPR reserves.'

The unbeaten run was good for confidence but not good for my legs, which were slowly turning blue. Let me explain. As you may have gathered from aspects of my match-day routine, I am superstitious. While I have tried to cut down on my superstitions I have not really succeeded. When my grandson, Charlie, came to his first full game all the family was on tenterhooks. They know if anyone new comes to a game and the result goes against us I usually ban them. Fortunately QPR won.

A lot of football people are superstitious, but I have to admit I'm a bit of a bad case; you might call it a sad case. I used to put a new razor blade in on a Friday morning, and if we won on a

Saturday I kept that same blade in until we lost. If we lost I put a new blade in the following week even if I didn't need one. If we won I used to wear the same shirt, same suit, same tie, same underwear. At Rotherham I remember having the same jockstrap. We went on an 18-game unbeaten run, I used to whistle it to me. At Huddersfield I had a lucky pair of underpants. We went about 17 games without losing, a run that culminated in winning a Wembley play-off final. The lads threw me in the bath afterwards. They may have been celebrating, but maybe they just wanted to make sure the pants got a wash before next season. I would also try a different route to the ground if we lost, except when I got to Leeds I ran out of roads to use.

So what has this got to do with cold legs? At the start of the season, when it was hot, I wore shorts. As our unbeaten run continued I continued wearing shorts. Gradually the mercury dropped, but we still didn't lose. By the time it was November, and we were playing evening midweek matches, I was absolutely perishing and really feeling it where I had a hip resurface. Sharon thought I was bonkers, and to make it worse I began thinking about wearing some tights (not hers I'd like to stress). It's not that I'm a cross-dresser or anything, but in my playing days I once copied a tip from Jimmy Robertson, the old Spurs and Ipswich player who was at Crewe with me. Jimmy said he often wore tights as it prevented muscle injuries. Older readers will recall Keith Weller wore some in a televised game around that time. I thought, 'Why not?' I scored a goal, but then pulled my hamstring. So much for tights.

So I had slightly mixed feelings when Tommy Smith scored our 90th minute equaliser at Portsmouth in mid-November. It was great to nick a point – one we deserved – but as I lay soaking in a hot bath at 1am, still trying to thaw out despite two hours in the warmth of the coach and my car, I did fleetingly think, as I pondered the weather forecast for the weekend (two inches of snow), 'Would it have been so damaging if Tommy had missed?' Then I thought, 'What am I thinking? I hope I'm still shivering like this in February'.

Our run didn't quite extend that far, but it did get deep into December. Cardiff City had briefly overtaken us in the league but we beat them on a marvellous afternoon at Loftus Road with Adel scoring twice to give ourselves a bit of breathing space. It was the sort of result to give us momentum but the next game at Hull was called off because of bad weather, we struggled even to get a training session on as there was snow everywhere. By the time we got back into action after a fortnight's break we were caught cold and run ragged by Watford at home. We lost 3–1 and it could have been six though we had a cert penalty early on which the ref missed – which didn't surprise me on the day.

Still, at least it meant I could finally put those trackie bottoms on. At last.

Chapter Seven

The Referee's Always Right?

It is a great profession being a referee. They are never wrong.

Arsène Wenger

IN THE MID-70S THERE WAS AN OCCASION WHEN A PART-time referee went to ref a match on a military base in Lincolnshire. The conditions were awful and, to make matters worse, the pitch sloped uphill. The home side, kicking up the slope, raced into a 3–0 lead before they had a certain penalty to make it 4–0 before half-time.

The referee thought, 'If I give this then the second half'll be a massacre, kicking downhill they'll get another five or six. I won't enjoy that.' So he didn't give the penalty.

In the second half the visiting team came back and scored four goals, winning 4–3.

When the game finished the referee headed quickly to his car, pausing as he passed the club secretary to say, 'Put my expenses into the club funds.' It was the only way he could think would compensate them.

Yes, I was that referee. It was while I was playing at Scunthorpe and reffing in the lower leagues. So I know refs don't always get it right, and then when they get it wrong it's sometimes – only sometimes, mind – for the very best of reasons.

I always try to bear this incident in mind when I'm cursing the latest decision to go against my team.

It is not always their fault, the way the laws have to be applied now means they are not allowed to use the 18th law: common sense. I grew up watching my dad referee around Sheffield; he used to talk his way though games, managing the players. Some refs now seem to regard themselves as above that.

I am worried about the standard of officials. We seem to have gone back ten years. We have a generation of referees coming through who, as Bill Shankly used to say, know the laws but not the game. Most of them have never kicked a ball, not even at a decent youth level because to get to the top as a ref now you have to start young. They get all the simple decisions right, but because they don't understand the game they get big ones wrong. Usually it is the controversial and most important ones. They are manu-factured referees, but why am I surprised? Mike Riley was just like that, and he is now the ref's chief. It is as if he is cloning himself.

A good example of refs not using common sense, and being bound by the laws, cropped up when Jose Mourinho was fined and banned by Uefa after two of his Real Madrid players were sent off in a Champions League tie. Real were 4–0 up at Ajax when Xabi Alonso and Sergio Ramos started wasting time and got themselves a second booking. That meant they were suspended from a group game that was meaningless for Real as they had already won their group, and would start the knockout stage with a clean slate. If refs applied common sense neither the players nor the managers would get away with it. A ref should know which players are close to suspension, so he can react accordingly. With Real the ref, Scotland's Craig Thomson, should have realised what was happening. Four-nil up with a few minutes left there is no need to waste time. He should have said to them, 'I know what you're doing, you can take all night but you're not going off. I'll just keep adding on time.'

Everyone does this. If you have an easy game coming up and a vital player in danger of missing it you get that suspension out of the way. One of my players once had that threat hanging over him, he knew we had a game the following week against a team struggling at the bottom before, another seven days later, facing our toughest rivals. He decided to get a booking and take his suspension for the first game. But he had to work for it – a bad tackle didn't get him a card so he kicked the ball away when the ref was walking towards him to make sure. In the end we won both games, the first without him and the second with.

There's a few refs you can still have a conversation with. After QPR lost against Watford we lost again, at Leeds. The cameras caught me in the tunnel afterwards having a go at the referee, Scott Mathieson – he's one you want when there's 30,000 screaming – as I thought he'd missed the worst tackle of the game by Bradley Johnson on Jamie Mackie. Our lads were incensed and Clint Hill got himself booked because of that, which wouldn't have happened if the ref had seen Johnson's foul. The cameras also caught Scott having a go back – he replied if my lads had made as few mistakes as he had we'd have won. For once I was almost lost for words.

It wasn't Scott that I had the hump with most though, or even our lads though we started slow and made a terrible error for their second goal. What really annoyed me was the way Leeds celebrated. Some really went over the top in the tunnel and the dressing room so I just said to them, 'Let's see where you are at the end of the season eh? I just hope you need a result on the last day because you're at our place.' The only consolation of the trip was the chance to stop over in Harrogate with James, Sarah and new grandson, Charlie.

We had a couple of good wins over Swansea and Coventry, both of whom were in the promotion frame, but then had more bad luck with officials when we lost at Norwich. We were up against Grant Holt. He's a really good pro who has worked his way up from playing in the Northern Premier League with Barrow to the Premier League, but he can be infuriating to play against. Holt is one of the most professional I've seen at getting decisions from referees. I noticed he'd won a penalty against Sheffield United the previous week and in the paper afterwards one of their players said he'd admitted he'd tricked the ref. So before going to Norwich I cut the bit in the paper out and highlighted the comments about him and made sure the linesman got a copy before the game.

Our referee was Jon Moss. Last time I'd given him a low mark and said he wasn't fit enough to referee at Championship level and was guessing decisions as he wasn't up with play. Somehow he heard about it, I suppose, because when I handed the team sheets in he made some comments about his fitness. I thought, 'We'll do well to get something today.' As luck would have it at 0–0 Holt was put clear and Matt Connolly pulled him down. It's never a goalscoring opportunity as Holt would have been caught long before he could get a shot in. He was still 50 yards from goal and he's not much quicker than me – and I'm in my sixties. It wasn't a surprise when Moss sent Connolly off, but it was when Moss was promoted to the Premier League list at the end of the season. The good thing is he lives in Leeds so he couldn't referee me when I went there.

I never had much luck with refs against Norwich while I was at QPR. The following season, when both clubs had been promoted, we were winning one-nil when Joey Barton, who had scored, was sent off for putting his head towards Bradley Johnson. Johnson, who'd not been spotted by the officials having a go at Joey just minutes earlier, went down but nothing happened for a minute or two until Holt drew the ref's attention to his mate who was still rolling around. Then the linesman, who'd kept his flag down, suddenly thinks he's seen something. The ref speaks to him and Joey is sent off. We lose 2–1. I was fired before the next league game.

Looking back at this I was unhappy about a conversation I had before the match with Phil Dowd, the fourth official. The referee was Neil Swarbrick, who I once gave a mark of 100 after a poor game in the Championship with the comment: 'I hope this will get him into the Premier League.' More fool me because it turned out Swarbrick had been told this and remembered it because he had mentioned it to Phil. I'm not in any way suggesting it influenced his performance, but he obviously had it on his mind before the game. The next season QPR got a couple of fortuitous decisions at Norwich and took a point. Some might say that proves these things even up, but not for me, as it was a different manager benefiting.

Marks, incidentally, are allocated on a form every manager fills in after a game. We are asked to judge the ref in various categories relating to their control of the match. There is also a space for comments. Some managers don't bother but I usually use this to try and be constructive. I've had good feedback from the referees' society over my input, though I realise it goes in one ear and out the other most of the time.

I used to think officials were biased against me personally, because I had been critical of them in the past. I felt this especially when I was in the top flight with Sheffield United, but after other newly promoted clubs, like Blackpool a few seasons later, had similar misfortune I realised big clubs tend to get more decisions for two reasons. One is that the bigger teams tend to have 70 per cent of the game against smaller sides so inevitably they will have more penalty appeals and suchlike. Refs are only human, they will make mistakes, and the odds are that mistake will favour the bigger team, as the majority of penalty appeals will be made by them. It also means when a smaller team has a good penalty appeal rejected, probably their only appeal of the game, it is more noticeable – and more crucial as they may not get another chance.

But there's another reason the fact refs are only human benefits the bigger club. They know, deep down, if they give a decision in favour of Manchester United few notice. If they give a bad decision against them it's worldwide headlines. That's bound to be at the back of a ref's mind; he will want to be absolutely certain of his decision. Clearly Rob Styles wasn't when he failed to dismiss Gabriel Heinze and award a penalty after he had fouled Luton Shelton, of my Sheffield United team, at Old Trafford. Steve Bruce said, after his Wigan team had been done at Stamford Bridge, that as a Manchester United player he used to get the sort of decisions that were now going against him when he took 'little Wigan' to the big clubs. This is one reason I think we should have independent timekeepers. Everyone knows referees do not add as much time on in the first half as the second when there is a lot of pressure at certain, bigger, grounds to add time on when the home team are losing.

The big club syndrome is frustrating though. The 2010 FA Cup tie with Aston Villa, a match of crucial importance to Crystal Palace, was a case in point. We were 2–1 up with three minutes to go and the assistant Trevor Massey gave a corner instead of a goal kick when the ball had come off Nathan Delfouneso's legs.

In the TV interview I said the officials must have thought, 'We don't know which way to give it, so we'll give it to the Premier League team as they are losing.' The FA told me that questioned their integrity. I pleaded guilty and was fined.

When I got home that night, Sharon reminded me that in our game in the previous round Palace had taken the lead against Wolves from a corner that shouldn't have been given. I suppose I should have remembered that myself but as always it's what you see in front of you that you react to.

We went to Villa for the replay and at nil-nil Martin Atkinson awarded a corner instead of a goal-kick after the ball went off James Milner. Coincidence? They scored. Coming off I approached Atkinson. 'Are you 100 per cent sure it was a corner?' I asked.

'I wouldn't have given it otherwise,' he answered.

I wonder what he thought when the replay showed it was a goal-kick, but I don't think they give a damn. Both officials got Premier League games the week afterwards.

I don't think referees understand how important the first goal is. Although we got an equaliser we'd given it everything and lost to late two penalties – both correct decisions.

I do think refs could do with some help. I'm so glad we now have goalline technology coming in. If the resources are there, why not use them? It would have saved us a few years ago at Bristol City when we scored the 'ghost goal'. We'd just taken Freddie Sears on loan to Palace from West Ham and he scored a great goal only for the officials – all of them – to miss it after it bounced back off the back stanchion. It would have put us one-up. How did they miss it? Even the body language of the players gave it away. Guess what happened? City scored a last-minute winner and I had to walk down the pitch to the tunnel – which is in the corner at Ashton Gate – without reacting to 14,000 Bristolians slaughtering me, knowing it was a goal.

When it happened I asked Gary Johnson, their manager, to let us score, but no chance. I said to him, 'You'll regret it, what goes around comes around.' He never did anything after that at Bristol – now he's managing Yeovil. Simon went over the top, calling them cheats and so on in the boardroom, which didn't go down well. The goal caused such a stir even Gordon Brown, the Prime Minister, mentioned it when I went to a reception at 10 Downing Street sometime later. 'Unlucky that goal at Bristol,' he said. I was there with Sean Scannell, it was an event to promote the importance of apprenticeships and he had won the Championship Apprentice of the Year award.

I actually felt sorry for the officials; Rob Shoebridge was beside himself. I said to them, 'Do you know how hard my players have worked today to get nothing? Do you know what sweat and toil they have put in? They haven't been let down by a brilliant bit of play from the opposition, or some tactical genius, but by you four in this room.' These things can have consequences. If Palace had not got a draw at Hillsborough the last day of that season that result at Bristol would have sent them down. And what about poor Freddie Sears? He was 19 at the time; a goal would have given him the confidence to have a good spell with us. As it was he never did score at Palace and he only scored three goals in as many seasons from that day.

Bristol City was never a happy hunting ground for me. The previous year Palace conceded a late equaliser after referee Richard Beeby played a ridiculous amount of injury-time. I said to the lads after the match: 'I'm going to get fined now, watch my interview.' I went on TV and straight away they asked about the equaliser coming after so many extra minutes. I said, with a smile: 'I thought it were a bit out of order when the referee punched the air when they scored.' That cost me two grand in fines but I loved it and so did the players. It was one of the funniest things in my career, and I'm sure Richard laughs about it now.

Despite my lack of fortune I enjoy going to Ashton Gate. I have always felt Bristol City is a proper football club. Steve Lansdown, the chairman, has really had a go over the last few years and I look forward to going there when I move to Cornwall, as it will be my local Championship club.

I don't think the fifth official is much of an improvement when it comes to spotting such goals. While you have humans you will have human error, we just want goalline technology. Not for offsides or penalties, just goals. It's either over the line, or it isn't.

The role of fourth official has improved matters. They do talk to the referee and tell them about things they have not seen, and you can let off a bit of steam with them. When they first started they were so petty you could be six inches out of your technical area and they'd be jumping on you, or two of you would stand up and they'd be demanding someone sat down. But there was a meeting with Keith Hackett, who was in charge of the refs, and they stopped treating us like schoolkids. Now there is some banter. One week at Leeds there was a foul that was not given. I said to the fourth official, 'He's got to see that'.

He replied, 'If it's any consolation, Neil, I'd have given a foul.'

What can you say to that?

They can interfere though. The number of times I've been unhappy with a linesman and I've shouted to a sub, 'Get down there, get behind him and watch his offsides – see if he knows what he's doing.' Or I'll send someone down with instructions to tell the linesman to look for something or other. The fourth official will say, 'You can't do that,' So now I have to whisper.

One ref I can't forgive is Styles who I thought gave several bad decisions against Sheffield United when I managed them in the Premier League, ultimately contributing to me losing my dream job when we went down by one goal on goal difference. I then encountered him at Palace. When he held his hand out in the referee's room before the match I said, 'I'm sorry, Rob, but I can't be a hypocrite.'

I went back to the dressing room and said to the boys: 'Sorry, lads, I couldn't shake his hand, you won't be getting much today.' Surprisingly we still got a draw.

Not that I always bear a grudge. Graham Poll is the ref who cost me the chance of leading the Blades out in an FA Cup final and for years I couldn't stand him, not because of his error, but because of the way he smiled about it afterwards. When he did his three-card trick at the World Cup three years later, I thought to myself at least he maybe now understood the pain a manager feels after a mistake has cost him something he has worked so hard to try and achieve, because I don't think officials usually appreciate the hurt they can cause. However after he'd stopped reffing I bumped into him at a Football Writers' Association function at The Savoy. Someone suddenly thrust a hand at me and said, 'Hello, Neil'. I accepted the hand, shook it, then realised it was Graham Poll. I didn't really know what to do, but life moves on. It turned out he was a QPR fan and he had been taking his kid to watch us play and suddenly saw me completely differently.

Or at least that was the impression he gave that night. Imagine my surprise when Poll took the opportunity of my departure from Leeds to write a newspaper article full of cheap insults, dragging up a load of old nonsense from years before, and saying he was glad I was retiring. As I put in my own *Independent* column, it is a shame he wasn't brave enough to say that to my face, but he obviously couldn't resist a headline for his paid-for column.

The last time I was in trouble was at Millwall with Leeds in November 2012. The FA charged me after I told my players not to shake the hand of Mark Halsey after the match. He had dismissed Luke Varney soon after the break for what he said was 'a deliberate elbow'. As far as I was concerned, it was nothing of the sort. At the end of the game, which we lost to a late goal, I wanted to ensure my players didn't say anything which might get them in trouble as our thin squad could not afford another suspension, and I didn't see why they should be shaking his hand in any case after he cost us the game. I forcefully told them to stay away from him and he reported me to the FA for being disrespectful.

What annoyed me was what I perceived to be the hypocrisy of the charge because I'd felt Halsey had disrespected me at half-time. I had asked why, having played advantage after a bad foul by a Millwall player, he had not gone back and booked the culprit. In front of three of my staff, and some of the players, he said (and I've toned this right down), 'You didn't say anything about not booking Brownie two weeks ago, you weren't moaning then.' It did take me back a bit but I didn't have an issue with it until he went crying to the FA. I thought that was petty and showed a lack of class. It cost me two grand.

It was odd that Mark reported me but not the racist abuse that Dioufy had told him during the game he was receiving from some Millwall fans. It was only after a Sky documentary exposed it that some fans were convicted.

You may recall a few weeks later Sir Alex Ferguson ranting and raving at Mike Dean and a linesman after Newcastle scored a controversial goal at Old Trafford. It was far worse than what I'd done, but Sir Alex was not charged.

Being charged after that match at Millwall rankled as I'd made an effort to curb my behaviour and not been charged for several seasons. Getting older helped, you get slightly less selective with your memory because we all remember the ones that cost you, and forget the ones that don't. When I went to Fratton Park early on with Leeds we scored a goal that was over the line but wasn't given. In the old days I'd have been apoplectic, and I'd probably not have noticed that we got away with a penalty when Tom Lees handled in the box and the ref missed it.

I do think the relationship between managers and players, and referees, has got better in recent seasons after a period in which it had noticeably declined. There is more communication between officials and clubs now. Early in the season referees will visit the training ground to talk about any new initiatives, what they are looking to crack down on, and explain some decisions. At QPR Peter Walton, the Premier League ref, and Keren Barratt, a former ref who became an assessor before managing the select group officials, dropped in. We removed the mirrors and told the chef not to use any garlic so they felt at home, and then we all watched a video presentation in the canteen. There was a bit of banter as a couple of the incidents they showed involved Joey Barton. He was forced to try to defend his antics.

Peter told us about a game he reffed, Everton-West Ham, when Frédéric Piquionne celebrated scoring a goal for the Hammers by running into the crowd. It was a stupid thing to do because he had already been booked and, explained Peter, he had no choice but to give him another yellow card. It's a Fifa directive. Like it or not, players and refs have to obey it. In the remaining five minutes Everton equalised. Had West Ham won at Goodison

Park that season they may have gone on to stay up. There was a question-and-answer session too and at the end I thought both sides had a better understanding of the other. Hopefully that will continue now the League Managers' Association, and the referees, are both going to be based at Burton, at the new FA coaching HQ.

The big issue that season was women officials after Richard Keys and Andy Gray were fired by Sky after making some disparaging comments off-air about Sian Massey. While I was sad to see them lose their jobs because I have always got on with them personally, I did feel they had made an error of judgement.

I can remember a time when I would have laughed at the idea of a woman official myself. 'No chance, they don't have a clue about football!' would have been my response. Well, I was wrong. I actually find women officials are usually better than their male equivalents, maybe because players seem to show more respect towards them. I cannot remember the first time there was a woman linesman for one of my matches as manager, which tells you what a good job they did because I can remember bad decisions against my teams, and who made them, going back decades. It is an indication of how used to having women officials I have become that after the Sky row broke out I remembered QPR recently had a female referee's assistant but I couldn't remember who, or when. I had it looked up and it turned out Sian Massey had done two of our games that season. I've always found Sian perfectly capable of doing the job and it was the same with Wendy Toms. Indeed, I don't think it will be long before we have a woman ref in the Premier League. And won't that make an impact in some of those countries overseas that watch our football avidly but don't give women full rights!

My own refereeing was never more than a hobby but I did

reach the international arena. Years ago, when I was still playing, I was on holiday in the Seychelles. Bob Matthewson, the former Football League ref, knew I was a qualified referee and asked me to run the line at an international against Reunion. Late on a player made a clever run at a free-kick, beat the offside trap, and scored. The defence questioned me but the goal was good and I thought no more of it. At the final whistle I jogged towards Bob only to see him sprinting towards me. 'What's up?' I said.

'Follow me,' he shouted running past.

We raced down a tunnel and through some big gates, which were quickly locked. Seconds later there were angry players hammering on the gate, trying to reach us. I'd thought nothing untoward was going to happen but Bob's experience had told him we had to get out quickly.

Imagine the fine the FA would slap on me if that happened at one of my games.

Chapter Eight

FA Cup Magic?

Some days I've found myself leaving home at three in the morning. I'm outside the training ground at five but they don't open until seven. I just sit there, listening to the radio.

Harry Redknapp

IT WAS A FRIDAY. MY QPR TEAM HAD FINISHED TRAINING AT Harlington and we'd all got on the bus to go into London and catch a train to Lancashire. I was on the phone, not really concentrating, but after a while I noticed we had gone past this big station. Then we pulled up at Kings Cross.

'Whereabouts is Euston then, driver?' I asked.

'I drove past it ages ago,' he said.

'But we're going from Euston.'

He looked down at a bit of paper. 'I've got Kings Cross on here.'

'Pull up on the side here,' I said. 'You ring your gaffer. I'll ring mine.'

I called Caroline, my secretary.

'Where's the train going from?' I asked. 'The driver says he's been told it's Kings Cross.'

She didn't know and she'd ring back. The driver can't get his office to reply. We waited, parked up on one of the busiest roads in London. I expected a traffic warden to turn up at any moment with a big smile on his face and a ticket in his hand. Fortunately Caroline soon called back. 'It's Euston.'

'Driver. It's Euston. Quick. Turn this thing around before we miss the train.'

And that is how QPR's ill-fated 2011 FA Cup campaign began.

I'm old enough to remember the FA Cup when it stood astride the fixture list like a Colossus. It was a special day at our house, just below birthdays and Christmas. Friends and family would come round from mid-morning and we'd watch all the build-up while munching on fruit pancakes. I can remember playing football in the street as a boy when all these double-decker buses came past full of people wearing yellow-and-green scarves. They were Norwich City fans on the way to play Sheffield United at Bramall Lane. They waved at us and we waved back. Everyone was friendly. I suppose nowadays they'd be more likely to get V-signs or a brick through a window. Norwich were a Third Division team at the time and they were on a cup run which had attracted national attention because they had knocked out Manchester United and Tottenham to reach the sixth round. The Blades hadn't been in the semi-finals since before the War but we thought this was our year as we'd beaten Arsenal and now we were playing a Third Division team.

It wasn't to be. Norwich got a 1–1 draw and when the replay came around we all sat at the kitchen table while my dad fiddled with the old wireless, seeking the commentary from Carrow Road. It was so exciting listening to it because in my imagination every shot was going in the top corner. Some probably did as it was a five-goal thriller, unfortunately Norwich got three of them and I went to bed disappointed. The Blades did get to the semi-finals two years later but lost to Leicester City after two replays. We didn't manage to get a goal in any of the three matches.

Not many years later I began playing in the cup but none of the teams I played for were very good at giant-killing and I never got past the fourth round. The pinnacle was a fourth round tie against mighty Newcastle United when I was with Scunthorpe United in 1974. We were leading up there but Terry McDermott scored an equaliser to force a replay. That could have been a cracker with a big crowd under the lights at the Old Showground. We'd have fancied our chances. But it was during the miners' strike and there was a three-day week. To save electricity we had to play on a midweek afternoon. The atmosphere was flat and they won 3–0, with Supermac – Malcolm MacDonald – getting a couple. Newcastle went on to reach the final where they lost to Liverpool. At least I played. I bitterly remember one year, at Rotherham, I was picked to play against Leeds United when they were the best in the land but the match was fogged off. We had a league game in the interim and the manager obviously didn't think I played that well as he dropped me for the re-arranged game, and the replay.

I've not been much more successful in the competition as a manager. I've sometimes felt the need to rest players because either I've not had a team I thought could win it, or there have been other priorities like staying up or being promoted. The exception was in 2003 when Sheffield United reached the semi-final, David Seaman made an incredible save from Paul Peschisolido, and Graham Poll provided the assist for Arsenal's goal. Sheffield United, would you believe, have not been to the FA Cup final in my lifetime. Isn't that terrible?

On the flip side since getting into the league I've never been a non-League giant-killing victim either, though I've had some close shaves. It was bad enough needing a replay at Huddersfield to beat Telford, and another at Bury to get past Tamworth but the most nerve-racking tie was very early in my time at Sheffield United. Rushden & Diamonds, now sadly bust but then a real force in the Conference, took us to a replay. We took the lead in extra-time through Shaun Derry of all people, but they forced an equaliser to take us into penalties. We scraped through 6–5. I felt sick all night. Losing that wouldn't have been a great start to my time at Bramall Lane.

But while the FA Cup has not been kind to me – I even went out in the qualifying rounds five times – it did put me on the map. In 1985 I was managing Burton Albion in the Northern Premier League. You don't get much attention from the national news-papers at that level, but we did. Our cup run started at a Bedfordshire village against a team called Wootton Blue Cross and our star striker Stewart Mell, who was a fireman, only turned up five minutes before kick-off, still wearing his uniform. I'd just persuaded the ref to take him off the team-sheet by getting one of the other lads to go into the toilet and pretend he was being sick when Stewart showed up. We had to go back to the ref and say we were going to stick to the original team-sheet. Stewart inevitably scored in our win, we then beat Stevenage Borough and Wycombe Wanderers, who were both still non-League then, on the way to knocking out Fourth Division Aldershot at their place on a magical afternoon. Stewart scored again, as did Nigel Simms who was a miner.

In those days the third round draw was made straight away and we all gathered in the club house bar there to hear it. Imagine the whoops when Leicester City, a top-flight side just down the road from Burton and with Gary Lineker and Alan Smith up front, came out of the velvet bag. We moved the game to Derby County's Baseball Ground and the press descended upon us, especially me, with my chiropody business. Come the match Lineker scored but we soon equalised. Then Paul Evans, our goalkeeper, who later became my assistant and best friend, was hit by a chunk of wood thrown from the crowd. He was wobbling about and even sick on the pitch, but Brian Hill, the ref, said we had to play on. We lost 6–1 and when I said there should be a replay the ref and their manager, Gordon Milne, dismissed the idea. Then John Sadler, who was a big name journalist at *The Sun*, took up our cause, describing it as a David and Goliath contest. The FA had an inquiry and ordered a rematch played behind closed doors at Coventry City's Highfield Road. It was a really weird atmosphere but we had a right go and only lost 1–0. A year later the board changed at Burton and I was forced out, but because of the cup run people knew who I was. I was on my way.

I have to admit none of this was running through my mind ahead of QPR's third round tie at Blackburn Rovers in 2011. While I'd love to get to Wembley, promotion was the priority then, it had to be, but we didn't even have enough fit players for me to rest some for the league which turned out to have serious consequences. We started training with five ruled out and lost two more during it. In addition Lee Cook and Fitz Hall were doubtful and Kyle Walker had gone back to Spurs.

I went over to see the kids. I picked out Michael Doherty, a midfielder, Bruno Andrade, a little winger, good lads both, then said to the coach, 'We also need a defender.' He suggested Harriman, a right-back. I shouted out 'Harry,' and all these kids looked over. I shouted again. Eventually one jogged across. 'Harry, you're with us tomorrow.'

I found out later his name was Michael, but from that day on he was known as Harry.

I sent 'Harry' off to join training. Then Jamie Mackie, who I wanted to rest, came to see me. 'I want to play tomorrow. I'm desperate to play, gaffer.'

'You need a rest.'

'I've seven days to recover. Please play me.'

In the end I figured I had to, I'd nobody else.

Maybe the subsequent problems we had getting the train were an omen because the tie was a disaster. Not because we lost the tie; the blow was we lost Mackie to a broken leg, a bad one. It wasn't a bad tackle, in fact Mackie was as bad as the other guy, but I could tell straight away there was something wrong. You always worry when a player goes down but some players go down if you breathe on them. Mackie's one who if he goes down, and stays down, you know he's hurt. He didn't move until the physio went on.

What happens then is Coxy talks to Sangi Patel, the other physio (who I brought over from Palace when they made her redundant), through a walkie-talkie, which frustrates me at times because I want to know what's going on, and most of the time they either can't hear each other or can't make their mind up. I'm asking, 'What's happening, is he injured, can he carry on?' and they don't know.

In this case there was a lot of background noise as the crowd started booing. They were frustrated as Blackburn weren't playing very well and though we had a weakened side it was still 0–0 and time was ticking away. They could also see El Hadji Diouf standing over Jamie, telling him, 'There's nothing wrong with you, get up and stop conning the ref.' That infuriated our players – and me when Coxy told me about it. After the game I told the press about Diouf's behaviour, and said he was 'lower than a sewer rat'. Eighteen months on I signed him for Leeds – but more of that later.

Jamie was carried off on a stretcher and taken straight to hospital. These days clubs are well organised with ambulances standing by and a hospital designated. It wasn't always the case. At Sheffield United we lost Rob Hulse to a bad leg-break at Chelsea and it was terrible how he was looked after. It took ages to get an ambulance and the stretcher-bearers had problems with stairs and a narrow corridor. We were so disappointed in the way he was treated we wrote a letter of complaint. Rob was in agony but there was no sense of urgency. It was all a bit ironic given the fuss Chelsea made when Petr Cech didn't have quick access to an ambulance at Reading the same season.

At least both men had an ambulance eventually. I was playing for Burton at Marine on Merseyside as my career was winding down and I went into a challenge with the 'keeper and came out with a broken arm. One of their guys said, 'Don't worry about calling an ambulance, I'll take you in the car, Walton Hospital's just a couple of minutes away.' What a mistake. I ended up in a two-hour queue while all these people in ambulances overtook me. They put me on a trolley in a narrow corridor: everytime someone came past they bumped the trolley and sent the pain jarring through my arm again, I was in agony. I had been given a painkiller, but I brought it straight back up so it didn't have any effect.

Fortunately Jamie didn't have to worry about any of that. After the game we went to the hospital on the bus to pick the physio up and we were told Jamie's condition was stable and we could take him back to London with us. He had a light cast on his leg and we stretched him out on the bus. He had it set the following day in London. That was much better as he was close to home and friends and family could see him and keep his spirits up because it was obvious he had a long road back to recovery ahead.

Bill Shankly was famous for ignoring injured players. He said players were no use to him injured and I assume he reasoned the cold shoulder would persuade them to try and get fit as soon as possible. I don't go along with that. I try and spend more time with injured players than the fit ones. Injuries are part of the game but they are still tough to accept. They affect you twice, you feel for the player, and you worry about the impact on the team. Jamie understandably got a bit low so we took him to a couple of games with us, Kieron Dyer the same. When Chris Morgan was injured at Sheffield United I used to give him a phone call here and there, just keeping in touch. I think they appreciate that.

It wasn't just the pastoral care that used to be different. The medical care could be hopeless. At Chesterfield when I was 19 years old I had a groin injury. Ollie Thompson was the physio. He used to have a heated lamp and he'd rub Deep Heat into your groin with a fag hanging from his mouth while it was on. Then he'd say, 'Go run it off around the track.'

'I can't, I'm struggling.'

'It's all in your head.'

I remember those words like I heard them yesterday. This went on for two months, it wasn't getting better. Some of my mates at the time were Sheffield United and Wednesday apprentices – we used to go to Heartbeat in Sheffield on a Saturday night for a dance. One of them said, 'You should see our physio. He treats people privately. He's doing another player from a different club at the moment.'

It was Bobby Little in Sheffield. He said he'd have a look, then he said, 'You shouldn't have been training, let alone playing, you've got a badly strained adductor.' Or whatever it was. 'You need to build that up with exercises. Have you got any to do?'

'No. They've got me running and jogging around the pitch.'

I went to see him two or three times a week for three weeks, it was all I could afford as it was expensive. Then I went back to Chesterfield and the manager said, 'You've recovered. Ollie's done well to get you fit.' I should have kept my mouth shut, but I didn't. 'I wish he had.'

'What do you mean?'

'Well, it weren't him that got me fit.'

He got it out of me, where I'd been, and instead of being impressed that I'd paid my own money and sorted it out myself to get fit he never talked to me again. I got a free transfer at the end of the season. That was a good lesson: keep your mouth shut.

I used to get injections to play that you wouldn't have now – I had one to play that FA Cup tie against Newcastle for Scunthorpe. But I've been lucky really as an ex-pro, being a winger you didn't get the same physical contact and unlike a lot of former players my knees and ankles are OK. I've had a resurfaced hip and assume I'll need the other side done eventually, but that might not be anything to do with football. Believe it or not the football legacy I have is with my thumbs. I used to land on them when I was crossing and being tackled, and I was constantly knocking them back. They were dislocated sometimes and now they are arthritic.

Modern physios do proper courses and are qualified, but I know some players at QPR thought Nigel was not good enough even though I disagreed. It was the same at Huddersfield, at Plymouth, everywhere else. Whoever the physio is there's always players who will use the physio as an excuse if they can.

Clubs used to push players into playing when they weren't ready but now most medical staff don't give players back unless they are fit. But however good the rehabilitation programme is there is no fitness test as demanding as actually playing a game which is why you sometimes get players who break down as soon as they return, like poor Kieron Dyer did at QPR. He worked his socks off for four months to get fit and only lasted a few minutes. I could have cried.

Just as I spend time with players who are injured I also take care to keep in touch with squad players who are not in the team. Like the injured, they need the attention. When I was a player, at Chesterfield and Rotherham, if you weren't in the team you were a leper, we used to say, 'You in the leper colony today?' You felt ostracised.

I always tell players why I am dropping them though I forgot a couple of times with QPR; I assumed they would realise the regular first team player was coming back, but I should have told them. I think you get more respect then even if they don't agree with you. They'll argue.

'You're wrong,' they'll say.

'I don't believe it.'

'So-and-so's playing worse and he's not been dropped.'

You have to answer them the best way you can. That's as hard a part of the game as there is for managers, after telling kids they are not getting a pro contract. That is tough, but I think it is the manager's job, not the youth academy guy. I found out Chesterfield were letting me go at the end of my first season in senior football when a team-mate rang to commiserate. He'd read in the local paper that I'd been given a free transfer. Not only had Jimmy McGuigan not told me, I'd not even seen the paper myself. When I got into management I said I wouldn't do it that way.

I've had kids in my office with tears streaming down their face and me telling them, 'It's not the end of the world. Managers make mistakes. You can go to a club lower down and in a couple of years you can be back at this level. If you have the dedication you can prove me wrong.' To be honest, I can't think of any that have, but there must have been some.

I take the job home – I'm terrible after a loss – but that part of it, seeing the devastation on the faces of boys just starting out, stays with me for days afterwards.

Chapter Nine

Where's Flavio?

Sometimes I am still at work at three in the afternoon.

Paul Merson during his brief spell as manager at
Walsall

THE TRANSFER WINDOW OPENED IN JANUARY 2011 AND I'D
lined up a couple of deals, one of them Kyle Naughton, a full-back
to replace his Spurs team-mate Kyle Walker whose loan had ended.
On the phone, at the training ground, I spoke to the club, the
player, and the agent. The pieces started to come together. Then I
went into London to have lunch with Amit, Ishan and Gianni. Amit
said the deals are OK with him, but we had to get Bernie Ecclestone's
permission. I got in a taxi and went to Bernie with Gianni. We
talked for an hour, he said it's OK with him, but we have to get the
OK off Flavio because he'd promised he won't do anything unless
Flavio agreed it. 'OK,' I said wearily. 'Where's Flavio?'

'He's on safari in Africa. He's out of reach.'

Momentum is important in football. Teams lose confidence
much more quickly than they build it. You can have a long

unbeaten run lasting months then you lose a couple of games and immediately players start to question things: their own ability, their team-mates' commitment, the manager's decisions. So when you have momentum it is vital to keep it going and if it does start to slip a new face can sometimes give it a lift. That's where the January transfer window, often a nightmare for managers, can provide a boost.

QPR went into the window top of the Championship but our form was wobbling. I wanted to bring in a few players to give us a lift that would take us all the way to promotion in May. You don't want too many loanees at a club, because at the end of the day, however good a character they are, it is not their club and results are not going to matter as much to them as to someone who is employed by the club. However, sometimes you need to strengthen and there's no other way of doing it. You can get players who wouldn't be available on a permanent transfer, or who you couldn't afford otherwise, and in the Football League, with the emergency loan system, you can fill a gap when someone is injured.

It's not always easy though. A lot of the players loaned by Premier League clubs are young, but the Championship is a hard league and it's difficult to bring a young kid in. It was different with Walker, who had been on loan to us from Tottenham, as he'd had a season at Sheffield United under his belt already. He'd been brilliant for us, especially going forward, and would have liked to stay but Tottenham wanted him to go to Aston Villa to get Premier League games. Villa were also going to pay a big loan fee which probably helped make up the mind of Daniel Levy, Spurs' chairman. That's right, contrary to what you might think many loans are not free.

So I tried to get Kyle Naughton who had been at Leicester on loan. Like Walker I knew him from Sheffield United. Spurs wanted a loan fee, and a bonus if we got promotion. The problem was Leicester City were also willing to pay it. The good news was Kyle wanted to come to us so Tottenham said they would let him come if we came up with a proper deal. I offered so much a game, a fee and a hefty bonus if we got promotion.

They accepted that, but Leicester came back in with a larger loan fee, the same per game and a bonus if they went up. Leicester were well off the promotion pace so I wasn't surprised they were prepared to offer so much if they went up, because they probably wouldn't. There was also Rodolph Austin, the Jamaican midfielder I'd been to see playing in Norway, in my sights. We'd have to pay a loan fee for him but that would be knocked off the £1.5m asking price if we then bought him. I said to Gianni, 'You must try and get hold of Flavio.'

'Don't worry, I'll sort it out with Tottenham in the morning. By 11 o'clock he'll be our player.'

'He won't if we don't come up with the money.'

The following morning I called Kyle's agent. He said Tottenham had been told we wouldn't pay so Naughton was going to Leicester. I rang Spurs to be told Gianni rang an hour earlier to say we can't pay a loan fee. I got to the training ground, Gianni was there.

'Have you spoken to Flavio?'

'No. Tottenham have rung me. The deal's off.'

Gianni often got criticised, but he made life at QPR so enjoyable for me and I'll always be grateful. I found him a wonderful man and I'll always class him as a friend. But there were times he drove me mad. I said: 'No, they haven't. You rang them and said we can't pay a loan fee. We're five points clear, six with the goal difference, we've just lost Kyle Walker and we can't pay a loan fee for a player who's worth £5m to get us up. What on earth is going on?'

'I don't know. I can't get hold of Flavio.'

'What is the point of trying to get players if we can't get hold of Flavio in a situation like this for a player like that?'

I found out later Flavio had told him he couldn't do it, and he wanted to keep that away from me. I was absolutely furious. I was supposed to be dealing with Amit from day one when I came to the club but the takeover hadn't happened. I could have bloody screamed. Kyle Naughton went to Leicester; Austin stayed in Norway until I brought him to Leeds.

This was the day we nearly missed the train to Blackburn. When we finally got on the train I phoned Kyle. He said he would still love to come to us, but Tottenham were pressuring him to sign a new contract and wanted him to go to Leicester. Obviously I felt the agent was pushing him to go to Leicester for whatever reason.

I said, 'Give me an hour.' I called Gianni. He still couldn't get hold of Flavio. I called Amit; he said he couldn't do anything without Flavio's permission. In the end I had to tell Kyle, 'Thanks for hanging on, son, sign for Leicester and good luck to you.'

I was absolutely disconsolate. Kyle would have been perfect and I simply could not understand why a club in our position, with our supposed wealth, couldn't invest that amount of money at such a crucial stage. I turned to Mick Jones and said: 'I've never felt like this. We're six points clear, we sign Kyle Naughton, a good striker and another, and we're certs. Promotion is worth £60m. We've just thrown it away because we can't get hold of someone on a bloody safari. It is doing my head in. If I could leave now, I'd leave now, I would honestly.'

Then to top it off I found out Ishan had been asking about Yakubu and Stefan Moore. I texted him and said, 'I don't want Yakubu or Stefan Moore.' All this did my head in.

After Blackburn we drew at Burnley. That meant we'd taken two points from nine. We'd lost Walker and were hit by injuries. The pack was closing in, the fans and media were beginning to wonder if we would blow it. We needed the lift you get from a new signing. I was desperate for Wayne Routledge at Newcastle. His agent said he'd come but it was dependent on Newcastle getting in the players they wanted. I was also waiting for Ishmael Miller. For weeks at West Brom they'd been saying he'd come.

I spoke to Derek Lambias, Newcastle's chief executive. He wanted us to pay Routledge's wages which were a lot of money. We offered to pay three-quarters of it and top up most of the rest up on a pay-as-you-play basis. Then Newcastle said they weren't sure they wanted to let Routledge go and manager Alan Pardew wanted to speak to him, but Routledge's agent told me the lad was in London and wouldn't be going back up. I wasn't surprised; he'd only started four games in four months.

We had a board meeting and I said, 'Look, if we can sign Miller and Routledge, plus the defenders Pascal Chimbonda and Danny Shittu, we have a 90 per cent chance of going up. If we don't it's 70 per cent.' I personally didn't think we'd win our next match against Coventry if we didn't sign Routledge. We needed that fresh impetus. Crucially I knew Flavio liked him. That helped. The board agreed as long as we got rid of some players to cut the wage bill. I agreed, though I didn't have many players to let go as I didn't want to be left short. I spoke to Newcastle again. This time Lambias said they would let Routledge come without a loan fee as long as we agreed to buy him in the summer if we went up. That helped, as it was clear after the Kyle Naughton fiasco the board didn't want to spend anything on transfers or loan fees until they knew we had money from promotion.

They agreed and we managed to get Wayne five minutes before the deadline for him to play against Coventry. The delay was because Routledge wanted a clause inserted stating if we got promotion, and other clubs came in for him as well, he could go to another Premier League club if we couldn't agree terms. Of course I agreed – it also meant if we went up but Routledge didn't do well we could just offer him less money knowing he wouldn't want to stay then. I thought it was a great clause.

We also got Ishmael in, though there was a complication there too. I was going to sign him to the end of the season then I got a call from Dan Ashworth, who now works as the FA's director of elite development at Burton, but was at West Brom then and did the transfers, saying I couldn't sign him on that basis because John Carew had gone to Stoke and if they had injuries they might need Miller to go back. We agreed a 93-day loan with a clause enabling West Brom to call him back after 28.

I was told Ishmael was not fit, but he said he'd like to be on the bench against Coventry. Wayne went straight in. I felt he needed a little more confidence in himself getting into the box and having a go, so I gave him a pep talk. 'Don't play as an out-an-out winger, go all over the place and enjoy yourself. They said Walcott couldn't score and he's got ten this season playing like that – you can score eight goals for us between now and the end of the season playing the same way.'

It was a Sunday afternoon televised game and we started well, then Gorkss and Connolly made a mistake and we lost a goal before half-time. On the touchline I said to Curly, 'If we don't score before half-time we'll not win'. Then their lad, from only their second chance, went through with only the goalie to beat. If he scored it was all over, but he put it wide.

We made the most of the reprieve. Adel picked the ball up on the left, went inside two players and scored a brilliant goal. We were buzzing in the dressing room and I told them it's just a matter of keeping it going. Adel played a ball from the left wing with the outside of his foot 50 yards into the box to pick out Routledge who had drifted in off the right wing. Wayne took a touch with his left then finished with his right. It was an unbelievable goal and it won the game. Though I would have loved to sign him myself I was pleased to see Wayne settle down at Swansea the following season and to play with such confidence. I always love the way he runs straight at the opposition when he picks the ball up.

Ishmael was also lacking in confidence, which was hardly surprising as he'd not really had a long run in the team at West Brom for years. I had always fancied him; I tried to get him from Manchester City when I was at Sheffield United. When I met him I said to him, 'I'll make you a player, son, you're going to enjoy yourself playing with me.' I looked into his eyes and I could tell I would get a lot out of him. I put him on as sub for half-an-hour before the end against Coventry and he was superb. Having those two around lifted everyone, we were buzzing but I knew without those two coming in it could have gone rapidly downhill.

Getting players in meant I had to trim the squad. I'd promised Leon Clarke if he wasn't in the team by January I would let him go even though I didn't want him to. Gianni then arranged with Maurice Lindsay at Preston for Clarky to go there but I felt we should have got some money for him. We agreed we would get an amount on every game he played, and a bit more if they stayed up. At least it gave us a bit towards the players we brought in. I also let Mikele Leigertwood, who wasn't getting many games as Dezza was doing so well, go to Reading to the end of the season and I managed to get shot of Rowan Vine to Milton Keynes for a few weeks.

Pascal Chimbonda, who had been released by Blackburn, and Danny Shittu, a former QPR player who had been on a short-term deal at Millwall, also joined which gave us some defensive cover. Danny's a big lad and a nice lad but I found out when we played Millwall later on that maybe because he's such a gentle giant when the crowd are giving him stick he struggles. Steve Morison scored, and then Danny got sent off for bringing him down. (Morison battered us; I tried to sign him for QPR, and later signed him at Leeds.) I didn't realise that's how Danny was, so I learned something that day. It cost him too as Gorkss took the opportunity to get his place back. Football's like that sometimes. It was the only time I saw the atmosphere of a game get to Danny like that. I hadn't expected it; how ironic now Danny has gone back to Millwall and is one of the best players in the team. We had a laugh about it when I was down there with Leeds recently.

Through all this testing period I was so grateful to have Mick Jones at my side. Football is a rat race. If you don't have your own people around you, good people you can trust, you get stabbed in the back. I've been with Mick for the best part of 20 years and yet I asked him to join me on a hunch because I'd never worked with him. He was managing Peterborough and I was managing Scarborough when I met him. We had a drink after a game and I thought, 'He talks a lot of sense.' Early in my first full season at Notts County, Peterborough sacked him. It was very early, they'd only played two league games and he'd won one of them. I asked if he would be my assistant and he was with me through two promotions there, another at Huddersfield and a fourth at Plymouth. We seemed to be a good combination. Then Dan McCauley fired me at Plymouth and offered Mick my job. He took it – he still had a hankering to be the No.1 – and we didn't talk for a few years. It didn't work out for him. That can happen, there is a big difference between being No.1 and No.2; you have to make the decisions, and you can't be frightened of upsetting people. The previous season I remember making one at Doncaster. I'd brought on a teenager, Lee Hills, to replace Claude Davis who was injured. But at half-time I knew I had to change things tactically – we were behind and a mess. Lee was the fall guy. I called him over and said to him, 'Lee, I'm sorry son, I don't know how to tell you, but I'm going to have to sub you.' I told him it wasn't about him, it was about the team, but I could see it hurt. However we got a draw, so it was justified.

While I went to Oldham, Bury and Sheffield United, Mick went to Brunei and Telford. Then Telford went bust. Meanwhile I'd been thinking about my old mate Brian Clough and how he fell out with Peter Taylor and never got round to making up before Taylor died. Cloughie regretted that to the grave. So I rang Mick, asked him to join me at Bramall Lane, and he came. Since then we've been to London with Palace and QPR and back to Yorkshire with Leeds.

People ask what Mick does, especially chairmen who are always trying to make sure everyone is earning their keep. Well, he's my sounding board, my second sight, someone who isn't afraid to offer a dissenting voice but won't get upset if I ignore it. Someone who provides a link to the players, who knows what I want and what I like. Someone I can trust, who I know I can moan to and it won't go any further. All managers need someone like that. Every day there's something I want to talk to him about. And on matchdays he sits in the stand because he can read a game well.

My other main assistant was Kevin Blackwell. Blackie was brilliant and we had some great times and laughs. I signed Blackie as a player at Scarborough and he helped us overtake Barry Fry's Barnet, who had sold him to me, and go up. He was then with me, initially as a player, increasingly as a member of the coaching staff, at Notts County, Torquay, Huddersfield, Plymouth, Bury and Sheffield United, by which time he was my No.2. Then he went to Leeds, our big rivals, and I only found out when the press rang me. After nearly 20 years together. I didn't talk to him at the start – I'm not the sort of person who can hide his feelings like that – and although we now talk quite frequently it's fair to say that our relationship has never quite been the same since.

Curly – Keith Curle – is another one who's been with me at several clubs. He was a very good player and when his career was winding down I tried to get him to join me at Bury as I'd heard he wasn't a bad coach. I knew he wanted to do that, and figured I could get him to play centre-half as well. He stayed at Wolves then, but a few years later I got him to Sheffield United as a player with the promise of doing some coaching. He then had some management stints at Mansfield, Chester and Torquay, but was out of work when I got the Palace job so I hired him because he was an excellent coach. He went with me to QPR and after we got fired became manager at Notts County where he made a great start but unfortunately lost his job before the end of the season during his first bad run. I thought he would have received a bit more support but that doesn't seem to happen these days.

I also had David Kelly at Sheffield United. He was well respected by the players, a decent coach and a fabulous person. That's important. If you are going to spend ten months of the season working alongside someone you want to like them. Another was Stuart McCall who was at Bradford when I was at Sheffield United. When Blackie left for Leeds I got in touch with Stuart as I knew he wanted to be a coach. He was a lovely lad, a nice family man. He wasn't a shouter like Blackie was, and Curly to an extent, more a talker. He learned a lot and he's done well at Motherwell since.

I had Jeppo, Ronnie Jepson, coaching at Leeds. He played for me at Huddersfield and I signed him again at Oldham, he was also my reserve team coach at Palace and QPR. He's had a spell as manager, at Gillingham. Perhaps surprisingly he's also worked a lot with Stan Ternant, but I don't hold that against him!

As clubs get bigger it becomes harder to have the close-knit staff you need. When Manchester City came to QPR they were spilling into the corridor. At QPR we went to visit Tony Fernandes' motor racing team both at a Grand Prix and at their Norfolk base. I had a good chat with Riad Asmat, the team manager. We had a lot in common and I have to say I admired the way the way he managed to get a good team spirit, considering the size of his staff. They had 45 staff at the GP and another 200 back in Norfolk. Even a club the size of Leeds only has a dozen football-related people on a match day: four coaches including me, five medical and fitness-related, a liaison man, an IT man and a kitman. In many ways that's better than having dozens of staff. I like to know who's alongside me and know them well, not for them to just be someone I only know by sight.

Chapter Ten

Where's Adel?

A manager can't give players what they haven't got. The job is to make them find what they need inside themselves.

David Beckham

ONE SEASON AT SHEFFIELD UNITED WE FOUND OURSELVES without a fit keeper three days before a match at Burnley, an absolute nightmare for any manager. We rang round and eventually managed to get two goalies in on loan: Lee Baxter, the son of Stuart Baxter who's been a big success managing in Sweden, and Alan Fettis, a ginger-haired lad from Hull who had played for Northern Ireland a few years before. We didn't know much about either player and as form is usually as reliable a guide as anything I decided to pick whoever performed best in training. Baxter was sensational, stopping everything, so I played him.

It's not the best decision I've ever made. He threw one in to give them a goal's start but we then played really well to go 2–1 ahead. Then he chucked another one in. Next they got a penalty, not his fault this time, but he didn't redeem himself by saving it either. At half-time I had to take him off and bring on Fettis. He kept a clean half-sheet, but we didn't score at the other end so we lost 3–2. Only one game, did it matter that much? Yes. We missed the play-offs by two points; Burnley survived by two points.

That's why playing those Fantasy Football games is a million miles from being a real manager – you never get those off-the-wall problems you're confronted with in management. Fortunately that was a bit of a one-off, unlike the call to say a player's got a sick child. You have to remember players are human. Most can block out everything when they go on the pitch but others, if they are worried, will not perform as well. Plus if you make them play some'll resent it, which can cause problems down the line. You are much better off being an understanding gaffer – they'll pay it back with interest in the long term. It all depends on the player, which is why you need to know them inside out.

One morning, just as I was setting out to the training ground, I received a call from Curly. We were due to travel to Hull that afternoon.

'Gaffer. Clint Hill's little girl has been to hospital with sickness and diarrhoea. Clint's been up with her half the night and looks shattered. He doesn't want to come with us.'

'Put him on the phone to me.' I know what Clint is like; he'll go through a brick wall for us. 'Clint, the family comes first. If you want to, get off home now, but we need you tomorrow so if you need an hour or two to get your missus sorted out, to get help, then come up in the morning.'

'I'll ring the missus after training, gaffer – she thinks I should go up with you today.'

We decided to play it by ear. Another dilemma sorted.

We got the bus to the station and the train to Hull. Usually we have a carriage to ourselves but something had obviously gone wrong with the booking as on every four-person table there was a stranger. Heavens knows what they were thinking as we piled on. They are all polite and that, as people are on trains, but I had to ask the guy on our table to move because I wanted to have a private conversation with Mick and Curly.

Hull were a decent side with a chance of the play-offs and a manager, Nigel Pearson, I rate even if he is a Wednesdayite. We started well but ten minutes before the break Adel completely lost it. He was unhappy the ref hadn't given him a foul, and then he thought a couple of players didn't pass to him quickly enough. He argued with Dezza on the pitch. Then he waved to me, signalling he wanted to be subbed, rolling his hands over. I ignored him. Curly was watching. 'He wants to come off, gaffer'.

'Just ignore him.'

'What do you mean?'

'Ignore him. If he wants to come off let him come over here and ask.'

At half-time I told Curly to get onto the pitch quick and make sure he escorted Adel off to avoid him arguing with the ref, his team-mates or the Hull fans who were on his back. I didn't want him sent off.

In the dressing room Adel put a towel over his head. I went over to talk to him, try and calm him down. I told him, 'You're captain, you can't come off just because their fans are giving you stick.' Then I told the lads to give him the ball earlier. I knew some were unhappy with him, but I'd already explained to a number of them we just needed to keep him on board to get us where we wanted to be. No one else would score the goals to take us to the Promised Land. If they wanted to have a verbal with Adel we'd all lose.

In the second half Adel did OK, but nothing special and we had to settle for a draw. We got back on the bus for the four–five hour journey home (we went up by train, back by bus) and I could tell there was a bit of an atmosphere. So I went back to check Adel was not sitting on his own, I saw Ali nearby, and a group playing cards. I sat down and began talking about the game. I said in a light-hearted way, 'You should all know there was no way I'd take Taarbs off, he's another career I've resurrected.' That's an old line of mine, any former player reading this will know I've said that about dozens of their team-mates over the years and I used it a few times about Adel. Back on that bus I also made the point of saying something favourable about Adel, then I told a few stories about my playing days to relieve the tension.

Next day I was in at Talksport doing a radio show when my phone flashed. It was a text from Adel. 'Gaffer. I'm very sorry for what I did yesterday. It was just because I feel we can win the game in the first half. I know I have to control myself. I am working on it.'

That summed him up. It wasn't like an English player having a strop, this is how he reacts. People forgot he was only 21 and every team we played against was going to try and kick lumps out of him. We had to take the rough with the smooth.

On Monday, before training, I took Dezza and Clint aside and showed them the text. All weekend Dezza had been fretting about how Adel had let the team down; that sort of behaviour is completely alien to a pro like Dezza. I had to reiterate to both of them that while it would be easy to fall out with Adel they couldn't afford to if they wanted to play in the Premier League. And looking back, they both went on to play a lot of Premier League games with QPR, having barely played in it before in Dezza's case, and never in Clint's.

Then I spoke to Adel on his own and told him how disrespectful to me the incident was. I said I classed myself as part of his family. 'Would you treat your father like you did me?'

'No, gaffer. I'm sorry.'

'The answer I want, and the way to apologise to the team, is to get us all three points tomorrow against Portsmouth.'

Needless to say, he scored the first in our 2–0 victory, and made the second. Clint scored that goal and as he ran back after celebrating he gave me a wink and a nod. We both knew neither of us would ever come across another player like Adel in our careers. A few weeks later Adel was voted the Football League's Player of the Year. He deserved it. It was easy to forget, given his role in the side, that this was his first full season playing regularly at any club. He said to me at one stage: 'I've never played this many games in my life, gaffer.'

Adel topped a shortlist that featured quality players Grant Holt and Scott Sinclair. Shane Long, Danny Graham and Jay Bothroyd, who was picked for England earlier in the season, didn't even make the short-list. All three were signed by Premier League clubs the following season. It shows there are some quality players in the Championship.

Adel does, though, take some looking after. He's the youngest of six. The little one in a big family has usually been spoilt, or had to look after himself. I don't know which it was with Adel but sometimes I think I can guess.

The day before the awards night we were playing at Doncaster. Despite having a virus all week Adel travelled and intended to play. Then on the morning of the game he got a phone call saying his cousin had been shot dead in Marseilles. I could see he was distraught and I sent him straight back to London. He was in no state to play and why would he be after a shock like that? It was our 38th game and the first he had missed all season.

The week after was an international break. Adel had been called up by Morocco so I told him to take some extra days and see his family. I gave the other players a few days off and took Sharon out there too. I tried to sell it as a mid-season break, but then had to admit I wanted to watch Adel's game and look at a player or two in the Olympic team.

I saw that game in the flesh but Adel was playing in Algeria so I had to watch on TV. The atmosphere looked incredible but Adel looked a lost lamb. They didn't play to his strengths like we did. I met his latest agent after the game and said, 'He needs a year with us, a year with me, before he starts going on to other things. Otherwise someone won't tolerate him and if he has two bad games he'll be dropped and he won't get back in.'

I saw Adel out there and he said he'd be back on the Thursday.

'Have Saturday off if you want,' I said, 'because we are not playing until Monday against Sheffield United.'

'No, I'll be in Thursday.'

I usually do the press on Thursday. As Adel had won the Football League award Sky wanted to talk to him and so did the newspaper press. Come Thursday morning there was no Adel to be seen. Me and Derry did the TV bit. I had to apologise to Sky, tell them I hadn't a clue where he was, that he'd rung in sick. Friday we didn't see him. Then he came in Saturday and trained well. Sunday morning we were going to do set-pieces, but at half-ten Nigel Cox phoned and said he'd got a message from Adel who'd told him he was not feeling well, had stomach pains, couldn't get out of bed and so on. We left messages for him to ring. He didn't call anybody. I texted him saying, 'I hope you are OK, I hope you didn't feel too much pain when you were out on Saturday, smoking your Shisha pipe and eating with your mates.' I felt let down. I wanted him ready for Sheffield United.

I decided to play Hogan Ephraim instead, who scored the winner at Donny when Adel was missing. We did the set-pieces with Hogan involved. I told Dezza and Clint I was going to play Hogan, but added, 'You know me, I might change my mind.'

Meanwhile Nigel went to his house. Knocked on the door, no answer. He spoke to the neighbours, they had not seen him. Nigel fixed up a scan for Adel on his stomach – Adel said he'd got pain everywhere. On the Monday Adel rang Nigel. He said he has still got pain but he didn't want a scan as he needed to sleep – 'because I'll be playing tonight'!

Just before six I saw him coming into Loftus Road and I had a chat with him. 'If you're tired I don't want to risk you getting injured, how do you feel?'

'I want to play.'

'But we'll regret it if you get injured. Why don't you sit on the bench? If we need you I'll bring you on.'

'No. I want to play.'

Then Paddy Kenny came in. I said: 'Paddy, you're just the man. Adel wants to play.'

'I'd play him, gaffer. He'll win us the game.'

'That's it, Adel,' I said. 'You're playing. Paddy, you sort it out with everybody else. If he plays crap it's your fault.'

He didn't play crap. We played really well and won 3–0. The television cameras were there too. But it was sad to see how far Sheffield had fallen, only 413 away fans attended.

The day after I had a meeting with Flavio. I needed to take William with me as Amy was out with Sharon. QPR had arranged to send a car at 5.30pm but it didn't turn up. I rang Gianni.

'The car is coming at 7.30.'

'You can't just change things like that, why didn't you tell me?'

'Flavio rung to say his flight's delayed. It'll be 7.30.'

So William had to go round to a friend's house as Amy and Sharon weren't back until late. Before the car arrived I got a phone call from a good friend who said he had a contact in QPR who had told him when we won promotion I'd get the sack. I said it wouldn't surprise me. Nothing does. I didn't mention it to Flavio. What was the point?

For Adel to be missing training was damaging, to him and the team. Matchdays are the main event at a football club, but you spend a lot more time training than playing, and if you don't get that right the results won't come.

Some managers do the coaching themselves, like Roy Hodgson, others leave it all to the coach and just observe, like Sven Göran Eriksson. I do a bit of both. I like my coaches to coach, to put sessions on. I couldn't put a session on like these lads do now, it's fantastic, the movement, the repetitiveness, what they do. For example, I'll tell Curly, or Jeppo, 'I want forward play today with crosses coming into the box and defenders defending.' He'll set it up with tramlines either side for the wingers to operate in. A defender will then play the ball into the forward who will lay the ball back to a midfielder who'll play it out wide, and they'll vary the types of crosses coming in. Then we'll take the defenders out and just have finishing to give the forwards a confident end, and the goalies a good work out. I'll be watching, sometimes I'll step in.

I've always said to the coaches I've had, 'Look, I'm not belittling you when I jump into your session, it is just how I am. When I see something I'll step in.' They accept that. I'll jump in a lot if I have just gone to a club and want them to know how I play. Sometimes it is quite elementary stuff. You'd be surprised even at the top level how many defenders don't get told how to defend; because they are top players people assume they can do it but I've found defenders who haven't got a clue coming from top clubs. Armand Traore, in my opinion, would be a good example. Sometimes they are not aware of what position they should be in, in relation to where the ball is, or they won't be in line with the rest of the back four. But I don't suppose you need to defend at Arsenal, they go forward that much.

If we've played on Saturday the lads will be back in on a Monday. We'll have a warm-down and the players who didn't have a full game on Saturday will have a practice match. If there's no game on Tuesday night Tuesday will be a very physical day aimed at keeping their fitness levels up. I'll give them the day off to recover Wednesday before building up to the weekend game on the Thursday. Rest is as important as training. A lot of managers do double-sessions but I've never been that way inclined. When I was a player I used to hate doing a session, having a break, showering, getting changed, then having to go and warm up again and do something else, not just mentally but physically. I would rather do a long session. If I feel we need to train harder we do a three-hour session, then rest.

The lads get a lot more rest with me. The layman might say, 'They can't be fit enough, the team that trains three times a week will be fitter,' but I think that's rubbish. People have them swimming in the morning, or boxing at four in the afternoon. I don't believe in any of that, and my teams have always had a reputation for being one of the fittest around. A lot of it is in the mind, you have to give them the ingredients, but once you have that hard work out of the way, that first two or three weeks pre-season, then the resting is as important as the physical work. You can do too much. It is not just physical, it is mental. You can bore the pants off them like Capello did when he took England away to Austria before the 2010 World Cup. When players are cooped up together for a long time if there's no humour, no rapport, they go stale.

Thursday is the technical day, working on patterns of play, how we will play against the opposition's strengths and on their weaknesses. The coach will do a session then set up an 11 v 11. I often take over then. I think that is where you do organise your team. I wouldn't really describe myself as a coach, but my coaches have always said, 'You'd be surprised how much coaching you do.' I don't put elaborate sessions on, but in an 11 v 11 I can spot things I don't like and coach them to play the way I want them to, defensive or attacking. I don't do too much shadow play, where you walk through moves, as it bores you to death. It needs to be repetitive to work, but if you go on too long the players switch off. Also you have to cater for the lads who are not in the 11. It is a long season and you'll need them.

In 11 v 11 the reserves are the opposition. If we are playing someone like Nasri, or Mata, one of the reserves will be told how to play like them and the full-back will be told how far to track him if he comes inside, and when to pass him over. Once, at Sheffield, we were one short, so I was Michael Owen when we played Liverpool in the Carling Cup semi-final. I scored too. My defence obviously didn't heed the lesson because unfortunately so did Owen, in extra time. It proved to be the winner.

These days I'll often ask the captain and other senior pros their opinion. I used to ask Joey at QPR. He'd give you an opinion on most things whether you asked him or not, but there were times when I did pick his brains. I don't normally go overboard about opponents, it is more about what we are going to do, but an exception is Stoke as they are such a special case. You have to be very organised against them; people need to know what they are doing. When QPR played there in the Premier League we spent four days on the training ground planning, looking at how we were going to play them. We had a goalkeeper slinging in throws into the box to duplicate Rory Delap's long throws. We told our best header of the ball, Heider Helguson, to keep himself free and just target the incoming ball while everyone else picked up. Then we looked at how they play, how their wide players get forward to get balls in, and how we could catch them on the break.

After training the players get a personalized DVD from the IT guys. Full-backs will get one of the opposing wingers, centre-halves will get the strikers, midfielders will get the midfielders, the goalkeeper will get one about crosses, corners, penalties, things like that. A lot of the lads will watch them on Friday so it is fresh in the mind.

Friday we'll do set-pieces. They are a big part of the game and it's amazing to think clubs didn't used to bother much with them. My first manager, Jimmy McGuigan at Chesterfield, really worked on them, defending and attacking them, but that was unusual at the time.

At the back of your mind you know the lads who are not playing will be sitting down talking and not paying attention while you do set-pieces. Often you let them go with the reserve coach or somebody and do a session. Of course, if one of them comes on as sub you'd like them to know what the signals are, but it's the lesser of two evils because they will be brassed off as they are not in the team and they can be a distraction. After the session we will watch a DVD compilation of the opposition's free-kicks and corners. There is so much information about now. Everyone knows everything about everyone. Nothing is secret for long.

The atmosphere in training is a good assessment of the mood of the club. There are a lot of opportunities to build team spirit but there is also always the possibility of a confrontation developing.

Such as the week when Pascal Chimbonda had a complaint.

'Gaffer, Curly make me take my hat off before training. Why? It is so cold, I'm used to training with my hat on.'

'Don't worry,' I said, 'leave it to me. I'll sort it out.'

Curly's like that at times, but Pascal just wants some attention. He's not playing and he's probably not happy. I spoke to Curly.

'I don't want anybody wearing a hat,' he said.

'Let him wear a hat. There's not long to go, it's not worth the hassle.'

Then I told Pascal in front of all the other players: 'You can wear a hat anytime you want, nobody else, just you. I authorise it because you are used to wearing a hat, OK.' And I winked at the other lads. I could tell he wasn't sure how to take it. The other lads were clever. They didn't make a fuss, they just ignored it.

I like the banter at training. I always say it's what I'll miss when I retire. I sometimes adopt a player as my favourite. It was Phil Jagielka and Michael Brown at Sheffield. I'd call them 'son' and if it were raining I'd let them stand under my umbrella. You have to pick the right player. They were good players, and popular, so everyone was OK with it.

Then there was a time at QPR when I told the first-team squad to lie on their backs in a row. They wondered what I was up to. I walked across their stomachs in my boots and told them, 'I can tell who's doing their abdominal exercises.' I took it easy, taking the weight off and when I finished a few said: 'You should have walked without stopping, boss,' as they jogged away laughing.

'Right, back here now, we'll do it again.' This time I walked across without mercy. And this was before my diet.

Chapter Eleven

On The Road

As I mulled it over, reliving every kick, I could hear the players laughing and playing cards. They soon forget, but it's a seven-day punishment for managers.

Andy King

I PLAYED MORE GAMES FOR SCUNTHORPE UNITED THAN any other of the eight Football League clubs I graced in my glittering career, and at times it has seemed the club's been taking revenge ever since. One of my worst defeats was the 4–0 drubbing Scunthorpe inflicted on Crystal Palace at Selhurst Park in my last season there. So what happens a year later, when QPR are top of the Championship and Scunthorpe are bottom of it? Well, there was an improvement. They beat us 4–1.

The build-up wasn't the best; we had more problems with Taarbs. He rang on the Thursday to say he was struggling to get in. I told him to come in on Friday. Friday he rang Curly, said his father's in tears and he had to go home and see him. I told him he had to come into training. I had my doubts about playing him at

Scunthorpe anyway with the pitch and everything so when he got in I told him he could fly to Morocco immediately, but must be back Monday so he can play Tuesday at Barnsley.

We went one-up after seven minutes at Glanford Park and had enough chances to put the game to bed but missed them all. Then for some reason Clint Hill gave a stupid free-kick away, then he didn't mark his man and it was 1–1 at half-time. Danny Shittu and Fitz Hall were having terrible games so I took Danny off, put Clint in the centre and brought on Pascal Chimbonda at left-back. I thought that would give us more drive on the flank. But Chimbonda didn't pass the ball more than ten yards, just gave simple passes to the nearest man all the time. Then Rob Hulse conceded a silly foul and topped it off at the free-kick by not marking his man who got a header in, Paddy made a mistake, Pascal was not marking anybody and it was 2–1. They got a world-beater for 3–1. Then Clint, instead of kicking the ball out for a throw-in tried to shepherd it out – a cardinal sin in my book, the kid did him and it was 4–1.

I was furious but there was no point in bawling them out. How often did Paddy and Clint play that badly? It had to be a freak match. In the dressing room I said, 'That's got to be a one-off – there were so many bad performances – so just forget about it and relax. We have seven games to go.'

Twenty minutes down the road from Scunthorpe Heider noticed we'd left Paddy Kenny behind. Heider's got a stutter and one of the staff said, 'He noticed 15 minutes ago, he's been trying to get it out ever since: P-P-P-P-P-P.' We all laughed. That's football humour for you. Heider laughed too. He was one of the nicest players I have ever managed and one of the most underrated, a gem of a lad. We went back for Paddy but there was no rescuing the sweep for the Grand National, which we'd left at the hotel, so we didn't know who'd won. It was a nightmare day all round.

That sort of result you want to go home and forget about, but we had decided to stay up because we had Barnsley on the Tuesday. We would have got back late Saturday night and had to go back north again on Monday. That drains players physically and mentally and I thought we'd be better off staying up than doing all those miles.

The travelling is the worst part of the job. It sounds nice: away from home, on the bus, staying in a hotel, but it's not. The hotels are fine – though I've been in some ropey ones in my early days as a manager and as a player – but I'm not one for being away from home. You miss your family, and you get bored. I'm no computer whizzkid but I've started taking one to watch DVDs on, as a change from watching the TV on the bus or in my room. It's monotonous and I've been doing it a long time. Having played at Hartlepool, and managed Torquay, I know what it feels like to spend hours on a coach. It is one of the reasons my teams now get the train when we can. I remember travelling to Torquay from Hartlepool in the early Seventies. There weren't so many motorways then and it took for ever. Torquay used to play Friday night and we were given the choice between travelling the day before or stopping down after the game. We always chose stopping as that meant we could stay overnight and go out on the town after the match.

There were no iPads, iPods, PlayStations or even Walkmans in those days, no TVs on the coach either. The main activity was cards. One player at Hartlepool gambled away his Ford Anglia on a trip to Gillingham. He ran out of cash, so he threw the keys in. You might think being a team-mate the winner wouldn't take it, but he did. Heaven knows what his wife said when the guy who lost it got home. Len Ashurst was furious when he found out and he banned cards. I recalled that when I went into management and I've always kept my eye on card schools. The one good thing about long trips is the adversity gets the camaraderie going but you can't tell me people are going to play well after losing their car to a team-mate.

When all is said and done though, we have it lucky compared to the fans. We're in a comfortable coach with a telly. If the weather's bad or we get delayed it is inconvenient but no more than that. The fans are the ones who suffer in those circumstances. I'll give you a couple of examples from recent seasons when no one seems to have thought about them.

When my Palace team lost an FA Cup replay at Aston Villa some genius had decided that 10pm that night was the perfect time to start roadworks by the M6/M42 junction at Birmingham. They clearly were not a football fan as not only were 4,000 of our fans hoping to head south at that very time, but there were a similar number of Reading fans on the way home from playing at West Bromwich. Even when we got there, on the team bus having left some time after the final whistle, it took us an-hour-and-three-quarters to go eight miles: eight miles of bumper-to-bumper traffic as three lanes were squeezed into one. So what huge construction project was so urgent it had to be started then? Two blokes walking – not working – in the coned-off area. Clueless. We got back to the training ground at 3.35. Some of the lads then faced another hour's journey home before being woken up by the kids at seven. At least the players had that day off. The fans would have got back in the early hours then had to get up to go to work. I just hope none of them had a job where being wide awake at work mattered, like a bus driver or paramedic.

Then there was a trip to Leeds with QPR in the depths of winter. The pitch was fine but the weather was so bad the police said only essential travel should be undertaken. Obviously for a lot of football fans watching their team is essential travel – especially if they had already forked out for tickets. I spoke to a couple of lads a few days later who had got home at quarter-past three in the morning – from a 3pm kick-off. The snow had been forecast, so the match could have been postponed well in advance; you can't tell me football is worth people putting their lives at risk for.

I should know that better than most. I finished my league career at Crewe Alexandra. I was living in Sheffield at the time and it was a glorious journey to Cheshire over the Peak District. Then winter arrived. The road was so notorious there were lights at the bottom of the hill to warn people when it was impassable. However, the farmers I used to chat to when I stopped for a sandwich in the High Peak said it was just the authorities being over-cautious and the road was always passable. Of course, they had tractors. I had an Austin A30. For my younger readers, the Austin's top speed was about sixty mph. Downhill. With a following wind.

One night I drove over for a match with a team-mate who lived in Notts, only to find it called off for snow. I had a sandwich and we drove back. The lights were flashing, but I ploughed on. Soon I was literally ploughing on, through drifts of snow. I blasted my way through the banks but they started getting unnervingly big, almost as big as the car. Then we came across a wall of snow, about ten feet. We didn't even have a flask of coffee between us let alone blankets and a spade. It was very dark and very cold. Our jokes had a nervous titter to them, as they do when you are bricking it inside. We didn't have enough fuel to just sit there with the heater on all night, and there was no chance of anyone being as daft as we were so there was little prospect of someone coming along to rescue us. I executed a 10-point turn very slowly and we bashed our way back. When we saw those lights at the bottom of the hill it felt like reaching the cup final.

I like my players to live near the club. Commuting long-distances is not good for footballers, even in good weather. I found that out for myself as a player. When I was at Hartlepool I had a little sports car and used it to drive from Sheffield, where I lived, to Hartlepool where I had digs. I had sciatica come on and for about five or six months it was agony, and when I drove I had to put my arm under my thigh to ease the pain. In the end I went to see a specialist. He did all sorts of tests, then he said casually: 'What car do you drive?'

'An Austin Healy Sprite.'

'Oh. Just change it then, you won't have a problem.'

I thought to myself. 'I'm paying money to see you and that is all you can come up with. What rubbish.'

But I borrowed a car for a couple of weeks, an Escort. Within three or four days I never felt another twinge. 'All these months of agony,' I thought, 'and it was so simple.'

That came back to me at QPR. Because of the size of London some players lived a bit too far away. Fitz Hall came right round the M25 to get to the training ground and I began to think it was not a coincidence that he kept getting back and hamstring problems. In the end I said, 'Your contract is up at the end of the season and you really have to think about moving, because these niggles you are getting have got to be related to the driving you are doing.' He got a flat near the training ground and the injuries stopped.

When I went to Scarborough we often trained in Sheffield because it was more convenient for the players. The first time I met the chairman, some time before I got the job, I had told him he'd never get a decent team if he insisted the players lived in Scarborough. But when we got into the league and went full-time it was different. We were then their main employer. I moved to

Scarborough and so did the players, except those in Hull, which was only 45 minutes away.

Personally I like to live no more than 15 minutes away from the training ground. At QPR I was half-an-hour away, in Richmond, because of William's school, but Loftus Road was closer. At Palace I was five minutes from our Beckenham training ground. I lived just outside Oldham when I was there. I discovered the delights of the West Country when at Torquay and Plymouth. The closest was in Sheffield when I was two minutes away, but then we moved the training ground to the other side of Sheffield. I delayed the change as long as I could, as I knew it would add 30 minutes to my journey.

I don't think players should do more than 30 minutes each way. At Leeds I have people driving in from Manchester. They rely on the M62 all through winter. If they are late it is their fault, they still get fined, it is they who have chosen to live where they are.

After that dreadful result against Scunthorpe I found myself wondering if taking QPR back down south might not have been the best option. Avoiding hours on the road was the thinking behind staying up in Yorkshire that weekend, but what seemed a like a good idea when I planned it sitting in my office did not look such a good decision in the wake of a thrashing. With all the players cooped up together there was a danger of the result festering. We tried to relax. The lads played golf and went in the pool on the Sunday. I got out of their way and nipped down to see James and Charlie in Leeds. It helped me and the lads seemed fresher by Sunday night too.

Come Monday morning the first task was to find Taarbs. Caroline had booked him on the 12.30 train but didn't know where he was. I then found Adel had rang Paul, the press officer, and asked him to get a copy of every one of his games and he'd pick it up at 1.00 from the training ground – so he's obviously not going to get a 12.30 train. I rang Paul and told him, 'Don't you think you should tell me things like this? I need to know where he is.'

I got Caroline to speak to him and suggested instead of getting the train we had a car waiting at the training ground to bring him straight up otherwise we might never see him again. Caroline rang at quarter to two; of course he's not there. I told Caroline the car's just going to have to wait. At quarter past two he turned up. I told Caroline, 'Don't let the car leave without him.' She called back; Adel needed to go home to get something and wanted the car to meet him there at four o'clock. I told them to make it earlier to beat the traffic and send the car with him. The car followed Adel, to his friend's house, not his, left with him at quarter to four and he eventually arrived at our hotel at half-seven. He wasn't the only arrival. After the way we defended on Saturday I had decided to recall Matt Connolly and Kaspars Gorkss and play them in harness as they play well together. I rang Connolly who'd lost his confidence with a bad performance last time he played. That had knocked him back weeks but he'd been smiling in training so I thought he was ready.

'How are you feeling Matt?' I asked. 'Are you ready to play?'

'Great gaffer. I want to get back in.'

'Get up here then, you're playing Tuesday.'

While Taarbs and Connolly were coming north, Jamie Mackie and Peter Ramage were heading south. They'd both been injured so bringing them along made them feel involved. Mackie went back to continue his rehab while Ramage went back to play in a reserve game. I told him, 'Have half-an-hour, then the following week have a full game.' Then if I needed to use him I could. You have to ease players back gently.

It soon turned out they were not the only ones going back. I brought in Pascal Chimbonda because I thought he'd be good cover with his experience and versatility but it was not one of my best decisions. He was not a good influence and the weekend highlighted that. All I could hear on the bus on Saturday was 'Why are we not on our way to London?' On Monday morning he was moaning, 'I wish we were in London.' Then someone asked Nigel Cox what time kick-off was and I heard Pascal shout, 'Never mind kick-off, when do we get back to London so we can go out?' That did it for me. I said to Mick, 'It's not going to be a nice job, but I'm going to get rid of him today.'

I waited until everyone had their lunch then I called him in. 'Look Pasc,' I said, 'I'm not having you on the bench today. In fact you don't want to be around so I've booked you a train ticket and I'll get one of the staff to take you to the station. We have only got six games left and now Ramage is fit I won't be using you, so as far as I am concerned you can stay at home now.'

'I'll come in training.'

'I don't want you coming in training. I don't think you are a good influence.'

'What on?' he said.

'On the other players. I don't think you are a good influence if you're not playing. All I've heard is "Why aren't we in London? I want to go home." Well now you can go. You get on that train and if I need you before the end of the season I'll give you a buzz.'

In the afternoon I got a call from Jeppo saying Ramage had done well and was OK. I was glad to hear it. When we got to Barnsley, I spoke to the lads before we got off the bus. 'Listen lads,' I said. 'You've seen Pascal's not with us tonight, but let me tell you a story. When I was at Sheffield United I spent £1m on Ade Akinbayi and £1m on Geoff Horsfield and then we didn't win for about four games. We had six games to go. I knew if I carried on playing those two we wouldn't go up. So I made a decision l was going to play Neil Shipperley, who was overweight according to everyone else, couldn't run, etc, etc. But I knew he was a team player and a fabulous person. I called him in and said, "Neil, you are going to play the next six games irrespective of how you play." We went up and Neil was instrumental in that. Now I know Pascal Chimbonda's not a striker, but the same principle applies. I didn't want those two involved but if I'd been a younger manager I wouldn't have been able to drop them having spent that money. Having been around I thought, "To hell, if I don't do it now we're not going up." I thought the same today about Pascal. I've done it for a reason. You've all tolerated him but it's enough for us all with Adel without anybody else and we all know Adel's not the same animal [I said this in front of Taarabt]. I want us all together tonight; we're going to need that. I read in this morning's paper, and it does sum us up, "If you spend all your time worrying about the clouds, you forget about the sunshine." I thought that was great. So let's get out there and think about the sunshine.'

We got off and I said to Mick, 'That's better, they're all our lads here and we'll need them in the trenches tonight.' That was absolutely spot on. Adel scored a wonderful goal after 47 seconds but sometimes the saying, 'you can score too early' is true because Barnsley then put us under so much pressure. Fortunately we defended magnificently, everybody, and I mean everybody, defended from the front. Gorkss had one of his best games since I'd been at the club and Matt did well too. Barnsley got onto the referee as well, the players, and then their staff at half-time. Tony Bates was referee. He doesn't give much either way and he's usually consistent, but the second half was a nightmare. Nathan Doyle did Taarabt with a terrible tackle from behind. It took both his legs. I thought it was a red card. I'm waiting to see what colour card the ref produces when he makes a sign with his hands to signal a ball. I thought, 'I better get Adel off before he's injured. If that's not even a foul it's going to be open season on him.' I thought I'd be putting his career in jeopardy leaving him on and I've never felt that before.

When I went in to see my son James who'd come to the game the assessors were there. I shook my head and I think they knew. I like Tony, he's one of the better refs, but it was a bad day at the office. I've never seen him like that before. They got to him, but it didn't affect the win and it felt fantastic coming off the pitch. At Oakwell the away fans are in the corner and they were loving it. When we went over to clap them it felt like we'd won the FA Cup. For me there was relief as well, after the thing with Chimbonda, losing badly at Scunthorpe and the other clubs mouthing off about catching us.

Then it was back on the bus and this time the miles just flew by. They always do when you've won.

Chapter Twelve

Half-Time Wisdom

Anyone who uses the word 'quintessentially' in a half-time talk is talking crap.

Mick McCarthy, after a contribution from
then-player Niall Quinn

WHAT YOU SAY AT HALF-TIME IS THE MOST IMPORTANT five minutes of a manager's week and you have to choose your words carefully because no two players are alike. Some you have to bully to bring the best from them, some you have to put an arm around. When QPR played at Nottingham Forest that season we were struggling to contain them and one reason was that Rob Hulse was being dominated by his marker, Wes Morgan. Rob wasn't holding the ball up which meant we weren't relieving pressure on the defence so we couldn't get into the game. At half-time I went over to him and told him to pull his finger out. 'You're not doing enough. You're letting us all down. Morgan's got you in his pocket. He's strolling out there. He's got the big cigar and everything. Impose yourself on him.'

'What do you want me to do, gaffer? Twat him and get myself sent off?'

'No, you pillock. I don't want you to twat him, but I do want you to let him know he's in a game.'

Looking back it was funny, I'm sure Rob also laughs at it now. But it worked because it got a reaction. He didn't thump Morgan, though he did get booked for giving him a whack early in the half. I didn't mind that. It showed he had changed his approach. He played much better in the second half, we got into the game and won a good point.

A manager is a psychiatrist as well as a tactician, talent scout and all the other things. So much of football, any sport, is in the mind. The mental side of the game is becoming more and more important. The week before we went into administration at Crystal Palace the players were attacking matches without any negative thoughts in their heads. We were heading for the play-offs and the vibe was positive. A week later we'd lost 10 points and were in a relegation scrap. The players were the same but suddenly they were fearful of making errors and that affected their performance. In circumstances like that, especially with a young team, you can change the game in your favour at half-time, but you have to choose your words carefully. I don't say that much because it is important what you do say has maximum effect, especially when you've not got long to make a difference, like at half-time.

At soon as the whistle goes for the break I get straight into the dressing room then listen to the players coming in, moaning or making good points. If we're doing well they all want to talk, if not they all shut up and it's quiet, unless there's arguing going on between players over something that happened in the half.

I never say much then, I go off with Mick Jones – who's been sitting in the stand to get a different view – and Curly and get their opinion. I listen to them and then tell them what I think. By now the physio will have checked the players and he'll tell us if anyone has a problem, if anyone has to come off, has a tight hamstring, or something else we need to be aware off.

Then I'll go in and talk about how we're going to defend better, or get more crosses in, or if they have a danger man let's go ten against ten and man-mark him. You get people come back at you sometimes, but in general, while they might not agree with you, they listen. Every manager has a situation where a player may say 'I don't agree with this or that' but not often. Usually they are not challenging your authority, it is more a case of them being constructive and I don't mind that. Sometimes there is a genuine reason for something not working on the pitch. They might say, 'Gaffer, he's making a different run so we have to pass on and not stay with him', or, 'They're blocking at corners.' You may not have seen that. They don't answer back much; over the years one of my strengths has been is that I can spot things. If someone does disagree you try and explain why you want something done. If they persevere you just tell them to shut up.

I have been known to throw or kick something at half-time, but not often; if you do that it loses impact. I've not thrown proper crockery, I'll throw a paper cup or a drinks bottle, but I'll have had a look at where the shower is and I know it won't hurt anyone or break anything. I might look angry but I never completely lose control. It's a controlled rage, especially as you get older.

And you have to be careful what you kick. With Burton at Macclesfield once, the ref played seven minutes' injury time and they equalised to make it 1–1. I was furious at my defenders for not getting rid of the ball in the build-up to their goal and while rollicking them decided to kick what I thought was a cardboard box for effect. It was actually a scrap of cardboard covering one of those old fashioned metal anvils used for hammering studs into boots. It didn't give an inch. I can't describe the pain, but I couldn't show the players. I had to close my mouth and bear it. I walked into the shower room and bit my wrist so hard I drew blood. I'd had an operation to remove a hammertoe and only just come off crutches. It was agony.

Other times I'll take a different tack. I'll tell people at half-time in an even game, 'Which way do you want to go now? Remember last week beating so-and-so and how you felt, do you want that feeling again? Or the other week, when we lost to so-and-so, and you felt like death warmed up, when you came back in here and knew you should have won, and you felt like that all week. Do you want to feel like that, or feel like you did when you won?'

The time was approaching when I would need to make a telling half-time intervention. Despite getting the points at Oakwell things were still a bit tense as QPR closed in on promotion; Flavio had been interfering again. Before we went to Scunthorpe, on the Friday morning, Gianni came into training as white as a sheet.

I said to him: 'What's up? What's happened?'

'I was summoned to see Flavio last night at half-seven. I turn up at the restaurant and Pini Zahavi is sat with him on one side, Kia Joorabchian, Tevez's agent, on the other, Avram Grant's there as well. They are all talking about players, some that might cost him £20m.'

I was dumbfounded. I didn't know then that Kia would become a large player at QPR when I left.

'I've told them all I don't want to go foreign until Christmas,' I said. 'I want us to give the players time to establish themselves, to settle the team in. You've been fantastic to me but we both know Flavio is going to be difficult to control with all these agents talking telephone numbers from abroad. Stall him as long as you can because I'll do only this as long as there's no interference.'

It's not what I had been promised. Amit had assured me he would have the majority shareholding in a couple of weeks, but that didn't happen.

After the Scunthorpe game I didn't get any calls until Monday, then Flavio came on. He'd heard the result and he was obviously panicking, he always did after we lost a game. Bernie Ecclestone also called. 'We can't afford another result like that, Neil, blah, blah. Flavio is not happy either. It cannot happen.'

I'm thinking, I know they don't understand football, but does anybody want a result like that? You don't plan for results like that. I said, 'Bernie, you've got to leave it with me, let me deal with it. There's six games left, we'll get ups and downs, so will the other teams.'

'But how did that happen against a bottom of the league team?'

I think I said something like, 'It's like when you put wet tyres on a Grand Prix car, you don't know what's going to happen.'

Obviously we then get that good result at Barnsley. I went straight down to Cornwall to join the family who had gone down there. Bernie rang on the Thursday, he said, 'Well done' and all that, then he said, 'Do you want me to come and give a talk to them on Monday [before our next game, v Derby]?'

'No. I appreciate your thoughts but I don't want to change anything. I'm superstitious like that.'

It was an excuse. I'd heard about him and Flavio coming in and doing talks and I didn't want that. I'd heard that if we did go up I'd be losing my job. I'd kept hearing all the time about Flavio wanting someone else in if we get to the Premier League. He didn't want me to sign any players. I tried to re-sign Helguson, and give him a deal which meant if he played 20 games he'd get a further year on the wages for whatever league we were in. He'd been fantastic for me. I spoke to Gianni and he'd agreed, but Flavio said no. Obviously Flavio was running the show. He began ringing me and talking about players who, in his view, were not good enough. I just bit my tongue but it meant, despite our league position – clear at the top – I wasn't really enjoying it. I was doing it for the fans really; they'd been superb with me. They'd had 15 years of bad times and deserved some good ones. 'What will be, will be,' I thought. I knew Sharon would be quite happy if I got the sack, packed it in and we all went to Cornwall for good, whatever other offers might crop up. That meant I could be quite sanguine about the situation.

After Barnsley I gave the players Wednesday and Thursday off, then Adel said he needed Friday off. We were not playing until Monday so I said, 'OK, I'll see you all Saturday, everybody.' Of course, Adel was nowhere to be seen come Saturday. I found out he'd been with his Moroccan friend from Arsenal, Chamakh. Then he rang up and claimed I'd said 'come in Sunday'. He'd put weight on as he was not training and it was not good enough. I had a one-to-one with him on the Sunday and told him what I expected of him.

When the game arrived Adel's lack of sharpness showed. Robbie Savage, who's more than a decade older, man-marked him and Adel didn't work hard enough to lose him. I had to pull him off after about 65–70 minutes. When he came off Coxy, like a stupid physio, gave him a bottle of water that he deliberately threw down in disgust. All the while the TV cameras were on him. I didn't say anything at the time, but later in the week, during a staff meeting, I said to Nigel, 'If you ever give another bottle of water to Adel when he's been substituted I will ram it down your throat.' I think he understood. We laughed about it later.

Giving a player a bottle of water shouldn't cause an issue, in fact it's good practice to keep players hydrated, but Adel had become a problem. When we trained on the Thursday I decided to finish it off with a forwards drill, three against two, so Adel could get a few goals and get him back into it. I put this session on and everybody was superb apart from Adel who didn't give a toss. He toe-poked the ball away, turned round and passed the ball out, never really tried. I was disgusted with him, but I kept it to myself.

The following day we trained before setting off for Cardiff. They were in second place just behind us so it was an important game. I called Adel into my office and laid it out to him. 'I put Thursday's session on just for you and you repaid me by showing how much disrespect you have for me. If you want to go at the end of the season that's fine by me, just don't show me that disrespect after what I've done for you this season. Nobody else would have done what I have done for you. To treat me with contempt like that was disgusting. I expect better.' I added: 'There are four games to go. You have to accept that if you aren't playing well or are being marked out of the game I have to be able to substitute you without you throwing a tantrum. And you've put weight on.'

One of the players – Mackie or Derry – had lifted his shirt up the day before and he looked all floppy, puppy fat. The fitness guy confirmed he'd put weight on. He didn't look after himself. He wasn't professional enough. By then I doubted Adel would be with us next year and was just concentrating on getting us over the line.

I sent him out, and then I called in Clint Hill, Tommy Smith, Heider Helguson, Bradley Orr and Paddy Kenny.

I said to them: 'Shaun Derry was annoyed yesterday and wanted to have a go at Taarbs, the way he played and trained, but I'm not having any of you lot, if you're not having a good game, having a go at Taarbs. It's an easy get out. You've got to concentrate on your own game. We have four games to go and we have to win one of them. You've got to encourage him as much as you can. He is one of the main reasons we are where we are and you have got to tolerate it for four games. You must know how difficult it is for me as a manager.'

They were brilliant. Then I saw Derry. He had been saying to Curly the day before, 'It's not right, Curly, I have to do something.'

Curly said, 'I played with [Georgi] Kinkladze at Manchester City and it was exactly the same. In training he was a disgrace but in matches you just give him the ball and that is what we are going to do.'

Shaun strutted off. I could tell he was in a bad mood. He hadn't been spot on in the last couple of games and, like a lot of players, if he's not on his game he will, at times, blame someone else. So I collared him, and before I could say owt he said, 'It's all right gaffer, I know what you're saying. I just have to get my head around it and I will do.' So off we went to Cardiff, the lid just about on.

Ninian Park was a real old-fashioned football ground but Cardiff's new one has been well designed and also creates a good atmosphere. There was a full house in and it was rocking. I could see one or two of our lads were nervous and after Jay Bothroyd scored a fantastic goal after six minutes, I thought, 'with all their strikers we'll have to hang in now.'

They could have had three or four then Taarbs pulled one out of the hat. A corner went back to him and he bent it in the far corner. It was a fantastic goal. He was the only player on the pitch who could have scored it. I was standing on the side by the half-way line. The noise was bedlam. Then Adel scored and it was like putting an earplug in, to one side was total silence. All you could hear was our fans on the other side. You could *hear* the quietness elsewhere. It was weird.

But then Gorkss let Bothroyd cross it from the left and Craig Bellamy scored. At half-time I had work to do. I waited a few minutes as usual, and then got into them.

'We're giving them too much respect. Forget the fact they have Bothroyd and Bellamy and all that. We're top of the league, not them, we should go and play. Show them how good we are. We're not closing down enough, we're not passing early enough. We're not playing as a team. We're huffing and puffing because of where we are in the league table. Do you not realise a result here virtually guarantees promotion because it stops them from getting three points? We have to get a grip of ourselves. It has to start from the first tackle, the first header. And we have to get Adel on the ball more in dangerous areas.'

Then I took Adel to one side and said to him: 'We need a bit more magic from you.'

We started a lot better in the second half and Taarbs scored from a good ball from Routledge to level. It was a great point for us, looking back it was the point that won us the league. The dressing room was buzzing afterwards. I was really proud of them. I actually had a tear in my eye and had to stop talking to them. Mick pulled me to one side and said, 'Don't worry about that, gaffer, I don't blame you.'

My teams have often got better in the second half. At Sheffield United we were known for coming stronger in the second half, no matter what the result was we always got better which was good to know as a manager, and the fans got to realise it too which made them get behind us. It made a virtuous circle. Once, when William was five or six, we were losing 2–1 at half-time and Sharon went off for a cup of tea inside with Amy and William. They were talking to someone inside about how disappointing the first half had been and William chirped up, 'Don't worry, my dad will give them a bollocking at half-time and we'll win.' And we did.

William's heard it for himself, when we had a pre-season match at Luton with QPR. We came in at half-time 1–0 up but I wasn't happy and I let them know, using some choice language. Then I saw Will there. I said: 'I don't want you repeating anything you've heard in here.'

'It's all right, Dad, there's nothing I haven't heard before.'

All the players started laughing.

Chapter Thirteen

Don't Believe All You Read

The press in England make from a little mosquito a big elephant.

Ruud Gullit

AS IF THERE WASN'T ENOUGH TO CONTEND WITH AT QPR that spring, what with Flavio interfering, Adel playing up and a title to win, there was a Football Association investigation hanging over us. Ali Faurlin had joined the club in the summer of 2009, several managers before I arrived. He had a good season and we decided to extend his contract at the start of my first full season. That was agreed in the October. However, it seems his contract was partly owned by a third party, which was illegal under FA rules brought in after the Carlos Tevez affair. There was also a claim that an unlicensed agent had been involved. I wasn't responsible for transfers or contract negotiations so it all came as a bit of a shock to me when the FA charged us with seven counts of breaking regulations. This was bitterly ironic as far as I was concerned; the third-party regulations had only been brought in as a result of Tevez playing for West Ham – that season he kept them up virtually single-handedly at the expense of my Sheffield United team.

Obviously some in the media thought this irony very funny but I wasn't seriously worried as I had sat down with our barrister, Ian Mill, after we were charged. He spent an hour going through all the charges, what they meant, what we had or had not done, and satisfied everything I wanted to know. He thought we might be fined for breaching a couple of regulations, but there would be no points deduction whatsoever. I trusted him because he knew his stuff, and he was also independent of the club. It was good to hear because there was some speculation about points deductions in some tabloids. The players had been fairly relaxed about it, ribbing Faurlin as players will, but I could tell it was at the backs of their minds, nagging away – in the circumstances it was amazing they had maintained their form, especially Faurlin who was bound to feel responsible even though it was not his doing. I went over the charges with them, told them what the barrister had told me, and that we should let him deal with the case while we concentrated on our job: winning games.

The FA had announced the hearing would be on 3 May with the verdict two days later. The Championship season ended on 7 May so while I was confident about the verdict I was obviously aware it would add a bit of pressure on the panel if we had already clinched promotion. We had the chance to do that on Easter Monday, against Hull City, and should have done as we scored a good goal through Routledge – but then missed a sackful of chances. Gorkss made a mistake with eight minutes to go and they equalised but even then we thought we'd done enough only to hear, while the crowd were already on the pitch, that Norwich had snatched an injury-time equaliser to remain in contention. So we had to wait and I had a right go at Kaspars in the dressing room. I was kicking stuff, banging things, saying one or two things. I was gutted because we should have wrapped it up loads of times by then.

We had another chance to seal promotion before the hearing, away to Watford. But the day before the game there was a big double-page piece in the *Sun* from Shaun Custis, their main football writer, quoting an anonymous 'source' and claiming we'd be deducted 15 points. It was scandalous. There were no facts in it at all other than a 'source' within the FA. Like most of these 'sources' you see quoted, it was either a figment of the journalist's imagination or someone who didn't actually know what they were talking about.

It was the Royal Wedding day and as a Royalist I should have been in a good mood but I was furious. We were training before going to a hotel and when I got to the training ground Curly pulled me aside. 'The players have seen the papers and they're rock bottom, gaffer,' he said. 'I've never seen them like this. They've asked to speak to somebody at the club.'

'I'll speak to them.'

I told them, 'It's pointless getting somebody out here because you'll not know more than what I've told you. The barrister tells me he just thinks there will be a fine. I can only tell you what we're told – and you all know what QPR is like.' Hopefully that was comforting. I added: 'You cannot use this as an excuse. Stop messing about with these draws and get a result at Watford. Focus on that.'

Talksport rang and asked if I could go on with Darren Gough and Adrian Durham. I agreed. I said, 'The story is atrocious. They said a source at the FA – we all know what that means, I have a source who tells me their source is in the *Sun*'s office.'

It is ridiculous they can get away with that. Just because they had no back page that day they ruined all my preparation. There are a lot of other things I'd like to have said but I had to bite my tongue – Ishan had said, 'Don't make any comment, the club thinks this article will help, not hinder us.'

When you are at a club in the spotlight, such as QPR, there is something wrong about you in the tabloids almost every day. I used to get upset and ring up, but age makes a difference and, except for extreme cases like the points deduction story, I don't bother any more.

The biggest things that bug me with the papers is when a story comes out with 'a source', like that story, and those columnists who give you stick but never have the guts to talk to you in person. It is not as if I am unavailable. I give press conferences at least twice a week and, because I realise journalists have a job to do, I usually ring them back if they call me. But there are a few columnists out there who hide behind their laptops, rehash old tales, and spout the first thing that comes into their head.

Over the years the football writer's job has changed. To get on now young journalists have to create headlines and there is a difference in the questions they ask. They used to look for angles and talk about football, now it is all about headlines and personalities, no one ever asks about the game. Often you can tell within a couple of minutes a journalist has already done his story and is asking questions to back it up. But if you are clever enough you give the answers you want.

When I started we had the press guy on the bus, I would talk to him in confidence and because he wouldn't let me down I would give him everything. I still tell the local guys everything. I tell them 'I'll give you things you won't get anywhere else. But if you let me down once, I'll never give you anything again.' But they don't go on the bus any more. That stopped at Huddersfield. I got on well with Mel Booth, the local reporter, but by then no one did it any more.

Those days seem long gone now. There are still a few journalists you can trust like that, but there is generally a lack of trust between us (players and managers) and the press. You are always thinking, 'How will they interpret that?' It's sad. You know certain tabloids will produce headlines that do not represent what you said, and then the journalist says, 'I didn't write the headline.' That may be true, but it is a cop-out. They can influence it.

In response you have to try and shape coverage to your ends. When you start out you do anything to get the club publicity. I once abseiled down the Grand Hotel at Scarborough, a stunt to do with the Army, but the local paper's deadline meant they needed to take a picture before we were given any training. I was persuaded to do it. Having to let go from the top of that hotel was the most terrifying thing I've ever done.

Every manager uses the media. Sir Alex is the top man at it, but when you have the best team you can do that. There are certain times in your career when the media can help you with a particular game. You used to talk about the referee beforehand to put a bit of pressure on him, or make him aware of something, but the FA got wise to it and you can't do that now. You can raise or lower expectations within the fans, media and your own players by how you talk about a game, or season, coming up. Some managers go as far to tell lies about injuries and tactics. I was told Glenn Hoddle did this as England manager. During the 1998 World Cup he told the press Sol Campbell had a knee injury. Sol then went in to see the press who, naturally, asked him how his knee was. Sol looked blank. The press explained Hoddle said he had a knee problem. Sol paused, smiled, and asked, 'Did he say which knee it was?'

I don't lie as such, but you can be misleading – a little white lie as my mum and dad used to say. You might say a player has only a ten per cent chance of playing, when you know he's actually got a good chance. Most managers do that. On a couple of occasions I have told a player I am leaving out that I will tell the media he has a slight knock. The player usually agrees as he doesn't want people to know he has been dropped. It makes it easier for me because I am then not asked why he's been dropped, and makes the player look better.

I don't plan press conferences the way Jose Mourinho has said he does, I think I'm better speaking off the cuff, but I do have an idea of what I want to say. I'm fortunate because I'm relaxed both with the cameras on me and at talking to newspaper reporters. I know who the snakes are now. It's experience. We had a press conference soon after the John Terry-Anton Ferdinand racism allegation and when we finished a young reporter asked if we could have 'a quick chat off the record'. There were some of the biggest snakes in the trade there. I looked around the room and said to him, 'Off the record? With this lot? I'd be hung drawn and quartered.' All the journalists laughed, they knew I was right.

I appreciate what they do. I like reading the papers myself, I always have done. I look at several every day, you get bits of gossip about who might be available, who's done what, whether there's a press campaign developing over tackling or something – which can influence refs and the FA. On a day off, or matchday mornings, if it is a nice day I'll sit in the garden and read a few.

I'm actually a journalist myself, of sorts. I've written a Saturday column for *The Independent* since I was at Sheffield United and it has been nominated for a journalism award in the past. The reason I have stayed loyal to *The Independent* – and I've had offers of more money elsewhere – is because I can trust them not to take my column out of context, not to put a misleading headline on it. They have never tried to stitch me up. There are times when something has happened with my club and they will want me to address it. That's fair enough, they'd look silly if they employed me to write a column and I avoid the difficult things. But it gives me a chance to say what really happened without it being twisted. So it works well for both of us.

I enjoy doing it and it's enabled people to see another side of me, to see I'm not just some ogre ranting on the touchline. That aspect is only 90 minutes in my week, and I may only be ranting for a couple of minutes in it, but because that is the bit people see on TV they form the wrong impression. I get letters from people saying things like 'I've never liked you, but I do enjoy your column.' And people sometimes stop us in the street and talk to the kids about things they have read in the column.

Like quite a few managers I also do some electronic media. While at Sheffield United I started doing some radio. I used to do a Christmas Show. I'd ring up managers, and ex-players, and we'd have a chat about what they were doing and play a few of my favourite Motown records. I enjoyed it so much when I had a spell working for Talksport I did a Christmas Show for them too. For Talksport I worked with Alan Brazil, which was good fun. I think he liked working with me because I used to bring the packing up – that's a packed lunch to posh people – which Sharon made.

I do some television punditry, especially if I am between jobs. It keeps you in the public eye, brings in a few quid, and allows you to go to matches without people thinking you are after the manager's job. You don't want to get over-exposed though. After I left QPR Sharon did suggest I start turning things down because, she said, 'People will get fed up with looking at you.'

I enjoy making people smile when I'm on; people take themselves so seriously. I want to do some TV work when I finish but I don't want to do too much. Otherwise I might as well keep on working. I try and be constructive with what I say when I am the pundit. I try and put myself in the seat of the manager. I think it means more to people in the game if it is a fellow manager commenting, or a former player like Gary Neville, whose punditry I like. You take it more to heart, so you have to be measured.

There are two forms of TV punditry: covering a live match at the ground, or sitting in the studio watching games then commenting on them in the evening in a highlights show. That can be a long day, but there are worse jobs than watching football match after football match. Besides, there's usually another manager with me to keep me company. Working with someone like Gordon Strachan, who can be very funny, helps the afternoon pass quickly.

The live game is fine if you are in a studio, but potentially less comfortable if the TV company are doing it pitchside, as ESPN did with their FA Cup matches. I did an Arsenal-Aston Villa tie for them a couple of years ago and it was absolutely freezing. Fortunately I had plenty of layers on including long johns, scarf, jumpers and overcoat, even a pair of old sheepskin gloves. They had taken the precaution for the game I went to of placing the presentation desk in front of the home end. A few weeks earlier they had been at the away end in a game when Leeds were the visitors. I'm told the supporters' vocabulary in shouting over to Robbie Savage was post-watershed and a stray ball whacked towards them in the warm-up hit Martin Keown on the head.

It used to be a real special match if your club was on TV, now it is so commonplace I think everyone is used to it, though the first few times QPR were on Adel Taarabt was so poor, trying to do it all himself, I began thinking about leaving him out when the cameras were there. The money is welcome of course, and it has transformed the Premier League, but I do feel sorry for the fans when games are moved to inconvenient times for television.

I never played in a live televised match and I'd been managing for years before one of my teams played in one. I'm told it was the FA Cup quarter-final against Tottenham in 1991, though it might have been the Division Three play-off final against Tranmere Rovers the year before. TV showed highlights of Burton's FA Cup tie against Leicester, and another FA Cup tie between Notts County and Manchester City got a lot of coverage. They filmed us training in the snow when, from behind me, with the cameras running, my only two goalkeepers went whizzing past on a sledge. They could have both been crocked. I was horrified but had to pretend I knew it was happening. Now there are even plenty of Conference games televised and they have access to dressing rooms and everything.

You do have to be careful when cameras are around because you can forget they are there. I did a fly-on-the-wall programme at Sheffield United. It was quite good but all the attention afterwards was on my swearing. I'm told you can still find film of me rollicking the players on YouTube. So when I joined QPR and discovered they had a film crew everywhere doing what became *The Four Year Plan* I was careful as to where and when I allowed them to film. They were nice guys, but I wasn't in control of the editing which can totally change the way you are perceived.

When I arrived I didn't allow the director, Matt Gentry, access into the dressing room, but the more I got to know him the more I felt he was all right. So in the end I let him in the dressing room at certain times.

The final film was quite an eye-opener. If you've not seen it yet, you should. I watched it with Sharon. She said she'd watch the first five minutes with me over a cup of tea, and was still there at the end, the tea going cold. We all sat there, mouths agape. At the end there was just silence. It made me realise what an achievement it was to get success in spite of all that happened. I was glad it happened because I don't think anyone would have believed the circumstances I was working under without seeing the film. I didn't realise myself quite how difficult it was for the managers who preceded me. Nor did I know all that went on behind the scenes when I was manager. There's one part where we've been held to a draw in the last minute by Bristol City and Flavio is filmed saying, 'The coach is effing rubbish. He doesn't want to win games. He has no idea.' I'm glad I didn't know that was happening.

Television coverage has probably saved me a fortune in recent years. There was a time when I was up in front of the FA commission so often we were on first-name terms. Now with all the cameras you know before you speak to the media what actually happened when you talk about an incident and a referee's decision. Before I had to guess, and when they showed it and I was wrong I looked daft. Now, if the officials were right I keep my mouth shut, if they were wrong I can just point to the evidence. It's taken some of the emotion out of it, which is when I tended to talk myself into trouble.

I have been banned a few times and it does make life difficult. There are managers who prefer to sit up in the stands and take in the play but I want to be on the touchline. The players I've managed over the years need reminding about their jobs and you can't do that from the stands. You can send a message down by phone but it never gets on as quickly or carries as much weight as when you are shouting it yourself.

However, when you are managing a top Premier League side

the players don't need someone in their ear all the time. The manager does his work before the game and at half-time, rendering touchline bans meaningless. If the FA really want to impose an effective punishment they should copy Uefa and bring in stadium bans. While I wouldn't like it for personal reasons I think it would make managers think twice. It hurts to miss a match, I've done more than 1,250 and I can only think of a couple of occasions when I was too ill to get to the game, I have to be at death's door to stay away. It is the same with players. I've long argued players who dive should receive retrospective six-match suspensions. That would soon cut it out.

The drawback is managers might become reluctant to talk to the media after a game for fear of punishment – a case of shooting the messenger you might say, but it would be more a case of self-protection. I don't really see why saying something about a referee to TV, or in a press conference, should result in a touchline ban anyway, it's not as if you have done something wrong on the touchline. The punishment should be appropriate.

I've started using technology in the post-match press conferences. In our promotion season at QPR we played at Portsmouth and conceded a penalty. Paddy Kenny made a brilliant save but the referee ordered a retake as the linesman said Paddy had moved early. Well, he might have done, by an inch or two, but if you ordered retakes for that every kick would be retaken. At the same time Kanu's great size 15 boots were encroaching more than a foot into the box. Kanu did the same at the retake, which Portsmouth scored. If you're going to order a retake for what Paddy did, there should be a retake for what Kanu did. It is gaining an unfair advantage. A year earlier Leicester had scored against my Palace side from a rebound when one of their players encroached so far into the box he'd almost been ahead of the taker.

So at Portsmouth I asked Andy Belk, our IT man, to freeze-frame the moment on his computer and took Andy into the press conference to show them my complaint was valid. We scored a last-minute equalizer so no harm was done, but I did say to the linesman afterwards, 'If you flag for something like that you are in the game for the wrong reasons'.

It can be a problem for teams, whether going for promotion or fighting relegation, if television coverage means you keep playing a few hours, or days, behind your rivals. I'm a big lover of Saturday afternoon games but sometimes you can go months without a home Saturday 3pm kick-off. Several matches in our promotion were televised and we had mixed results so I was quite happy that Watford game that followed the scandalous *Sun* story wasn't among them. It would feel more like an ordinary match.

As was becoming commonplace Adel was a problem in the build-up. I gave them two days off after the draw with Hull but when we came back in on the Thursday there was no Taarabt. Eventually Caroline got hold of him – he had to answer the phone because she was getting a ticket for his girlfriend to go back to France. I took over the call.

'Adel. Where are you, Why are you not in training?'

'I didn't know we were training today, gaffer,' he said all innocent.

'Adel, do you really think I'd give you all three days off in the middle of the week?'

'Sorry, gaffer.'

Let's be honest. Before QPR I would not have tolerated Adel at any time but for some reason I just knew if I persevered with him we would get promotion.

At Watford we had a meeting with the players. I said, 'Just get on with the game, a point will do us,' but I'd begun to wonder if things were conspiring against us with the Faurlin issue. First Tevez, then this, neither of them my doing. I didn't deserve it. We'd also lost Clint Hill. He had bits floating in his ankle and he saw a specialist at the start of the season who said, 'You could probably play five or six games, or it might even last the season. See how it goes.' He had only missed one match, which was unbelievable. The pain he must have been in some games. Half the people in my squad wouldn't have played half those games, the pain he's suffered. Sharon's always said she hopes William grows up to be as fearless as Clint.

We put in the team-sheet. The lads went out for the warm-up then about 25 to three the dressing room door opened and Curly came running in. 'Gaffer, Paddy's no good. He's gone for a shot and he feels his shoulder will go anytime.'

Bloody hell. Paddy came in and it was obvious we would have to go with Radek Cerny. I didn't go straight to the ref; I didn't want Watford to know. We left it to quarter to. Then I went and saw the ref. He was warming up. I told him, and then explained what had happened to Malky Mackay, their bright young manager. I told him he'd be glad Paddy wasn't playing and we changed the team-sheet.

Then with 20 minutes gone Fitz's hamstring went again. So we'd lost Clint, Paddy, Fitz, and there's the points things looming over us. If you are as superstitious as I am you do begin to wonder, but I told myself, don't let it affect you. We made some changes but I didn't bring Taarbs off this time as I thought he could win the game for us. We'd played him further forward rather than let John Eustace mark him. I thought about bringing Hogan on for Tommy, but I told Curly I fancied Tommy to do something so he stayed on. Sometimes you get these hunches right. Thirteen minutes from the end Tommy came in from wide left, crossed a great ball and

Taarbs finished it. Our great following behind the goal went mad. It was nerve-racking, with five minutes' injury-time with the game end-to-end, then Tommy himself scored and we'd done it.

The euphoria was overwhelming. Me and Curly had a great hug. Malky came on and said 'Well done'. I hoped the fans would stay off the pitch as we'd promised Watford we'd come off after five minutes so they could do their lap of appreciation. But some got a bit carried away and ran on. You could smell the booze on a few of them. I didn't enjoy that, or when they got a bit physical. We tried to get off quickly. The guy with the microphone started having a go at me for our fans being on the pitch when they want to do their lap. I said, 'You should thank me, I'm getting us off in five minutes and we've just won promotion.'

The lads went out in Mayfair. Amit looked after them all and they had a fantastic night. I was invited but Sharon and the kids were at Vicarage Road and I'm so pleased they were. I took William on the bus back to the training ground with me. He loved it. When we got home, we all got in our pyjamas and watched Sky Sports News at eight o'clock while I had a cheese sandwich. Amy opened a bottle of champagne and I had a glass; I hadn't had a drink until then, I just wanted to take it in, I didn't want to miss anything.

It was unreal, like looking from the outside. There was the FA verdict to come but they couldn't take it away from us. The players deserved that championship. To get that result at Watford after the players were so flat on the Friday was incredible. I thought, 'Even if the FA take some points away I hope we win the championship.' We deserved it. We won it fair and square.

I can still picture being in the dressing room, stood there while the lads were jumping on the table and the champagne corks were popping, I seemed to be out of it. I was stood there, looking at my team, all the different characters, how they had come together, what they had done over the season. It was an amazing couple of minutes but it seemed to go on for ages. I went through all of them, their strengths, what they have had to overcome, and the rollickings I'd given them. I was so proud to have put this group of players together, and also to have given QPR fans – who had not had anything to cheer about for many years – what was a truly remarkable season.

After a few minutes of celebrating I sat the players down and I thanked them. I started talking and began to go through individuals, but then I started filling up and I had to go into the shower and leave them to it. All the work I'd put in since joining – it was worth it, for this moment.

Chapter Fourteen

Who Needs Awards?

For a long time people have underestimated that the most important single person in football is the manager.

Sir Alan Sugar

THE EUPHORIA OF CLINCHING PROMOTION DID NOT LAST long. The following day we had the club's Awards dinner at the Hilton. A lot of supporters pay good money to attend and I insisted Adel turn up. On reflection I wish I hadn't. He won goal of the season – most of the goals in contention were his – but came second to Paddy in both the Players' Player of the Year, and Supporters' Player of the Year.

I got all the players up on stage one by one to talk about them so they all got a round of applause. At the end I asked Dezza if I'd missed anyone and he told me Adel had taken off, presumably because he hadn't been player of the year. I then had to make some comment to the fans about Adel having to shoot off to be somewhere, but at least he had turned up. But I was so disappointed because I wanted to say good things about what he'd done for us, and his strengths. I had really looked forward to saying good things about him in front of everyone. I'd treated Adel like one of the family and he'd got us promotion. I wanted to thank him but before I had the chance he'd gone.

I went back home and found I had a text from Adel sent at 22.59. I spoke to Sharon, 'Adel thinks not getting the Player of the Year Award means he's not respected. I'll tell him how I feel.'

I texted back at 12.30: 'It will not be supporters who make your career but managers. When you left I got the players up one by one. I wanted to speak about you but you had left. Do you think I will win Championship manager of the season?? I will not be picked in the top three. Disappointed I will be but there are worse things happen in life. Thanks for the most enjoyable season of my life. Speak soon. Gaffer.'

His reply was brisk. I thought, I wonder if we'll see you at the ground again, but I left it there. As I said to the players, let's get over the finishing line and worry about Adel and next season later. I was told that Chelsea and one or two other clubs have been into him, hinting at a move. I hadn't a clue whether he was going to turn up at training or even come to the Leeds game, the last of the season. But that was the least of my concerns.

The ownership saga had taken a turn for the worse. I was told now promotion had been achieved Bernie and Flavio wanted more money for the club which Amit had no intention of paying – instead he wanted to be bought out. I was disappointed with that. I came on the strength of Amit becoming the majority shareholder; I liked him, I thought he and his family were super, but it looked as if Bernie and Flavio would be in charge and I'd be reporting to Flavio. It was not a prospect to look forward to.

Plus we still had the FA hearing to worry about. Norwich were also promoted; Cardiff were third, nine points behind us.

With our goal difference that meant we could afford a six-point deduction and still go up regardless of results on the final day. But I didn't want to just go up, I wanted to be champions, we deserved it.

The case was being heard Tuesday and Wednesday. I spoke to the barrister on Tuesday night and he told me the evidence was going well. Then on Wednesday night I heard it might not be announced until Sunday, the day after the season had finished. That meant we would not be able to celebrate at the Leeds game. Norwich had been able to celebrate going up and there was us, the best team in the league and we can't celebrate for sure. Then we heard we would still get the trophy, so we could celebrate, but since there was the danger we might have to hand it back those celebrations would be muted. The players were gutted again. Very flat. I told the staff, 'No long faces – if I hear anybody, coaches, physios, moping around, I'll jump on them.'

Thursday was press day and they kept asking about the hearing. I just kept saying the same thing and hoped they got bored asking; that the players had been magnificent, we'd been the best team, and we'd celebrate. They all picked up on the Tevez angle, which didn't surprise me though to my mind it was a different issue. But I couldn't even say that as the barristers told me it was to our advantage to get them linked in people's minds, as West Ham didn't lose any points. The press also asked about Mark Palios, the former FA chief executive who resigned after having an affair with a secretary. He had been doing the rounds on TV saying we should be deducted ten points. I said it's just cheap publicity, he should be used to it after the last few years.

Then I went to meet Taarabt's agents. I'd still not heard from the player. 'We want Adel to stay with QPR and play in the Premier League,' they said.

'Well, he can't carry on like this. He has to apologise to me as well, he's been so disrespectful.'

'He will, he's sorry. He's gone to visit his family.'

'Flavio wants to fine him £100,000 for not reporting, but I don't. I want him involved on Saturday.'

'He'll play. He wants everyone to wear T-shirts while warming up supporting the victims of the Moroccan bomb blast.' A bomb had gone off in a café in Marrakesh killing 15 people – only a few weeks ago Sharon and I had sat in the very same café when I went out to see Adel in Morocco. A shudder went down my spine when I watched news of it.

'That's fine, as long as Adel brings them.' I left with no idea whether he'd be turning up. Faurlin had not been training either as he had been giving evidence at the hearing. It was not the best preparation to play Leeds – who I wanted to beat because of the way they rubbed victory in our noses up there. They had a mathematical chance of the play-offs so they would be chasing a result.

That night I went to the Football Writers' dinner with *The Independent* and watched Scott Parker get the award for Footballer of the Year. What a professional he is, it would be wonderful to have him in my team. The contrast with the way Adel was behaving was so stark. Dean Smith, who was managing Walsall and doing well with no money, and Aidy Boothroyd, who'd just left Coventry, were on the *Independent* table and we had a chat. When we played Coventry at Christmas they were pushing for promotion, but a few months later Aidy was out of work. It showed how fickle football is. Changing managers didn't do Coventry much good; two seasons later they were fighting relegation to League Two, while Aidy was pushing for promotion to League One with Northampton Town.

I had a good night but with so much on my mind I couldn't really relax. Plenty of people offered their congratulations, but I couldn't even enjoy that knowing we could have the title taken away from us by the FA.

The following day at training there was still no sign of Taarabt. I gathered the players together. 'You'll have noticed Adel's not here. I don't know where he is and it won't surprise me if he doesn't turn up tomorrow, but if he does treat him normally one last time, don't have a go at him. We've done it all season and he's helped us get where we are.' They agreed.

I had been told an agent had rung Daniel Levy and asked if Spurs would take him back. Levy had obviously said no. I couldn't say I was surprised given the way he behaved that season. I loved him to bits but he had to change his ways or he would never play regularly at the top level. He won't find many managers prepared to tolerate him the way I did. I'm sure he can pick up money in the Far East just walking around and doing his tricks, but that would be sad when he has the talent to play among the very best. I'd had a chat to him a few weeks earlier and told him, 'You've got the world at your feet but if you don't change your attitude you haven't got a cat in hell's chance of being a top player. You could be, but if you look at Barcelona they all work their socks off. You have to contribute more; you can't not train for a week and disrespect your team-mates. You have to learn.'

That night the agent called to say Adel was coming, but the flight was due at Gatwick at 11am. I thought, 'It's a good job we're at home.' But it was a 12.45 kick-off and there was no chance of him getting to Loftus Road before 12.15. I said, 'You ring me when he's in your car. If I know he's on the way I'll put him on the bench, but I can't be made to look stupid.'

Saturday morning I couldn't get hold of Taarbs until the agent rang at ten past 11 to say he was in the car and on the way. Then I got a text from Taarbs. 'I want to play today.' I said to Curly and Mick, 'Just say I've no phone signal from now on, there's no way he can start. We'll put him on for half an hour and let him pick the cup up.'

I pulled Shaun Derry aside and told him what I was doing. I said, 'I want you to be captain, but when he comes on second half you'll have to give him the armband. He's been fantastic for us.' I wanted to see Adel lifting the trophy up and taking accolades for having an unbelievable season in a system that was suited for him. Dezza said: 'Gaffer, we're not going to remember the last two or three weeks, let's remember him for what a great season he's had.' The lads in the dressing room, the senior players, had been fantastic. They'd stopped any disagreements.

By midday Adel had still not arrived but suddenly the mood lifted. I'd just done a TV interview and was walking back through the tunnel to the dressing room when Terry Springett, one of our club secretaries who had been involved in the case throughout, grabbed me. She was crying and I wondered what was up when she blurted out, 'No points, two counts, both fines, they're announcing it any second now'. It was fantastic news. I gave her a kiss. Then I heard Gianni. He was shouting, 'No points, no points, no points. I told you I was telling the truth.' He was crying his eyes out. We had a big hug. I was absolutely delighted for him, as he had been put through the wringer.

I rushed to the dressing room to tell the players who were busy getting changed. The relief was unbelievable. They were all jumping up and down and hugging each other, half of them were in tears. It really sank in then just how much the threat hanging over of having points deducted, and losing our promotion, had affected the players. It was just jubilation. A moment in time none of us will forget.

Eventually we calmed down. I thanked them all for what they had done in the season, and told them we had got what we deserved. Then I said: 'We also have a game, if we go into it with the wrong attitude you might get injured. I don't want anyone injured for next season.'

Then I went to exchange team-sheets (including Adel on the bench) in the referee's room.

Richard Naylor, the Leeds captain, said, 'We'll give you a guard of honour.' The clubs haven't got on that well this year so I said to him: 'You won't be spitting on the floor in front of us, will you?' Everyone laughed, including referee Mark Clattenburg.

The atmosphere in the ground was incredible, the club had placed flags on each seat and the place was a sea of blue-and-white. It was happy, happy party time. It was 15 years since QPR had been in the Premier League, 15 years in which the club had gone into the Third Division and nearly gone bust more than once. Any supporter under 20 had never seen us in the top flight, now they'd be watching us playing Manchester United, Arsenal and Chelsea. We scored almost right from kick-off, through Helguson, and it all started again. Inevitably the strain of the week, and the waiting, took its toll on the players and Leeds were able to win the match but it was irrelevant. Our supporters didn't care and the other results went against Leeds so the points were no good to them.

Adel came on and Dezza gave him the armband. So it was Adel who lifted the trophy. I was covered in champagne then we did a lap of honour. A lot of us had our children with us and it was great to have William with me, in his QPR kit. That night I took the trophy home, I was determined not to let anyone else lay their hands on it. It is a special and beautiful trophy, much prettier than the Premier League one, and with so much history. Billy Wright,

Danny Blanchflower and Billy Bremner lifted that trophy. So I asked Sharon, did she mind if I slept with it that night? That was fine by Sharon, as long I didn't expect her to do the same. She slept in the spare room.

I managed to hold onto the trophy for several days. It would have looked great on the mantelpiece if only we'd had a mantelpiece big enough to put it on. I took it to William's school assembly, where only three lads admitted to being QPR fans, and one was William and another I think only put his hand up out of sympathy. There were even more Brentford than QPR. Then we went to the neighbouring infants school. The teacher said: 'This is Mr Warnock and he has brought a cup with him, having won the league. Can anyone tell me what football club Mr Warnock manages?' This bright little boy thrust his hand up. He said: 'Crystal Palace United, Miss.'

It would have been great to have had an open-top bus ride through the streets around Loftus Road and down to the Town Hall. Swansea did one and they only went up through the play-offs. I've been lucky enough to do it with Scarborough, Plymouth, Notts County and Sheffield United and those are the days you never forget. The fans and players deserved it but unfortunately no one wanted to pay for it. The club would not pay, and neither would Hammersmith & Fulham Council. So in the end Gianni, me, and some of the staff went to the Town Hall to meet the Mayor and council leaders and pose for some photographs. It was all a bit unsatisfactory and smacked of penny-pinching.

Another disappointment was being the only title-winning manager in the four divisions not to be voted manager of the year at that year's League Managers' Association dinner. Paul Lambert got it. I know Norwich had successive promotions, but they spent more money than we had and I don't think people really appreciated how tough it had been to turn QPR around. We'd nearly been relegated the year before. People looked at our owners and assumed we'd spent billions, but we had actually been very thrifty with our money. However, while I was disappointed I didn't walk out like Adel had.

Sharon thought it was amusing when I said Brendan Rogers and Brian McDermott had also been short-listed rather than me. I would imagine everyone present at that awards dinner knew I should have won it, including Paul Lambert, and that was the main thing. I know, with what I had to put up with that year at QPR, I was the best manager by miles. William cheered me up. He got me his own cup and presented it to me. But Amy said, 'Other managers don't like you, so what do you expect, Dad?' Clever girl.

Actually it is a myth that all other managers don't like me, but it is fair to say I'm not the most popular manager out there. Some find it difficult to separate how I behave on the pitch to what I am like off it. My mate Mick McCarthy said on a radio programme about me that I try and wind people up at matches, including other managers. Apparently even he nearly went for me once during a Sheffield United v Millwall match but Ian Evans, who was his assistant, held him back. When I asked him about it later he said I'd been 'Shouting stupid things,' telling players to get stuck into tackles and so on and for once it had got to him.

My bark is worse than my bite. I'm just passionate when the game is on. Dioufy said in an interview that he and I are 'the misunderstood'. And if I was that bad why have so many players, like Dezza, Paddy, Clint and Tongey, followed me from club to club? But I'm not that bothered. As Sir Alex Ferguson said, in the foreword to Kenny Dalglish's autobiography funnily enough, 'You only need six to carry your coffin.' In truth there are only two or three managers I cannot stand (it's well known who they are), most of the others I get on OK with and there are a few who are very good friends. Mick and I go way back – as an apprentice he used to clean my boots when I was a player at Barnsley and I never let him forget it. I regularly speak to Mick, Harry Redknapp, Alan Pardew, Brian McDermott, people like that. Then there is the new breed, young managers like Malky Mackay, Brendan Rodgers, Paul Lambert and Dougie Freeman who I've tried to help with bits of advice – not that they need much. I tipped one or two off too. I told Roberto Martinez to buy Victor Moses and David Moyes to sign Phil Jagielka. I told Arsène about Jags as well, though Arsène tends to keep to himself. I've been fortunate that I've been invited into his office with my family, and not many people see that side of Arsène.

A better night was an LMA function we had in London for the managers who had done 1,000 league games. We're quite a select band. There were 19 at the time, 15 still alive and about eight or so still working. What's interesting is all of us except Sir Matt Busby and Sir Bobby Robson – and even he had a year learning the ropes at Vancouver – started in non-League, the lower divisions or an equivalent in Scotland. Managing at a lower level gives you a grounding that stands you in good stead later on in your career, because you can remember things you did wrong in the past.

If, however, you are someone like Andre Villas-Boas, who was such an instant success in Portugal he got the Chelsea job within a couple of years of becoming a manager, then you don't have that experience to fall back on. So when he did have a sticky patch at Chelsea he couldn't look back at decisions he'd made in similar situations in the past, and remember what worked and what didn't. Instead he had to back his hunches in the full glare of a top-rank European club. I made mistakes at Gainsborough, Sir Alex made them at East Stirling, and Martin O'Neill made them at

Shepshed Charterhouse. The great thing is, at that level, not many people cared so there wasn't the same pressure to get instant results. The people that did care, cared a lot, and you had to respect that, but there wasn't the media interest that can make things so much more difficult.

Managers don't get much time these days and it's important that you learn from your mistakes. You will make mistakes, you will have sticky periods. That is when you learn the most.

Chapter Fifteen

Summer of Discontent

I always enjoy the summer. You can't lose any matches.

Roy Evans

THE PHONE RANG AT NINE. IT WAS GIANNI, WHO NEVER rang that early – I immediately wondered what was up.

'Are you OK?' he said.

'Yes, why?'

'We've had 40-odd phone calls and people coming into the stadium asking if you are resigning. It is the last day of selling season tickets at a discount.'

'I've told you I'm not resigning. I'll give it a go with whatever we have – but they'll be my signings.'

This was the second time in the summer of 2011 Gianni had called me to ask if I was going to quit. The first time he had heard a rumour that Mick, while on holiday in Portugal, had told people I was walking away. I wasn't, and he hadn't, but I could see why Mick may have said to someone I might. Mick knew what I was going through working with Flavio.

People think football managers have the summer off. I wish. I felt absolutely zonked after this one. Mentally it was more tiring than when the games are taking place, what with all the meetings and all the problems.

The work never really stops all year. During the season as soon as one match is over, win or lose, I was thinking of the next one; and, always, thinking about strengthening the side. When the season is finished that becomes the main focus, especially when you have been promoted. From the end of January onwards you are planning, talking to agents, scouring the papers for bits of info on who might be available, trying to extend the contacts of players you want to keep, and whenever you watch matches, in the flesh or on TV, you are on the lookout for someone who might be able to do a job for you.

By the time promotion was secured I had an idea of the type of players I felt I needed, and the individuals who fitted that profile. We were OK in goal, but we needed a new back four. Faurlin was Premier League quality but we needed competition for Derry in central midfield, I wanted a wide player with pace, a goalscorer (we all want one of those), and cover for Heider. Not much then! On top of all that I had no idea what was going to happen with Adel.

Drawing up a shopping list is one thing, buying the players on it is another thing entirely, especially at QPR where the ownership was up in the air all summer. It was very frustrating and I didn't feel I was being treated with much respect. One day I turned up at Loftus Road for a meeting with the board to be told it had been rescheduled to the following week, but no one had bothered to tell me. When we finally had the meeting I was told they wanted to put season tickets up 90 per cent, which was almost on a par with Chelsea, and keep the wage bill within limits I thought were suicidal in terms of building a squad to compete at that level. That was when Amit resigned from the board, citing the way Ishan had been dismissed earlier in the year and his disagreement with the proposed ticket prices. I lost a big ally then and the prospect of him buying the club receded even further, though Gianni insisted Flavio and Bernie were still trying to sell.

It got worse. Gianni told me they didn't want to pay bonuses in June or July, they wanted to pay them in August. I told them it was in the contracts they had to pay them. Rumour had it they didn't even want to pay wages until August. If that had come out in the newspapers we'd have been dead, no one would have signed for us. But if we didn't pay players' wages or any outstanding debts to other clubs we wouldn't be allowed to sign anyone anyway. The joy of getting promotion had faded fast, but I decided I'd do my best with whatever we had. I carried on trying to line up players even though I had no idea of my budget.

Unless they have ridiculous amounts of money promoted clubs are usually limited to picking off the best players from clubs that have gone down, players who are out of favour at Premier League clubs and can't find a more established top flight team to go to, and Championship players who want to make the step up. We needed to move fast as we were likely to be competing with Norwich and whoever came up in the play-offs for the same players.

But we couldn't because there was the ownership impasse. While we were paralysed, Norwich signed James Vaughan from Everton and Steve Morison from Millwall, spending £4m. Swansea came up in the play-off final and suddenly I had competition for Watford's Danny Graham who became my first choice when Wolves stayed up – which meant Kevin Doyle wouldn't be available. Graham's agent told me there was a clause in his contract, a £2.5m buy-out. I persuaded us to bid £2.5m but Swansea offered £3.5m. They must have been desperate because there was no need with that clause. It was not about who Watford wanted to sell to; it was up to the player where he wanted to go. That was originally us, but Danny was worried about the takeover, that Bernie and Flavio would let me sign him, but no one else. I understood where he was coming from. I had him in my house, he met Sharon, we got on well – but he signed for Swansea. I couldn't blame him. Everything was up in the air and Swansea was a steady club. So why wait and gamble? Inevitably next season he scored against us.

What made it all the more confusing is Flavio had two completely different approaches. On the one hand he wouldn't give me the money to buy anyone, on the other he kept suggesting players being hawked around by his agent mates, way out of our price range and not who I wanted anyway. One night Gianni and Pini Zahavi, the super-agent, came to my house. Zahavi started off trying to sell me Ben Haim, who was at Chelsea and Portsmouth and was on £36,000 a week.

'You have no one like him,' said Zahavi. 'He's tenacious. Watch him playing against Wolves for West Ham. He was fantastic.'

'I watched that game and he was fantastic, but that was probably the only time in 20 games I've seen him play well. And I don't think he is the type we want.'

Pini is a brilliant agent, and was only doing what you'd expect an agent to do, looking after his players. He did a great job trying to persuade me to take one or two of his lads. 'What about Tamir Cohen? He'll score goals from midfield. He was let go by Bolton but could play in any Premier League team.'

'I don't agree. All my reports and people I know, especially people at Bolton, say he is a good Championship player but not a Premiership player.'

'How about Pinto, he's an under-21 player with Portugal. He'll grace any team.'

'Playing for the under-21s doesn't mean anything. Michael Mancienne is under-21 captain for England but I wouldn't have him in my team.'

As a player I never had an agent. I didn't see the need. When I became a manager I looked after the two Short brothers, Chris and Craig. They'd been part-time at Scarborough; one of them was a bank clerk. I took them to Notts County and I looked after them as if they were my sons with advice and so on. Then one day an agent, Kevin Mason, rang me about a contract for one of them and I couldn't believe they hadn't come to see me. It shattered my illusions. I found out he'd been giving them pairs of trainers, tracksuits and so on to get in their good books. These days it's jewellery and cars to turn players' heads.

I think players need an agent now, one with an accountant on the payroll, because contract negotiations are so complex most players can't do it on their own. The financial side of the game is beyond the average person. The trick is finding a good one. I've known agents who are just in it to get a buck but others are genuinely there to help their client on a long-term basis. They realise if they do a good job in the long-term everyone wins. They speak to players week-in, week-out. I do my negotiations myself, but I should have had an agent because by trusting people I have been let down on a few occasions.

Agents also help players get a move (though not always one which suits the players more than the agent). Some will ring you up and tell you their player is the best thing since sliced bread and you know because of who's saying it that the player won't be any good. Others you decide to take a look because they have been reliable in the past.

Since English football struck it rich and became a global game, there are so many more players to consider and you do need agents to keep you in touch with who might be available. But there are still times when you deal directly with clubs. That summer Marco Branca, one of the main guys running Inter Milan, got in touch. He knew Flavio and said he would do me a favour, 'let you have a very good player on loan for a season'. It was Marco Materazzi, the lad who played for Everton and who was butted by Zinedine Zidane in the 2006 World Cup final. He was on £50,000-a-week and would be 38 when the season started – I was quicker than him. I ended up disagreeing with Flavio on this. I told him I did not want to sign players who had been recommended on the strength of a DVD. QPR went down that line before I came and would have got relegated if I hadn't turned up. I knew even if I signed players they wanted it would still be me who would be fired when results didn't work out.

I did finally get a budget: £10m to spend and £15m on wages. But then I had problems when I wanted to spend it. After Graham fell through I looked at Jay Bothroyd, of Cardiff, and Craig Mackail-Smith, of Peterborough. Bothroyd had issues living in London before but he has ability. Everton, Newcastle, Sunderland had already spoke to his agent but I thought he'd be a regular with us. He spent two hours at our house and I liked him. He was on a Bosman, which made him affordable – by now I knew I would have to temper my expectations.

With everyone except us buying players I was inevitably asked about transfers by the press. Flavio didn't like my answers. I received a note from his office telling me not to speak to the press again.

He'd read about an interview where I'd said 'I've been given 50 Italians and Brazilians but I'll only sign players I want to sign.' That was true, but I'd not actually said it like that. Flavio said, 'I've not told you to sign an Italian.' He hadn't, though the likes of Materazzi were mentioned and I know if I hadn't had been in a position of strength he would have insisted. But I was only in a position of strength before the season started as, if I lost three or four games, that would be my lot. I sent an e-mail back, explaining my situation, the comments, and saying I won't comment any more.

He rang me. 'You have done an interview on Sky saying we'll not spend any money if we get it for Taarabt.'

'It was a joke, Flavio. They asked if I'd get the money and I said "of course not".'

'Why do you talk so much when other managers don't speak to the press?'

'Because they don't get asked. They haven't got a sense of humour like I have and their interviews aren't as interesting.'

'You are only my coach, you should not be on TV morning and afternoon like Paulo was.' That was a warning shot. Paulo Sousa had been fired for telling the press he had not been consulted about Dexter Blackstock, then QPR's top scorer, being sent to Nottingham Forest on loan. Paulo then had to fight for a pay-off as they said he had breached his contract.

Gianni rang and said, 'Don't worry, that's how he is.' The following day Bernie phoned. 'Neil, I know about things in the press. Flavio told me.'

'Bernie, he went ballistic, but I was joking, they didn't show all the interview. I wasn't having a go at you.'

'I know that, Neil. Flavio doesn't understand English humour. Just forget about it. You know what Flavio's like, just go along with him and take no notice.'

I thought, 'That's easier said than done,' but I just said, 'OK Bernie, I appreciate your call.'

I have to say that I did like Bernie and Flavio when I was in their company, but Bernie had far too much on his plate with Formula One so he left everything to Flavio, which made it difficult for me. Meanwhile I sent a letter to Rebecca Caplehorn, who ran the financial side of the club, to cover myself after they had written to me warning me not to talk to the media.

'Please accept this letter as acknowledgement that I have received your letter dated 22 July, 2011. Thank you for advising me of concerns that have been raised about our club's transfer policies in the media. I fully understand the importance of a positive image and will continue to promote this in any future external, obligatory interviews. It might be advisable that the club formally advise that as manager I will only be drawn on issues that are under my remit as manager and issues such as transfers and ownership will be avoided. If during the season circumstances arise that the club wish me not to comment on it would be appreciated if I am given precise direction as to the club's desired response.'

I had realised I had better keep my mouth shut and not risk making a joke about anything. Of course that risked a story about me not talking.

The uncertainty at the top had a detrimental impact on transfers. We agreed a deal with Peterborough for Mackail-Smith: £2.5m and £500,000 on games. The wages were decent, but not over the top. He also had Everton, Swansea and Norwich after him but I was confident he'd sign for us. He's a smashing lad who can play either side and I thought he'd do well for us. Then he asked me, 'I have heard things are difficult with the owners. Can you work with them? Will you be here?'

What could I say? 'Of course I will be here,' I said. 'It's not easy. Flavio has a way of dealing with things because of the way he is but he and Bernie both have the club at heart.' But I knew when I was talking to him he didn't believe it. Eventually he signed for Brighton who had just been promoted to the Championship. They matched us: £1.5m up front, £500k on games, and £500k on promotion. I thought, unbelievable, we've been beaten to a lad by Brighton.

Flavio wasn't bothered. He had a better idea, Valeri Bojinov, a Bulgarian lad who was at Parma where he knew the people running the club. They paid £11m for him. Man City had paid £6m then sold him. In fairness to Flavio he wasn't bad but he'd been out six months with knee ligaments.

I figured I was going to be sacked anyhow, so I had to do the job as best I could. It was hard though, especially when doing interviews and the press asked about transfers. I'd say, 'It's not easy, but we'll be getting four, five, six in.' In reality it was proving extremely difficult working with Flavio, as other managers had found. There's no way I would have come in the first place if I'd not been told Amit was becoming majority shareholder, I would have stayed at Palace. Now I was at QPR I just felt I had to do my best for the fans, they'd been brilliant and if I left they'd just get loads of loan players from abroad. Flavio would get stitched up by his 'friends' who he thought wanted to help him.

More players went begging: Dominguez, a Chilean centre-half with Audax of Argentina who I liked and Ahmed Fathy, a versatile Egyptian who played for me at Sheffield United. Flavio did not want to pay a loan fee, but that is what clubs will expect for decent players.

Flavio gave a list of players to Gianni he wanted to get rid of, including Helguson who I wanted to keep. He wanted me to get six or seven out to bring four in, but it is not that easy to shift players. One day Gianni told me Rob Hulse, who was on good money, was going to Millwall for half his wages.

I said, 'What, the player's agreed?'

'Yes, everything's done, the forms have gone through.'

'I can't believe that. When I spoke to him he wanted to get into the team.'

Kenny Jackett, Millwall's manager, phoned the next day. An agent had been dealing with it, had sent all the forms through, all filled in. I said, 'Kenny, have you spoken to the player?' He said no, though he had to say that even if he had talked to him.

I found out Rob not only hadn't agreed to it, he didn't even know about it. He stayed, but Kenny got his man eventually, on loan in 2013.

All summer we were linked with players I either didn't want, couldn't afford or had never heard of. According to the papers we were close to signing Rafik Halliche of Fulham – I'd never heard of him. We were close to signing Carlton Cole for £6m – we never asked about him (I couldn't afford that if we had). An agent rang to see if I was I aware Tony Pulis had been asked by QPR how much he'd sell Glenn Whelan for. I fobbed him off and said he was just one of the names we'd discussed – we'd not mentioned him at all. I spoke to Gianni and he said it was an agent who'd rung us first. That happens, there are so many agents around, each trying to get a piece, they will sometimes play clubs off against each other to create a deal. I don't blame them, they are trying to make a living, but it makes life complicated for managers, as sometimes you don't know who really represents a player, especially foreign ones.

Even with an agent though, players can still cause havoc. I was once offered a player who I didn't want and said so, straightaway.

Later that day my phone pinged – the player in question had texted me, mixing up my number with his agent's, saying something like, 'Never mind – I might as well go and get that operation I need now anyway.' What a lucky escape, I thought.

I fixed up a meeting with Daniel Levy at Spurs in the hope he would let me have Kyle Naughton, who we'd tried to get in January, on loan. Daniel, who's a clever man, proposed we took Robbie Keane and Jermaine Jenas for £8m and he'd throw Kyle in. There's no way we could afford that, but I did say if he didn't get anyone for Naughton it'd do his career the world of good to play week-in, week-out with me.

As pre-season approached we had another meeting at which I was told the maximum contract was £20,000-a-week, no contract to be longer than two years, and not to sign anyone until the end of July as people will lower prices. I said all the best players will be gone. As if to prove it Norwich made their fifth and sixth signings, Bradley Johnson and Anthony Pilkington. The budget was meaningless anyway. I identified a centre-half, Ashley Williams of Swansea, but he cost £3m and they didn't want to pay it. I couldn't see the point of having a budget after that, when I wanted a player I was told, 'You can't sign him.' There was no budget; it was just a case of 'Ask Flavio'.

Word got out. When Mackail-Smith signed for Brighton my old non-League rival Barry Fry, who had become Peterborough's director of football, went on Talksport and a caller came on and said Fry had promised he'd only leave for a Premier League club. Barry replied, 'He was going to go to QPR, but they're not allowed to sign anybody at the minute.' He went on a little bit about our problems. I rang Barry: 'Don't go on about us, you'll get me in trouble, they've already given me a written warning.' He apologised.

I wanted to talk to Bernie about the situation, to try and get him to understand why we needed to spend. The last board meeting had lasted two hours. Bernie had come in for one-and-a-half minutes, and then went out to make a conference call. Then he came in for another couple of minutes. He was so busy. I liked him, but he's not really interested in football. He just passed it on to Flavio.

Flavio wasn't happy I wanted a meeting with Bernie and accused me of playing games with him. I wasn't, but I needn't have bothered. Bernie came in for five minutes and just said, 'Neil, I'm not going to put another penny into this football club, if I could get the money out I've already put in I would.' He proceeded to sit down and talk about overpaid players, and Taarabt in the press talking about going to Chelsea and Arsenal, and how the coach said he could go if he wanted.

I texted Taarbs to tell him to keep quiet but I got a text back: 'Coach you promised me if I got you promotion I could go, keep your word.'

I texted him back but I knew he was going to meet Flavio in Monaco because Flavio had told me Taarbs wanted to meet him and talk about the coach – me – and the transfer. Flavio rang me after to say he'd told Taarbs that he'd talk about the transfer, but not about me. He added that I'd looked after Adel in a way he wouldn't have done, and that he'd told Taarabt he didn't try hard enough and threw tantrums.

When Flavio told me that I felt better. He was right about Adel. That summer he had walked out of the Morocco squad for a derby game against Algeria after the manager told him he was playing right wing. He said he couldn't play right wing so the manager told him he would be a substitute. So he left. That's Adel.

Amid all this the fixtures came out. The night before we were all talking about who we would get the first game, Sharon and William both went for Bolton at home. James and Natalie said Bolton, but away. I said, 'It'll be someone like Wigan, or Norwich.' The phone went at half-seven in the morning: Bolton at home.

I'd allowed the cameras to come round at nine o'clock; they were obviously struggling to get anyone to do it. They said, 'Can we bring the Premiership trophy to get some publicity for Barclays?' So I ended up being filmed in the driveway with it. Some people are superstitious about trophies – in fact I'm one of them – but I knew this would be the closest I'd ever get to being with the trophy. It didn't mean anything to me, it was just a publicity stunt, but it wasn't easy being all positive and enthusiastic after the discussions with Flavio. I don't think anyone knows this side of football management. They can't teach you at the LMA course at Warwick University what happened that summer. I wonder if a manager with less experience, or less able to stand up for himself, would have coped. I've never known anybody like Flavio. He could be charming, like you were his new best friend, but any sign of weakness and he would have crushed me.

Chapter Sixteen

Time to Diet

Football management should carry a government health warning, like it does on a packet of fags.

Barry Fry

I USUALLY LOVE THE FIRST DAY OF PRE-SEASON TRAINING: the smell of freshly cut grass, the warmth of summer sunshine on our backs, and the eagerness of players old and new. Except that summer, as QPR faced their first season back in the top flight in 15 years, we had no new players and it was chucking it down. The training ground really was the pits on days like that, with the aircraft flying overhead from Heathrow next-door, the wind blowing, and us barely able to hear each other. Everyone was flat. We all knew we didn't have the backing we needed for an assault on the world's most demanding league.

Then came devastating news. I had gone for a bicycle ride to clear my mind and prepare for another bout of transfer negotiations. It was relaxing, I'd seen a kingfisher for the first time in ages and was feeling better. Then Nigel called. 'It's Paddy. He's been passing some blood in his urine so we took him for a scan. We've just got the results back. There are some abnormalities. It doesn't look very good.'

'What do you mean "it doesn't look very good"?'

'There's a tumour or something near his kidney and it looks as if there's an abnormality near his heart. There's nothing confirmed. That is a worst-case scenario, but the radiologist said, "It doesn't look good."'

'Does Paddy know?'

'Not yet, I've only told you.'

As he'd talked I froze. I was distraught. Not only was Paddy, I thought, the best keeper in the country, he's also the nicest of lads and I just didn't know how he would cope with it. I'd known him more than ten years – I signed him from non-League as a raw 20-year-old at Bury. The manager in me thought, 'that's our goalkeeper', but the human being in me thought of Paddy, and his family. As I cycled home he was all I could think about. We would have to tell him and I really wasn't looking forward to it.

The following day, after training, I called him into my office. The doctor and Coxy were there. Paddy was just gobsmacked, as you'd expect. He lost all his colour. When the doctor went out Nigel said to him, 'I'm on the phone 24 hours, just call me about anything.' There's not much more you can say.

We sent Paddy for another scan, a really in-depth one. Then we had to wait 24 hours, the longest 24 hours of the summer. Paddy said after he couldn't sleep at all, he was in turmoil. Then Nigel rang with fantastic news: the specialist thought the abnormality was the shape of his kidney, not a tumour. I just filled up. I rang Paddy straight away and I just burst into tears as I was talking to him. We were both so emotional.

Illness can be so arbitrary. A few months earlier one of my former players, Chris Armstrong, who played with Paddy at Bury and Sheffield United, had to retire because he had multiple sclerosis. I know just how cruel this disease is because my mother had it. As far back as I can remember she needed help walking and by the time she was in her early forties she was in a wheelchair. She died at 46, I was 13. As the youngest I was really close to my mum and it felt like the end of my world. MS is very complex and people are affected in different ways. My mum must have had one of the more severe cases. There has been a lot of research since and while no cure has yet been found the condition can be ameliorated and most people live to a ripe old age. It can, though, still be a terrible degenerative disease.

I hope Chris proves to only have a mild case. You couldn't meet a nicer lad, or a braver one. He had a bad knee injury at Sheffield United and was offered a substantial insurance pay-off to retire. I doubted he would play again and was surprised he didn't take it but he battled back, confounding everyone. He went to Reading, was their player of the season in 2008–09, but a few months later he was diagnosed with MS. Eventually he had to accept he couldn't carry on playing.

When you hear about someone like that it makes you realise how important your health is. Paddy's scare really shook me up. It really makes you appreciate how fragile life can be, one minute you are full of life, the next you are waiting for a doctor to tell you if you are going to live or not.

I was 62, with young children I wanted to see grow up, and a stressful job. I thought, 'No wonder Sharon wants me to pack up.' Management should carry a health warning, because it's not good for you. It's not just the stress, which can send your heart rate to frightening levels during matches, it's also the diet. Motorway driving and hanging around airports, hotels and railway stations is guaranteed to put weight on you, because most of the available food isn't the healthiest and there's a danger of eating to kill the time. I do see some other managers and think, 'They're not in good shape.' I played for Charlie Wright, an ex-keeper, a big guy in every sense. I looked at him in the dressing room and vowed I would not get like that. But it is so easy to do so when you are a manager. Just think of all the hotel breakfasts, where the food is unlimited, when you are sitting around for a while, chatting, grazing without thinking.

During my time in the game there have been quite a few health scares. Gerard Houllier and Joe Kinnear had quite serious heart problems, Sir Alex Ferguson and Harry Redknapp have needed minor heart treatment, and I also had a warning. When I was at Sheffield United, a scan picked up some problems around my heart in one of the valves. Fortunately it was picked up early, due to the scan, and I didn't need an operation. I was told to change my diet though. It was a time when I was eating a lot of motorway service station food. At night at home I would eat a lot of cheese and biscuits, and I also liked prawns, which you might think are healthy but actually contain a lot of cholesterol. I cut all that out, but as time goes on you slip back into bad habits.

My playing weight was about 65–70kg. According to the Rothmans books in 1970, when I was playing (infrequently) for Rotherham I was 10st 8lbs (67kg). That's fine for someone who is 5ft 9in, maybe even a bit skinny. By the time I retired, in May 1979, at Crewe, I had put on two pounds. Then I began managing. Twenty years later, when I joined Sheffield United, I was 85kg (13st 5lb in old money).

Another decade or so on we were gathered round the television watching pictures of QPR celebrating the title success when Amy said to me: 'Daddy, I don't like your other chin.' Then 'Dad, look at your tummy.' And when I looked at it, it looked massive. I realised

I was always finding a reason to avoid stepping on the scales. And I felt bloated. So I weighed myself. I was 94kg (14st 11lb).

The League Managers' Association provide check-ups for managers with Wellness International and I was overdue one. Very overdue. My last check-up was in July 2008 and I'd let things slip. What with administration at Crystal Palace, changing jobs and moving home, turning QPR around, I'd been busy. Plus you don't want to be told off, and maybe at the back of your mind you don't want to hear what they might have to tell you, so it is one of those things you keep finding reasons to put off. You shouldn't, because prevention is so much better than the cure, but you do.

But after weighing myself I thought, 'Right, I'll have my medical in August. I've until then to get fitter.' Sharon and I went on the Dukan diet. It was all protein to start with – I could have had egg and bacon for breakfast, fillet steak for lunch, and lobster for the evening meal, not that I did. I lost six pounds straight away. Then we started eating things we liked as well but in moderation, and added more fruit and vegetables. I have cut out the bread, pasta and so on. I have a lot more fish and salad, and love it.

I also cut down on the alcohol. Booze can be a problem in management. At Notts County I used to drink quite a lot, I still like a glass or two of red wine but I used to open a bottle of wine and end up drinking it all. In football there is that culture, everything is free in all the boardrooms and so on; it's very easy to get into a drinking habit. Sometimes people drink to forget things, or if you are depressed, and football is one of those jobs where you are bound to feel that way every so often because it is so up and down. That's another thing that gets easier to handle as you get older and have a better perspective.

Just as important as the changes in diet was the increase in exercise. I got on my bike and started pedalling round Richmond

Park. When pre-season restarted I went into the gym for a work-out after training – you have to do it then because once you go up to the office you've no chance of getting away to work out as the phone never stops. That's something I missed between jobs, not having a gym at my workplace.

I had thought if I could get down to 87-and-a-half kilos I'd be happy but by the start of the season I'd surpassed that and, Sharon told me, stopped snoring as well. I actually looked forward to my fitness test. It showed how determined I was that I took it in the middle of the transfer window. It would have been so easy to put it off again but by then I viewed the test as a reward for all my hard work during the summer.

I arrived after a morning on the phone negotiating with agents and when young Ellie took my blood pressure I said, 'It'll be sky-high this morning after all the transfer talk I'm involved in.' To my surprise, and hers, it was the best I'd ever had. I also provided urine and blood to measure my cholesterol and glucose. Then I had my chest shaved, 10 electrodes wired up to an ECG machine stuck on, and a gruelling 20 minutes on the bike. The previous time I had gone on the jogging machine, but I'm a not big fan of that, it's tough on the joints and having had a hip resurface I didn't think it was a great idea.

The bike's hard enough. They keep upping the resistance. The last two minutes were soul-destroying, I was hanging on as long as I could but what makes it really difficult is you have to breathe through a nozzle in your mouth so they can measure your lung capacity. It makes the mouth so dry.

But it was worth it when I got my results. All my test scores showed a massive improvement. I came out feeling 10 foot high. It gave me such a boost I carried on and before long my weight had dropped 10kg and my waist gone from 41 inches to 37. It really hit home when I went to pull on a pair of jeans I'd not worn for a while and had about three inches spare. I couldn't believe it. All those pairs of trousers I had let out over the years I had to have taken back in.

The hard part is keeping it up, but I've done it so far. At the end of the 2011–12 season I went for another check-up and my results had improved again. That encouraged me and I was able to keep my weight to about 86kg, close to what I was when I joined Sheffield United at the end of 1999. Some of the changes were much easier than I expected. I could never imagine using skimmed milk, I thought it was horrible, but switching was easy. I'm quite partial to a skinny cappuccino now, I even bought a little frother at home. Most mornings when we've not got a game I have fat-free yoghurt, bran and berries for breakfast. Lunch I normally eat at the training ground where the food is healthy. You might think evenings would be a problem when I went to Leeds and left the family in Cornwall but I became quite disciplined. When I'm with the kids I end up eating the rest of theirs, and we have pizzas, Chinese takeaways and all sorts. On my own I get organised more and buy good food. I've even become a decent cook. Maybe when I pack in I'll go on *Masterchef* and share my recipes with the nation. Then you can all have a body like mine!

Chapter Seventeen

Bargain Basement Billionaires

The glory moment is when you sign the contract. From then on the situation deteriorates.

Carlos Quieroz

I'VE BEEN AT CLUBS THAT HAVEN'T GOT TWO BRASS farthings to rub together, where you wonder each month if you are going to get paid, but I didn't expect QPR to be one of them, not with some of the world's richest men owning it. Everyone thought we were billionaires, including me at first. How naïve I was.

The month after we won promotion I received a call from a player who keeps an eye on these things. 'Gaffer, we've not been paid our promotion bonus. We've been told we've got to wait until August.'

I checked my payslip. That didn't add up right either. I rang Rebecca. She'd paid my staying-up bonus – for staying up in the Championship – but not the bonus for being promoted to the Premier League. I was only due a staying-up bonus as the club had asked me to have a low basic salary, and the rest in various bonuses including one for staying up. I'd replied, 'Of course, if we don't stay up I don't deserve it.' It was due when we got to 50-odd points back in January but I accepted it in instalments to ease the club's cash flow.

I made a series of calls. It was bad enough not getting a pay rise for winning promotion – I was signing players on more than me even with our paltry budget – now I was fighting to get my bonus. It was the same for the players and worse for the staff – who were on wages that were poor by Championship standards. Rebecca said, 'Flavio doesn't want any increase in wages,' but it was embarrassing. My job felt impossible. How do you keep staff and players happy when they are not even being paid what they are due never mind what they deserve? We didn't have a bus-top parade, party or holiday. Swansea and Norwich took their promotion winners away, we were the champions but we got nothing, not even a thank you. When we got to Cornwall in pre-season I took the staff out and told them I couldn't see any rises in the foreseeable future and they were welcome to find other clubs if they got the chance.

In the circumstances we did well to get away pre-season at all, even if it was only to Cornwall, and a tournament in Italy that Flavio had arranged and turned out to be something of a mixed blessing. At least being away lightened the mood. One day I got a text from Faurlin saying how much he loved me, and 'thanks for making me captain in a pre-season match', and how he'll repay me. Of course it wasn't from Ali, it was from Curly who'd got hold of his phone. I pulled everybody and said, 'Look Ali, I don't want you sending me messages like this', and I read it out in front of the lads. They all laughed.

Italy was good in terms of the matches – we played well beating Sporting Braga and Atalanta in a mini-tournament – but the organisation was poor. Bergamo, where Atalanta play, was more than four hours from our hotel and we had to travel there in the morning. After the tournament we had to stay for a present-ation that didn't start until 11pm, then got showered, at which point I asked about some food. No one had sorted anything. Gianni finally got some pasta organised at a restaurant nearby which we sat down to eat after midnight, before we drove back. The bus looked like the aftermath of a student party, there were players trying to sleep all over the place – Akos Buzsacky was lying on the floor, absolutely exhausted. The air-con didn't work properly – remember this is Italy, in August. We must have asked the drivers about ten times to turn it on but they obviously didn't want it on themselves. Eventually they agreed, but by half-two in the morning it was freezing and they didn't want to turn it off. We got back to the hotel about half four. I bet that doesn't happen to Arsenal.

Still, at least I was alive. I nearly broke my neck at Bergamo. They had these horrible dug-outs sunk into the floor and I was sitting there when there was a bad tackle. I got out to remonstrate but there'd been some rain and I slipped over and fell backwards and hit my head on some concrete. It hurt like hell but I didn't want anyone to see so I just said, 'I'm fine, no problem.' Sitting on the bus later on though I had a hell of a headache.

We had some new players in Italy. Hurrah. Not that any of them cost money. Flavio, because of the way he negotiates, was able to get Jay Bothroyd in on a good deal, guaranteeing him a third year – which was really important to Jay – if he played in 22 games in the second season. We got Danny Gabbidon from West Ham on another Bosman, a back-up goalkeeper in Brian Murphy from Ipswich, and Kieron Dyer. I like Kieron. He's been terribly unlucky with injuries but he's a good player. I thought if we could get him fit he'd be a real bonus. He had something to prove and I like that in a player. It was a risk, but we weren't in a position to sign players as good as him who were not a risk. Besides, Flavio knew all about his injury record and was determined to drive a hard bargain.

'I'm embarrassed to tell you this,' said Gianni to me one day, before telling me Flavio wanted to offer Dyer a really low basic with big money each appearance. Flavio also insisted on a 50 per cent cut in Dyer's pay if we were relegated, not that I expected him to stay as we'd agreed a £250,000 release clause if we went down. Somehow this all got agreed, or something close to it, and we arranged to meet up at the training ground to finalise things. I was about ten minutes away when I got a call from Coxy. 'There's a problem with Dyer's contract, gaffer. Gianni and his agent have been slagging each other off in the car park and Dyer's threatening to drive off.'

'Tell him I'm nearly there. I'll sort it out.'

A couple of minutes later Coxy called again.

'Sorry, gaffer. I tried to stop him, but he's gone'.

I couldn't get hold of the agent, but I got hold of Dyer and persuaded him to pull over and wait. When I arrived it turned out we wanted an option that if he was injured before January we could cancel the contract. They wanted an option that if he did well he could leave on a free in January. It seemed fair to me and, after speaking to Flavio and Rebecca we got an agreement.

As it turned out, Kieron did get injured, but they left it until the last day of January to cancel his contract. He did not answer his phone; they couldn't get hold of him, and so had to keep him on. Which made me laugh when I heard him saying how supportive Mark Hughes had been to him when he finally made his comeback in September. I suppose he had to say that, and I didn't begrudge him at all, with his attitude he deserves every game he plays and I hope he plays until he's 40.

And, incredibly, we even managed to bring in a player who had to be paid for, just. We verbally agreed a £1.25m fee with Blackpool for DJ Campbell. He'd not only scored goals for them in the Premier League, he was a QPR fan as well. Crucially Flavio rated him and wanted to sign him too. I had DJ round the house, he agreed terms, he passed a medical, he even trained with us. It was a done deal, or so it seemed. Then before a press conference the media guy said to me, 'Don't talk about DJ.'

'What do you mean?'

'We can't put it through yet, we haven't got enough money.'

We hadn't sent the letter to Blackpool making a formal bid as we didn't have the money to pay it if they accepted. It turned out there was no money in the pot until we were given the first payment by the Premier League. Meanwhile Leicester spent £5m on Matt Mills taking their spending to £16m. I could have got Mills for £1m a year earlier but they wouldn't give me the money. Jealous? Me?

More potential signings slipped away. Jonathan Woodgate went to Stoke, Ashley Williams stayed at Swansea. But the one that got away which really upset me was Naughton. I knew Kyle, he was quick and could play on either flank, we needed him and I thought after the way we had helped Kyle Walker develop (when on loan to us from Tottenham), coming to us would be good for all parties. Daniel Levy had assured us that he wouldn't do anything with Kyle without telling me, so you can imagine how disappointed I was when I had a phone call from Gianni telling me he was signing for Norwich. Daniel hadn't had the courtesy to ring me, which I found appalling, but that's football. I had done everything by the book, gone through the right channels, but it obviously doesn't pay to be straight. I should have rung Kyle direct. You've got to admire Daniel Levy, though; there's a man who is always looking out for the best deal for his club, and look at how well Spurs have done as a result. You only have to see how he handled Luka Modric – Levy kept a player who wanted to leave, got another year out of him, kept him away from any of their rivals in the league, and at the end of the season sold him to Real Madrid for more than double what they'd paid for him. There's many who could learn a thing or two from Levy.

I scrambled to try and rescue the deal. Norwich had offered Tottenham a loan fee and a bonus if they stayed up. I said to Gianni. 'Why can't we pay that?' I rang Kyle, who was on tour with Spurs in South Africa. He told me the club were pestering him to sign the forms for Norwich. I asked him to give me an hour. I rang Gianni and shouted at him. I said, 'Look, I've been after him for three months. You and Flavio know that. We have to match it.'

Gianni got back to me and said Flavio would do it. I got on to Daniel Levy and everyone else and agreed to put it in writing the following morning. Which is when the office told me we'd offered £1.25m for DJ Campbell but if they accepted it we'd have a problem, as we hadn't got the money. So inevitably at one o'clock there was still no offer in writing to Tottenham when Kyle called to tell me he had to go to Norwich because of the uncertainty at QPR. I couldn't blame him, but I was absolutely distraught after chasing him all summer.

Flavio, of course, had a solution. I was sat with Nigel Cox by the pool in Italy when Gianni came over and said, 'Flavio wants you to sign Marco Motta from Juventus.' Coxy couldn't believe Flavio saying this in front of him. 'That's normal,' I said. Motta's a right-back, good athlete, big lad, but I didn't think he was a good defender. We checked him out: in four years he'd not played 20 games a year. The money being quoted was ridiculous. Mick Jones had watched him and said, 'He's not for us, not defensive-minded at all. He's not better than Bradley Orr.'

I told Gianni we'd be better with Nathaniel Clyne from Palace, a young lad who would become a top player, rather than someone we don't know. He'd cost £2m including wages, cheaper than Motta, and we'd have him for 3–4 years. It didn't make sense. In the end we didn't sign either. Motta, incidentally, didn't get a kick for Juventus that season and they sent him out on loan to Catania at the end of the January transfer window.

And amid all this there was the will-he, won't-he future of Adel who spent most of the summer nearly signing for Paris St-Germain. After the end of last season, with the fiasco of his dash from the airport for the final game, I fully expected Adel to have moved on but there he was in pre-season training as if he had never been away.

We had a chat and he said he would like to go, and could I help him? He thought Paris would offer £8m but Flavio wanted £12.5m because Tottenham had a big sell-on cut. I said 'Flavio's dealing with it.'

'Yes, I know. I've been speaking to him this morning.'

'That's a good start,' I thought. Before I came Flavio was speaking to all the players, probably asking if the coach was any good. 'No? OK. I sack him.'

Adel didn't come to Cornwall. He hoped he'd be going to Paris. It looked like it when Gianni said a deal had been agreed for £10m, plus £2m if Paris made the Champions League. 'Adel has gone, definitely gone,' he said.

Then Flavio rang. 'It's £8m plus £2m, not enough.'

Then Taarbs rang.

'Gaffer, can you help me, I want to go. My family, this opportunity, this contract, is unbelievable, will you speak to Flavio?'

'That won't help you, he won't take any notice of me on something like this, but surely if QPR keep you you'll get a big contract?'

'I'll have to ask.'

Bernie rang me, and said that he felt strongly enough about the Taarabt situation that he'd be happier to see him sit in the stand rather than give the money to Tottenham. He even said he'd pay the money personally.

'That's great,' I said, slightly surprised, though nothing about QPR surprised me by then; but I did think Bernie was trying to help me.

The next day my phone started ringing during our match with Bodmin. It was Flavio. He obviously had no idea we were playing. At half-time I rang him back.

'Taarabt is coming to Italy,' he said. 'He is staying with us. He has been to see Bernie and I, he's told me he is going to be the best player in the Premiership. He will be the best player QPR have got, he's going to be our leader, our captain. I will sort everything out.'

'What did Paris St-Germain do in the end?'

'They only offer £4m and another £4m in another year. By the time we pay Tottenham it is a waste of time. You have Bothroyd, Dyer, we are talking to Gabbidon and Taarabt is staying.'

I turned to Mick and Curly. 'We've got Taarabt now, whether we like it or not.' I was pleased personally, though I knew if I dropped him for two or three games he'd be on the phone to Flavio. That's how he works; he rang Amit the previous year. Adel's a good player, but difficult and I knew he would have to really knuckle down to make an impact in the Premier League. But if we had sold him what would I have got? Maybe £1m max, which at the time I had hoped to use to get Naughton perhaps. Either way I was glad it was decided. If Adel was to stay he had to be the focus of the team, but it was no good me building the team around him; if he then left just before the window shut, I'd be knackered.

When we got to Italy I had a word with Taarbs. 'Don't forget where you were when I came. You were on a low wage, Tottenham had bombed you out, and every manager at QPR had bombed you out. I don't want you to be the person that gets me the sack. I know you and the agent have spoken to Flavio about QPR. I want you to be careful about what you say.'

'Yes gaffer, but Flavio . . . can you believe it? He told Leonardo [PSG's general manager and a former player with Milan and Brazil] to "F off" and put the phone down on him.'

'Yes, I can believe it.'

Then came something else I believed, though I didn't want to.

'Gaffer, Flavio told me I might still go to Paris but I had to play the three games in August before the end of the transfer window. He said, "The coach has only three games."'

'Great,' I thought. 'If that's the case I'm like a dead man walking.'

I soon realised word had got round. Dezza came to see me. He'd been promised a new contract, but it hadn't materialised, now he'd had a fantastic offer to go back to Crystal Palace that included a coaching role. I had to tell him I couldn't guarantee anything and if he wanted to go to Palace I'd make sure he got a free transfer for what he'd done. I was sure Taarabt had told him Flavio said 'the coach only has three games'. The whole dressing room probably knew. And if they did, how much authority did my word carry? Even Alex Ferguson struggled to impose himself when he said he was retiring at the end of the season – what chance did I have?

Amid all this gloom there was a ray of hope. Flavio told me a guy called Tony Fernandes, a Malaysian airline magnate who had lived in England and supported West Ham, was going to invest in the club and he might want to meet me. My first thought was, is he going to be Flavio 2 — and was that a good thing? Then we spoke and Tony was very positive. He said he was trying to buy the club with Amit and take Flavio out of the equation, which was great news to me.

In case I needed reminding of how great that news would be I watched an advance copy of *The Four Year Plan*, the fly-on-the-wall film about the Briatore-Ecclestone years at QPR. It was jaw-dropping. I still can't believe Flavio allowed it to be filmed. It was warts and all, but it showed everybody how tough it was to work with someone like Flavio.

Flavio got rid of four managers before me in the film: Iain Dowie, Paulo Sousa, Jim Magilton and Paul Hart, and a couple of caretakers in Mick Harford and Gareth Ainsworth. The really funny bit is when he sends Gianni down to tell Gareth Ainsworth to put Gavin Mahon on against Cardiff and he scores the winner. They are all jumping up and down and Flavio says, 'I told you so.'

I battled on. I had hoped to play our final pre-season game at home. Gianni fixed up Parma. Then I was told we'd pulled the plug because the ground wouldn't be ready and the police costs would be extortionate. I tried to get another game on, but it was impossible. Our first home game would be the first of the Premier League season, against Bolton.

As we started gearing up towards that another problem arose. In the Championship season two executive boxes had been set aside to be used by the players' families. Between them they held 45 people. They were talking about knocking the two into one but even in separate boxes it was great for building team spirit; if you can keep players' families happy and united you have more chance of keeping the players that way. Then three days before the season started I found out the players were only having one box with a capacity of 25 – one complimentary ticket per player. I asked Rebecca, why? 'We've sold the other half,' she said. This for a group of players who had got the club to the Premier League. Why didn't they at least ask if we wanted to buy the other box?

There are lots of little details about the way you look after players, which may seem small but they are very important. Managers realise this, they know how players think, but obviously people in the administrative side may not appreciate the big picture. For example, when I played at Chesterfield every player used to get a turkey and a bottle of sherry at Christmas. One Christmas they cancelled it and there was uproar. Yes, all players can afford these things but it is the little things that seem silly that keep the spirit up in the camp.

I went to meet Rebecca and Terry Springett, the football secretary. Sharon and Mick came along. Rebecca said, 'Bernie said we have to sell all the boxes.' Yet they hadn't sold them all. She was unmoved, and the meeting became quite heated. Sharon said, 'Who got us in here, in the Premier League? Neil and the players. Yet they've had no help, no reward, no bus ride, no party, no holiday. And now you are taking half the family lounge away. Have you any idea how that will go down?' In the end I had to stop Sharon. She wanted to have a real go at Rebecca, she knew how vital it was to the players and their families, but I feared it would end in fisticuffs.

I found out they had sold our box to the *Evening Standard* so I got in touch with the *Standard* and they were happy to have a different box. Eventually, the day before the game, Rebecca agreed to allow that for the moment. But by then the lads had found out about it and were up in arms. It undermined all the hard work we'd done in pre-season.

That wasn't all. Rebecca added there was an issue with my tickets; I might get three, possibly four. I've one wife, four children, and some long-standing friends I like to invite occasionally. As I contemplated QPR's return to the elite for the first time since 1996 I thought, 'I don't suppose Alex Ferguson has this problem.'

I used to think back to the days when I first joined Palace. I'd lost my love of football management, and Simon Jordan gave it back to me. Now here at QPR that love was being sapped away again. After the extraordinary season we'd had, finishing as champions, everything that had happened since then seemed like a slap in face.

Chapter Eighteen

Deadline Day Dramas

I hate the transfer window. It's such a minefield of possibilities.

Alan Pardew

WHEN THE FIXTURES CAME OUT IN THE SUMMER SHARON had studied them quietly.

'Oh dear. You've got two away fixtures at Christmas.'

'Do you really think I'll still be at QPR at Christmas? I expect to see Santa coming down the chimney in Cornwall. I'm surprised the bookies only make me second-favourite in the "sack race". It's a compliment really.'

'Who's favourite?'

'Steve Kean.'

'What odds are you?'

'Six-to-one.'

'Maybe we should have a bet.'

'Maybe we should have done,' I thought to myself 90 minutes into the season after we had lost 4–0 at home to Bolton Wanderers. It looked like a gentle introduction to the Premier League but I thought, 'If this is one of the easier matches it is going to be a long hard winter.' The only positive was that Tony Fernandes was present. At least he realised the scale of rebuilding required, and the urgency of completing the takeover before the transfer window closed. So far I had only been able to commit £5.5m in wages and spent £500k net in fees, which was nowhere near enough at this level. We spoke after the game and Tony said he was definitely taking over on the Monday. He said he would support me. He was optimistic.

Going into the match I knew we needed, for starters, two full-backs, another midfielder and a winger. I had to play Kieron Dyer at right-back and Clint Hill at left back. Poor Kieron broke down after two minutes with a suspected broken metatarsal. I could have cried for him. He was in agony; mental as well as physical I shouldn't wonder. All through pre-season he'd been there half-eight every morning, he'd trained, he'd looked after himself, he'd been superb in the games, then two minutes in it was all over. I know everybody watching thought, 'There he goes again', but he didn't deserve it. As for Clint, he got himself sent off in a silly tangle with Martin Petrov who provoked him then went down very easily when Clint reacted.

Not that it affected the result. We played well for 40 minutes, we had three good chances, put them under pressure – then from a throw-in they got Gary Cahill spare at the edge of the box and he scored a fantastic goal. Midway through the second half Kevin Davies, who's too experienced for us, got a free-kick, the wall was not great and Danny Gabbidon ended up scoring an own goal. Then we just capitulated. It made me realise I couldn't be sentimental, which I had been.

It was hard to show a cheery face when I spoke to the press afterwards but at least the fans never stopped cheering – except for giving Flavio some stick which he didn't like. Even at 4–0 down at home they sang my name which was remarkable.

The week did not improve. I had avoided Flavio's calls on Saturday, but spoke to him on the Sunday.

'How did you sleep?'

'Not that great, but I never do after a game,' I said.

'It was embarrassing losing by four goals. That Ali Faurlin was at fault for three of them.'

I hedged around his individual criticisms. I didn't want to talk to him too long. Then he said: 'Fernandes has not come up with any money.'

On the Monday it was Bernie's turn to call. He said there was a problem with Amit, who was supposed to be coming back into the club with Fernandes, so Bernie might keep the club after all. Then Flavio rang and complained I had been quoted in the paper saying we needed players – as if that wasn't obvious to everyone. I was at the hospital with William so I couldn't really talk. Finally, that night as I was watching Manchester City beat Swansea on TV, Tony rang to say Amit had agreed his differences with Bernie and we could announce the takeover on Thursday. I had heard so many different things by that stage I decided I wouldn't believe anything until it was signed, sealed and delivered so I didn't count any chickens.

On the Tuesday I was told I could start setting deals up to bring in four or five players. I wanted Scott Parker, Shaun Wright-Phillips and Nedum Onuoha for starters. Then I went to the dentist. After an hour I came out, turned my phone on and I had six missed calls from Flavio. I didn't want to ring him as I thought I would only get told off for something, so I spoke to Tony who said, 'There's a slight problem with Amit so don't call Flavio yet.'

It went on like that until finally the deal was done and dusted and announced on the Thursday. It felt like a ton weight had been lifted. The previous three months had been even worse than being in administration at Palace. It was difficult working with Flavio and Bernie, though they could be good company. Sharon first met Flavio when I needed to speak to him one night, and we dropped by on our way into London. When we came to leave after about forty-five minutes Sharon said, 'You know Flavio, you are nothing like I thought you would be, I quite like you.' He and I fell about laughing; Gianni didn't know whether to laugh or not. I've not seen them since – though I did catch sight of Bernie when I went to the Grand Prix with Tony – but I'm sure they appreciated the job I'd done as they were able to sell the club for a lot more money than QPR was worth when I first arrived.

The takeover also gave the players a lift. They had been really flat at training on the Monday morning after the Bolton game. Not that everything was fine overnight. I had to have a word with Adel.

'You're not fit enough for this league are you, Adel?'

'No, gaffer. Sorry, gaffer.'

'I'm going to give you an hour against Everton, then you can play in the [Carling] cup [against Rochdale] and at Wigan. Then you have a fortnight to get fit. I'm bringing four or five players in. If you're not fit you're not guaranteed a place. It's up to you.'

He said he had booked himself into a fat farm in France, not that he used that phrase. I guess it was more like a boot camp.

But then Taarbs got a bug, one of those fabled 'mystery viruses', and he wasn't the only one. DJ Campbell actually collapsed at training and Matt Connolly was struggling. With a small squad, and Clint suspended, we had few options so they had to travel to Everton. In the morning Connolly and Taarbs said they would start and see how they went, but Jay Bothroyd said he felt unwell too.

He still thought he could play but I knew Jay would be a waste of time if he was like that so I decided to play Patrick Aygemang, who hadn't started a league game for me since I came to the club. I didn't tell anyone until the team meeting at 12.30 when I asked Patrick how he felt.

'Fine, gaffer.'

'Good, you're playing today.'

He was as shocked as anyone. The final XI was effectively our Championship team, only Danny Gabbidon of the new signings played. It felt like old times, all my old lads out there at Goodison Park. There were hairs lifting on the back of my neck. I looked at their team, top, top players, and an unbelievable subs' bench with Mikael Arteta, Louis Saha and Marouane Fellaini on it. We only went out and beat them one-nil.

It was probably one of the most professional performances I've ever seen that group play. Derry, Faurlin, even Taarbs was superb. He only came in because of DJ's illness. Patrick ran himself into the ground, so much so he collapsed just before the hour. He went down, tried to get up, and went down again, writhing in agony. All the Everton fans thought he was conning it, but he was obviously in agony. He ended up going off on a stretcher. When he came off I stopped Coxy.

'Nigel, what's wrong with him?'

'His knee's seized up, gaffer.'

'It looks to me as if everything has seized up.'

We got on the bus at 20 past six and didn't get back to the training ground until ten, but it wouldn't have bothered me if it had been midnight it was so good. It was one of those trips home that will forever stick in my mind.

As we got off I turned to Ricky, who's our club coach driver, handed over a belt and said, 'Look after it, I'll want it back for

Wigan.' You see, as I got dressed to leave the hotel to go to Goodison Park I discovered I had forgotten to pack a belt. That would not have mattered the previous year, but having lost weight my trousers would fall down without one. So I rang Mick Jones. 'Mick, I haven't got a belt with me. I can't go around holding my trousers up with my hands. You'll have to find me one.'

Fifteen minutes later there was a knock at the door and Mick was there with a black belt.

'Where did you get it?'

'The bus driver's not very happy, but I told him needs must. I've requisitioned it for the afternoon.'

When we won, with me being so superstitious Ricky could say goodbye to his belt – who needed new players when I had the bus driver's magic belt? Well, I did. I knew we were not likely to repeat the Everton result every week. But it had shown we were not complete no-hopers and I was able to attack the rest of the transfer window with credibility restored, hope and energy renewed.

I needed that. If you asked any manager what change they would like to make to the way the game is run I bet they would tell you they'd scrap the transfer deadline. It is another advantage for the big clubs who can afford to stack their 25-man squad with top quality players in case they suffer injuries. Mid-size clubs can't as I found to my cost in the Premier League with Sheffield United when we lost Rob Hulse, our top scorer, to a broken leg after the window closed. A club of that size wasn't able to carry back-up of the required standard on the off-chance we'd suffer an injury, but the window meant when we did lose a key player we couldn't buy someone to replace him. The window doesn't help those back-up players at big clubs either; they would be better off playing matches. I much prefer the old system when we could do deals until a mid-March deadline.

The other problem with the transfer window system is the sheer logistics. It is an absolute nightmare for managers. Sometimes it even clashes with a match night, which makes it near impossible. And it certainly messes up your family life. The previous season I'd been having a Bank Holiday picnic with the family in Richmond Park when the phone went. I'd been chasing Tommy Smith, a clever, versatile player, perfect for a small squad, without luck. Suddenly there was the possibility of doing a deal. I left my sandwich half-eaten and dashed to a hotel at Heathrow to meet Portsmouth's administrator. Then it was off to see Amit to establish if we could afford the deal I'd discussed. The following day, the last of the window, I was busy securing Rob Hulse, from Derby, and Tommy. Tommy was at the training ground early to talk terms and have his medical – while his agent was in America . . . on deadline day. I was constantly on the phone, to Portsmouth, to America, to our directors. It was driving me nuts. At one stage I said to Mick Jones: 'Let's not bother, we'll work with what we've got.'

Mick calmed me down and I ploughed back on. With 90 minutes left it still wasn't done and I was getting worried, not least because we were at the training ground near Heathrow, but our secretary, with the contracts, was at Loftus Road. In the end we just got under the wire, but only just. The Football League took three days to ratify Rob and we had to make Tommy's deal a loan until January, making it permanent then.

At least I got them. A couple of weeks earlier I spent two days in my office, only leaving to go to the toilet, and home to sleep, and still missed out on Darren Ambrose. We'd agreed a good fee with Palace's administrator but QPR wanted to force it down even lower. I kept warning them Palace were about to be taken over and the new owners would never agree the deal. Darren had passed his medical, agreed terms, even lined up a box at Loftus Road for his family. Then the takeover happened and the deal fell through. I was furious.

When I was younger I'd have been distraught at losing a player after chasing him for months, but now I just think, 'What will be, will be.' Sometimes these things turn out for the best, a player we already have comes good or I sign someone else who does brilliantly. In this case we bought Tommy Smith who did well for us.

People say, 'Why don't you get your deals lined up sooner?' Well, it's not always that easy. The player you want may have other options he's weighing up, you might have other irons in the fire. It also takes longer to get a deal over the line these days. Contracts are more complicated; there are agents and lawyers involved. When I started it was a simple form, green I recall, only a couple of pages long. Now there are pages and pages. One player I signed at QPR wanted dozens of amendments to the standard contract. I leave that side to the chief executives now, I don't want to be involved. Medicals are also more detailed – these players are costing millions of pounds in fees and wages so clubs want to make sure they've not bought a dud. Chairmen and, at the clubs who have them, directors of football, get involved. There are a lot of strings to pull together.

In 2011 there were a series of special circumstances – the need to strengthen after promotion, Flavio's refusal to spend in the summer, and the late takeover – that made our deadline day horrendous. After Tony bought the club he said to me: 'Who do you want?' I gave him my list more in hope than expectation with Scott Parker at the top of it. Tony is a West Ham fan and he loved Parker as much as I did. He said: 'Go and get them.' It was the most fantastic thing I'd heard all summer.

I didn't get Parker. I tried; I really rated him and had written in my *Independent* column the previous year that he should be England captain at a time when he wasn't in the squad. I was so pleased for Scott when he did become captain, he is a very good player but, more than that, a fabulous pro, a really good influence in the dressing room. He's an old-fashioned player in the best sense. A couple of years later when Leeds beat Tottenham in the FA Cup he and Michael Brown kicked each other up hill and down dale for 90 minutes, but when the whistle went and we had won I looked across and saw Parker go over to Brownie and they gave each other a hug. I thought to myself, that is how footballers used to be, no diving, no conning the ref, no theatricals; just two footballers who appreciated each other's efforts. We've lost a bit of that with the influx of foreign players. There's more glamour, but we've lost a bit of the game's soul.

Parker was also wanted by Stoke but I thought because we were in London he'd choose us ahead of them. Even when Tottenham came in I was optimistic, as Daniel Levy doesn't like paying big fees for older players who do not have much resale value. But once Harry Redknapp managed to persuade his chairman to make an exception and meet the fee I knew we'd lose him. I have wondered since how things might have worked out for me if we had signed Scott.

Tony wanted a marquee signing, someone of stature who would prove to other players we were a club that meant business. Having failed to get Scott we went for Joey Barton instead. I knew he was in dispute with Newcastle and he had baggage, but he was a good player and thought I could work with him and bring the best out of him.

We signed Joey on Friday 26th. He didn't cost a fee because Newcastle United were happy to let him go for nothing but we had to pay top dollar on his salary. He became the highest paid player in the history of the club. We also signed Luke Young. It was disappointing that he wasn't able to play for us at Wigan the next day. Someone in the office got the signing deadline wrong. We lost, though we were a bit unlucky and Young's absence was not the only reason.

I hoped to sign Armand Traore in time to play at Wigan but Arsenal had an injury crisis and needed him to play at Old Trafford. As you'll recall, they lost 8–2 and it wasn't Armand's greatest game. The morning after I phoned Richard Law, who deals with transfers at Arsenal, and asked whether they would now pay us to take him off their hands. He laughed, but the fee was unchanged.

That started the most demanding period of my life in management. The next few days were exhausting and it was a real baptism of fire for Phil Beard, QPR's new chief executive, who came in a couple of days before his official start date to help out.

All Monday and Tuesday I was on the phone, trying to set deals up. I was hopeful about getting Craig Bellamy who was leaving Manchester City on a free. We'd offered a two-year deal, which had tempted him because everyone else was worried about his knees and offering one. Craig was still a very good player and I figured he would be good for us. At six on Tuesday evening he rang and said he'd heard Liverpool might be interested in taking him back to Anfield, but if that didn't happen he'd come to us. I also had Sebastian Bassong lined up to come from Tottenham, but that depended on Spurs getting Gary Cahill which was looking unlikely as Bolton wanted £15m for him. It's like being in a chain to buy a house, but with an artificial deadline. I started considering alternatives with Anton Ferdinand, Scott Dann and Liam Ridgewell in the frame.

Deadline day began slowly. I was talking to players and agents, Amit was talking to them, and the chairman was even doing it on the phone from Malaysia, where he was seven hours ahead. All of us were trying to sell the club to players. After the Ali Faurlin saga we wanted to make sure everything was done meticulously so sorting out the contracts took ages.

This is how the last hours unfolded.

2pm: The financials still needed settling with Shaun Wright-Phillips and Manchester City so I talked to Jason Puncheon's agent as a back-up solution. The agent was pleading with us, Puncheon wanted to come, but I didn't really want to deal with Southampton chairman Nicola Cortese who can be very difficult to negotiate with, as we'd found with Kaspars Gorkss at the start of the season. They spent three weeks signing Kaspars with Cortese going from one extreme to another, then Brian McDermott, who I'd previously recommended Gorkss to, rang to say he was interested. I got straight on to Gorkss, who was on his way to Southampton for talks, to tell him to change direction as Reading was a better bet for him, a lovely club and there was no need to move house. The deal took four hours and I was delighted he'd gone there instead of Southampton after the way we'd been mucked around. The move was good for both parties as Kaspars played a big role in Reading's successful promotion.

4pm: Wright-Phillips finally settled with Manchester City and we organised scans for him. Meanwhile the chairman had given me permission to buy Bassong and Ferdinand. We'd earlier cancelled the Ferdinand deal so I rang Niall Quinn, asked if we could resurrect it, and put an offer in.

6pm: Bellamy's agent rang. Liverpool had been in touch. It wasn't looking good for that deal. I pressed on, feeling like a character in a Brian Rix farce opening and closing doors as I went from executive box to executive box talking to players and agents, trying to hammer out contracts. At one stage we had negotiations going on in three different boxes.

7.45pm: Harry Redknapp rang. 'Sorry, Neil, I can't get Cahill, I don't like letting you down but we have to pull the plug on Bassong.'

I wasn't surprised, I was used to it with Tottenham having lost Kyle Walker and been let down over Kyle Naughton. I was disappointed because everything was agreed. Fortunately we could sign Anton up so I just said, 'Wish you could have told me earlier, Harry, but not to worry.'

8.30pm: Shaun had had his scan and was on the way to the ground. Anton was going the other way to have his scans. I was talking to Ferdinand's agent with Sky Sports News on in the room. I looked up to see Loftus Road on screen and Puncheon walking into the entrance. It was the first time I knew he'd be coming to the ground. I'd spoken to his agent and Jason had been told to wait nearby in case we could do something, but instead of finding a restaurant round the corner he came to the ground. We'd agreed a £150,000 loan fee but Southampton were yet to give us permission to talk to him.

8.45pm: I rang Southampton. They'd obviously seen the same pictures I had and now wanted £200,000. Now we had Shaun we don't really need Puncheon so I said to his agent, 'There's no way we're paying that. You asked him to come here, you told me he'd be close by, but he's come to the front door! They've seen it, assumed we've illegally tapped him up, so you'll have to pay it.'

9pm: Puncheon's agent told me Jason is so keen to come he will pay the extra £50,000 out of his wages just to show me what he can do for us. It's a fantastic gesture. I'm impressed. Everyone thinks players are 'take, take, take', but here was one so desperate to play for us he footed the bill.

10pm: I looked up to see 'breaking news' on Sky Sports News: 'Craig Bellamy signs for Liverpool.' Oh well.

10.10pm: Wright-Phillips was done, his forms were being sent. I was talking to Jason Puncheon. Then I got a phone call from Nigel Cox, the physio. He was with Anton on the way back from having his medical. Coxy explained in a trembling voice there'd been an accident and they were stuck in traffic. This is when being a London club can be a disadvantage.

10.20pm: Still no sign of Anton. It was 40 minutes to the deadline. I rang Nigel and went daft with him. I told him, 'If Anton doesn't get here in time I wouldn't want to be in your shoes. Whatever it takes, get here.'

10.40pm: Ferdinand ran into the building and he and his agent read the forms as quickly as they could. Everything was in turmoil as we tried to get them sorted. I'd had a go at the admin staff after Luke Young's registration was not done in time for him to play at Wigan but the girls were uniformly fantastic. In ten minutes, the deal was done.

10.59pm: Puncheon and I shook hands and we sent his forms off – fortunately, being a loan there was no medical required.

11pm: That was it, the deadline. I'd missed out on Scott Parker, Craig Bellamy and Sebastian Bassong, but in the last week I'd signed Joey Barton, Shaun Wright-Phillips, Anton Ferdinand, Luke Young, Armand Traore and Jason Puncheon. We'd not actually spent that much money, it's not that easy to attract expensive players to a newly promoted club, but they all had Premier League experience. It was not quite what I wanted but I hoped it would be enough to keep us out of the bottom three until January when we could strengthen again.

11.30pm: Sky TV were still waiting outside so I did an interview with them and some other media then headed home. On the way Craig Bellamy rang, thanking me for my interest and telling me he always wanted to go back to Liverpool. I wished him all the best. When he scored the Liverpool goal that took them to the Carling Cup final later in the season I did think again of this night, and what might have been if he'd joined us instead. Then I called Tony in Malaysia and left a message thanking him for his support. I'd already thanked Amit. I felt at least we had a chance now.

12 midnight: I got home. I felt like a zombie and I needed a break to recharge so I decided to join the family in Cornwall. I was too wired to go to bed and as it was an international week the players had a few days off anyway. I fed the fish, and set off.

2.45am: I pulled in at Sedgemoor Services on the M5. I'd passed a couple of services so I could stop there as they always do me a nice coffee. But a young man said to me, 'I'm sorry. We've just washed the machines down, it'll be 20 minutes.' I could have cried for a coffee.

4am: I arrive at our place in Cornwall.

8am: I'm woken by the kids. On my phone there's a text from the chairman asking why have I signed Puncheon? It was right at the death and I couldn't get hold of him, but I did clear it with Amit. It was only a short-term loan to January, so I was sure he'd understand. He was a versatile player so it meant I'd be able to let a few go out on loan, so long-term I think it was better for the club.

Later in the day I had to ring five players to tell them they would not be in my 25-man squad. It was difficult. I got hold of Rob Hulse and Hogan Ephraim, but I couldn't reach Petter Vaagen Moen, Danny Shittu or Patrick Aygemang, Danny was aware anyway, but it would be a shock to the other two, especially Paddy who started at Everton the previous week and played so well when he was on the pitch. I would make sure they appeared in our team photograph, but then I would try to get them loaned to Championship clubs to get them some playing time and to ease our wage bill.

Postscript: a couple of weeks later I arrived at the ground and Curly told me Patrick Aygemang didn't feel he's mentally ready to play in a reserve game. He had to play games to get people interested in taking him and he wouldn't be playing in the first team as he was not in the 25. I replied, 'Is he mentally ready to be fined a week's wages?'

This was not that uncommon. It is extremely difficult nowadays to get senior pros to play in the reserves (or the under-21 league as it is now). The number of times players have said to me they didn't think they would gain anything out of it, they would rather train. If the player was a seasoned, experienced pro I tended to go along with him, especially if, no disrespect, we were playing a lesser team with a lot of young players as I do appreciate how difficult it is to get yourself up for a game like that and if you are not up for it that is when you could pick up an injury.

Patrick played, and went to Millwall on loan soon after. Although he then returned to QPR he later went to Stevenage on loan and that became a permanent move for him.

Chapter Nineteen

Four-Star Gaffer, One-Star Facilities

In my office I often regret the fact that players do not sit in chairs fitted with a lie-detector and an ejector seat.

Gordon Strachan

WHEN I WAS A PLAYER INITIATION TESTS COULD BE BRUTAL; after my first training session when I joined Aldershot I was grabbed, stripped of my pants and trousers, and had black boot polish rubbed all over my parts. I can tell you from bitter experience it's not easy to wash off.

It wasn't that they took an instant dislike to me, it happened to everybody who joined. I can't imagine that now, especially not in a Premier League club, where it's a bit more civilised. I wasn't always greeted like that. Generally I would turn up, introduce myself to somebody, try and have a laugh. At some clubs you'd put your gear down and someone would say, 'You better not change there because that is so-and-so's spot.' But I was never one to grab the corner, which is often the prized spot, I was usually glad to change anywhere as I was often on the fringe of the team.

When I sign someone now I normally ask the captain if they can introduce them to the rest of the lads. If they are British, or have played here for a while, they usually know someone at the club who they've played with, or played against a lot. Signings from overseas may not know anyone, but pros are pretty good at settling into a new environment. The type of lads I try and sign soon take people on board – and once they see people in games and the contribution they make they are even more welcome. That is one of the best parts of getting a team together, seeing them all gel.

It can seem an intimidating environment, especially to a youngster. At Leeds Sam Byram was still getting changed at training with the juniors long after he had made his first-team debut. I asked him why he was doing it. 'I like it. I know them all,' he told me.

I liked the fact he hadn't gone Billy Big-time with his old friends in the youth team, but I said to him, 'You're in the first team now, whether you like it or not you're going to have to go in and talk to one of them.'

At QPR the new lads appeared to fit in well at first even though I hadn't had time to properly check out their characters the way I would usually do. There was certainly an immediate impact on training with an extra 40–50 per cent intensity. The existing squad wanted to lift themselves as well, to prove they still deserved a place in the team despite the influx of new players. You need senior players to set an example in training. I can remember as a young lad running around like a blue-arsed fly and saying something to one of the older boys who wasn't getting much of a sweat on. He replied: 'How many caps have you got?' Clubs like

Manchester United have stayed at the top for so long because players like Roy Keane, Ryan Giggs, Paul Scholes and Gary Neville don't let standards drop on the training ground. I bet Phil Neville had a similar influence at Everton.

I decided to make Joey Barton captain, so I had a word with Adel. He took it well. I said to him, 'You just have to concentrate on getting some goals. I've brought in some better players so you should play better.'

The first game of the new era was at home to Newcastle United, which meant the press wanted to talk about Joey, but we had to treat it like another match. It was not, of course, for Joey, but I had a chat with him before the game to ask him to curb anything that might lead to trouble and he was good as gold.

You could sense coming into the ground a fresh excitement. I was really excited myself. The training had been great even though I was telling myself, 'You always get disappointed when you feel like this.' I was also wary as I had picked five new players: Joey, Wright-Phillips, Traore, Young and Ferdinand, which was a risk as we'd not really had time to gel on the training ground. I went round the new players before they went out and said, 'You've nothing to prove, play to your strengths and enjoy it.' I said to Shaun, 'Get back to where you are smiling all the time and laughing and taking them all on.' We were fantastic, but we just couldn't quite finish off our approach play and drew 0–0.

The following week, at Wolves, it all clicked. Again we'd trained so well I worried it would go the other way on Saturday, but we started like a house on fire and Dezza nearly scored with a header. I'd said I'd show my backside on the town hall steps if he ever scored, as Derry goals are as rare as hen's teeth. Ironically he did get an important goal late in the season, a header against Liverpool, but I'd left QPR by then so I didn't have to risk arrest at the Town

Hall. We then scored twice in two minutes at Molineux before winning 3–0, and we could have won by six. Mick Jones said to me afterwards, 'We mullered them,' and we did.

However, no one read in the papers how well we'd done because Joey, having scored and played well, couldn't help himself, re-igniting a feud with Karl Henry. He even took it on to Twitter. I had to call him in on Monday and tell him: 'All weekend has been about you and Henry, nothing's been said about the game. These lads deserve the applause for the way they played. That's wrong.' He accepted he was out of order. Hopefully that put it to bed. Mick McCarthy had a good line: 'Opinions are like backsides, we've all got one but you don't have to share it in public.'

I also laid into Anton in the dressing room for running 45 yards to confront the referee about the Barton/Henry incident. It was totally irresponsible. Faurlin was booked too. I said to them: 'In January, when you've got five bookings and are sat in the stand, you are no use to us.'

Things were even sillier the following week with Traore getting himself sent off for two bookings, the second for making a stupid tackle in a daft position. We were one-down at home to Villa with a minute left. I had a right go at him as he came off, because I thought he'd learn from it. He's going to be a hell of a player, but he's so naïve.

We'd gone behind to a bad penalty shout. The young lad, Michael Oliver, gave it for a shirt-tug so slight most of the Villa players did not even appeal. I said to him afterwards: 'If you'd have given that against Man United at Old Trafford there'd be a riot. To give fouls for that sort of decision in the box you'll be giving 25 a game.' He also missed a certain penalty for us when Alan Hutton handled.

'Surely your linesman saw it?' I said to him after.

'It's not the linesman, it was me. I didn't think it was handball.'

What can you say? I thought it was hand-to-ball, not ball-to-hand. They can't be training them right even though he is one of our better young refs. Fortunately we rallied and got an injury-time equaliser. It felt like we'd won the game, but that is what we should have done.

Days later I was told that the ref accepted it wasn't a penalty but that was too late to help us.

At the next day's training I could see Joey was het up but that was because he hadn't played well, we weren't getting a lot of the ball and he went looking for it so we lost our shape a bit. He wants to do so well he gets worked up when he doesn't reach a level of performance. Twenty-four hours later he was flying again so I asked Shaun Derry what the difference was.

'Gaffer, you have to let him play golf if he doesn't play well. He takes it out on the golf ball.'

Which was exactly what Joey had done.

Before playing golf Joey had come to see me. He said he had a committee and there was a list of things they'd like improved.

1. An extra physiotherapist.
2. Two masseuses.
3. Someone to help the IT guy.
4. Plugs for the baths.
5. Better training.

I didn't accept his criticism of the training, but they were legitimate points about the infrastructure; at one stage we had to run an extension cable out of the window of a room with a power socket, hang it on the outside of the building, then in through another window to heat these portable baths we'd hired. But it is not as if we had not been trying to improve matters ourselves. I made suggestions; Coxy had put forward a paper to improve the physios' room with some new machines; Carl Serrant (fitness and conditioning coach) did the same with the gym. The previous regime just threw it all out as they were not spending any money. The new one was on our side, that was obvious; as soon as I mentioned it Phil Beard sorted out the problem with the players' boxes at Loftus Road. We had these hoardings in front of the dug-out which were horrendous, within two weeks Phil sorted that out. We also brought in security for the players coming from the car park.

I told Joey he had some good points but we had to walk before we could run. Before we did all that I had to try and get the staff who were here last year the raise they never received. I said we'd present his requests to Phil and look to implement things as soon as we could.

Training facilities are more important than those at the stadium really, it is where you do your daily work, but even they are not the be-all and end-all. At Scarborough we used to train all hours of the day, at whatever and wherever we could get. We often used the same facilities my Todwick Sunday league team had, a 50p meter and one floodlight outside the dressing rooms. We'd be in the gym between nine and ten at night as it was the only time we could get it. We also trained at York, Doncaster, all over Sheffield. But we won the league.

When I got to Sheffield United we trained at Millhouses. It was a nice area but it was rented. The roof leaked, and we had to put a tin in the physios' room to catch the drips. I helped develop a new training ground with an academy. It's a fabulous site though it is on Wednesday territory. Much of it came from grants and so on but we spent £3m on it and people said at that time we'd be better off having £3m for players for the team, but as a Blade I thought it was more important long-term to have an academy. Look at the players it has produced: Phil Jagielka, Michael Tonge, Kyle Walker, Kyle Naughton, Matt Lowton, Jordan Slew and others. When we got in the Premier League we were able to put pop-up sprinklers in. That was £25,000 extra. Previously the groundsman had to drag a hose pipe across the pitches, that's hard work. Arsenal's training ground has pop-up sprinklers everywhere – there's probably one that'll pop up if you want a drink of water.

Crystal Palace's training ground at Beckenham wasn't the greatest, and it needed a lot of sprucing up when I arrived, but it was in a lovely situation, I enjoyed coming into the training ground. At QPR all you can see is aircraft taking off. I can understand why Jose Mourinho took one look, when it was Chelsea's training ground, and said, 'We need somewhere else.' It's very windy too, which can be a problem both in getting your message across and players being able to do what you want them to do. It was OK when we were in the Championship but when we got in the Premier League and started bringing in players who had been at bigger clubs like Chelsea and Newcastle they moaned like hell. The problem with that is it gives then an excuse and you don't want that.

Leeds United was the first club where I had felt truly confident that I could bring a prospective signing to the stadium, or the training ground, and they would be impressed. The team may not have been in the Premier League, but the facilities were. There is a big swimming pool, sauna and steam rooms, a massive gym and rehabilitation room. There were also pitches galore in a lovely setting. I thought I had won the pools.

That all counts, because it makes it a lot easier to sell a club. It's all very well saying, 'We're going to build this, move there, do that,' but players, and their agents, will be thinking, 'Yeah, yeah, they all say that, what have you got now?' At Leeds the buildings are already there.

At QPR I had sympathy with the new players' complaints but it wasn't a good sign. The mood around the training ground remained good though and I had some fun with the lads when Match Attax came out. Remember the bubble gum cards we used to collect (and, for the older readers, cigarette cards)? They are still around, but without bubble gum or cigarettes. And now they grade the players with star ratings.

William had collected them for several years so when the new season's packs came out we bought a few. Being back in the Premier League QPR featured and Kenny, Helguson, Faurlin and Smith came out of the early packs. I gathered the players on the training ground and said, 'I've some good news for four of you lads; come forward Paddy, Heider, Ali and Tommy.' I handed over the cards, and a pen. They all signed for William.

'I know you're disappointed, ' I said to the others, 'be patient. I'm sure we'll get yours in the next few weeks.'

And we did, after a marathon packet-opening session with William. The manager has a card too and I was naturally delighted to see I was a four-star. I pointed this out to the lads, and then I revealed the ratings. 'Sorry, Adel, you're only three-star, so are you, Armand. Kieron, you're just a two-star. Luke and Joey, you are both fours but Fitz . . . I can't bring myself to tell you . . .'

'Someone's already told me boss, I'm a one-star.'

Maybe they are marking Fitz on his injury record. He's always knocking on the door asking why he is not in the team, and I tell him, 'It's because you can't play three or four games on the trot without getting an injury.'

It is just his body really, even though things have improved since he stopped spending so much time in the car commuting (after I told him to move house, as the travelling was affecting his back). This season was typical. He started the first three games in the Premier League but had to come off injured in the third. He got back into the side when Danny Gabbidon was injured, started against Villa, but 25 minutes before kick-off at Fulham the following week he came in from the warm-up early having damaged his hamstring.

We were already without Traore because of his suspension, we'd lost Connolly to injury and I'd let Clint Hill go to Forest on loan as a favour and couldn't call him back. I said to Fitz, 'You have to start off, we'll see how it goes.' Fitz lasted the 90 minutes, but the clean sheet had gone in seconds. We were three-down at half-time. We changed personnel to be positive; we were doing well, I'm thinking, 'If we can get a goal'. Then we gave away a free-kick 40 yards out, Joey was talking to Fitz and Andy Johnson made a good run off them and scored. Four-nil, end of story; then it was Raggedy-arse Rovers and we lost 6–0.

There was a fuss in the paper about Adel leaving the ground. He was seen at a bus-stop in his club tracksuit, but I'm not sure he ever caught a bus. There was a lot of rubbish written. One paper claimed he was having a pint in the pub, which wasn't very likely as he doesn't drink. I didn't have a problem with him. After being subbed he had a shower, and at Fulham the bench is across the pitch, he's not going to walk around there changed in the middle of the game with all the fans giving him stick. Derry didn't either. Derry watched the game on TV from the cottage but I can't blame Adel for not wanting to hang around in the away dressing rooms there, it's a dump, especially when you're 3–0 down and you've been hooked. But I told him that these things can get out of hand and he needed to be careful.

Too many players were poor at Fulham, but it is never their

fault, always someone else's, they never look in the mirror. That's how players are. It was the same when I was playing. OK, they were used to better facilities and staffing levels. We did need more staff, but it's not as if we were the Dog & Duck training on a park.

Nevertheless we had a meeting with them. As well as not having enough masseurs and physios, the training was wrong, the training ground was a disgrace, the food was wrong, the coach wasn't good enough, presumably the manager too, the kit wasn't so good, even the grass at Loftus Road was too long – we could fix that immediately and had it cut short for the next game, against Blackburn. Of course, if we had been winning, most of this would have been fine.

They wanted training more intense. Little things like warming up, starting at half-ten instead of coming out just after. We agreed. I said to my staff, 'OK, let's jump on it now. We'll be a bit stricter. If we are going away we all come back on the bus unless I get a good reason by Thursday. If we are playing in London you come to the training ground first to go to the hotel.'

The staff mentioned some players were not eating at the club; they went straight off, which I didn't know. So we told the players, 12.30 to 1.15 they stay and eat. We were trying to restore team spirit, to knit the group back together. I knew we'd get drubbings, though I didn't think it would be at Fulham. It was about how we reacted.

In the meantime I told Jay Bothroyd I was going to give him a rest – he was yet to score and it was getting to him – only for DJ to suffer a stress fracture of his metatarsal. Having already spoken to Jay I could hardly put him back in so I decided to recall Helguson. That meant I couldn't pick Taarbs because Helguson wasn't the most mobile target man and Adel won't run about a lot. The good thing is that meant a first start for Jamie Mackie since his injury in

January. When I told him he was gob-smacked and the squad gave him a round of applause. It was ironic it was against Blackburn Rovers. Heider scored, but we drew again: that was four home matches without a win. It felt like we'd been beaten.

However, from the first eight games we were 11th in the table, had nine points and could have easily won the three drawn home games. So it was interesting next season hearing Mark Hughes say after each game that QPR had played well but hadn't got what they deserved, but he was convinced he could turn it round. He had three points from the first nine games, was rock bottom, and had spent £30m.

However, after the game Joey tweeted that Adel was supposed to be a genius but he'd not seen it yet. He shouldn't have been doing that. He should have been concentrating on his own football. The last couple of games Joey had not been playing well himself. Since coming to London he had been inundated with requests from people wanting to talk to him, media people, and he had been doing too much. I spoke to him about it and he promised to cut down.

Some of the players who came in looked at Adel and didn't like what they saw because he didn't run his socks off. The senior players the previous season were prepared to look at the positives, but some of the new ones have played with people who were as talented as Adel and who worked harder, so they expect him to. But blaming him was just another excuse to cover their own failings.

Wright-Phillips was also not himself on the pitch, and I had a problem with him over a disciplinary issue off it. I've always fined players ten per cent for dissent leading to a yellow card. I know that might sound rich coming from me but it is a needless booking and if it results in a red card for two yellows, or a suspension, it can hurt the team. Wright-Phillips was booked for dissent so he was informed of his fine by letter, which is the procedure. Instead of seeing me, knocking on the door, and complaining, he Sellotaped the letter onto his back at training in front of all the players, treating it like a joke. It was a lack of respect and I was disappointed with that and I told him so.

That was the moment that I realised just how difficult it was for managers in the modern day to discipline players with such big egos, on such big wages. That was one of the most disappointing mornings for me at QPR. Inside I was disgusted with Shaun yet to him it was a joke. I kept thinking I was the manager that got him out of the hell of Man City when no one else would touch him, gave him a cracking contract, brought him back to his home in London and then was treated with such contempt. I didn't think I deserved it.

So we had a meeting with the players committee about discipline. With the wages they are on now they think a ten per cent fine for dissent isn't right. One minute they were saying they want more discipline, but the next they are making fun of it, which made me think they didn't give two hoots.

I made a couple of calls to Mick McCarthy and a couple of others to see what they did. The general view was that if someone got booked, but did not get suspended, ten per cent was a bit much. So I gave the lads a list of all the things they might be fined for: being late for training, late for meetings, late for the bus, wearing an earring, things like that. They came back with amounts – £200 for being late, that sort of thing – and we decided the fines would be deducted from their salaries and paid into a separate account, which would then be used for something charitable. The only thing I disagreed with was instead of a grand for each booking for dissent, the sum increased each time, so it was £2,000 for the second booking, £3,000 for the third and so on. The reason was these bookings are totted up – a player is suspended if he is booked five times before January.

I'm not a big fan of fines to be honest, and QPR was the only time I let the senior players decide the structure of the fines. You can't use finance now to discipline people – when someone's on £70,000 a week a two-week fine is a lot of money, but they are still going to be raking in more than three million quid in the year so it's not going to hurt them. So you only use them if there's no other way to deal with issues but the problem is, there usually isn't. The manager still has the power of team selection but if you've a small squad that power is limited, and some players give the impression they are not that bothered anyway.

Sometimes small fines are better. If I'm doing set-pieces or something like that and I see someone not paying attention I ask: 'What did I say?' If they don't know it's £20 into the kitty and it always brings a laugh. Sometimes they'll guess. They'll have heard one word. Then someone will stick up for him. Paddy Kenny does that occasionally. So I'll ask him what I said and he'll get it wrong so I fine him as well. But Paddy's funny because he'll normally back me: 'He wasn't listening, gaffer,' he'll say. 'Fine him.'

Chapter Twenty

Beating Chelsea

A manager is responsible for 10 per cent of wins and 90 per cent of defeats. That's how it works.

Didier Deschamps

ALTHOUGH NOT EVERYTHING WAS GOING TO PLAN IN QPR's first season back in the top flight, I was looking forward to playing Chelsea. I'd been told at the start of the season if we beat them Amit's father-in-law, Lakshmi Mittal, the steel billionaire, would give me a million pounds. Not many people thought we could beat them, but I did – and that was quite an incentive. I told my family, and Gianni, and they were all rooting for me.

I'm sure QPR fans were looking forward to the game as well. When they left the Premier League in 1996 Chelsea were just another team. Things were starting to happen there – Ruud Gullit had arrived – but they were yet to win anything. Fifteen years on Chelsea were one of the big clubs. Rangers' fans had had to put up with a lot of stick in the meantime; this was their chance to give some of it back. Going to the game the build-up was fantastic. There was a whole generation of Hoops fans who had grown up without matches like this and they were relishing it.

I was too, but our build-up had been difficult. We had Armand Traore and Danny Gabbidon injured and training had not been very good. The players had heard Adel was out the night before the games against Fulham and Blackburn and they had a meeting amongst themselves that had come to my attention. Adel said he wasn't out. He doesn't drink anyhow so even if he was it is not the issue it would be with some. You have to give him the benefit of the doubt, but all week it had been festering.

Then there was selection and tactics. We were a bit at sixes and sevens. Joey and Dezza wanted to play three in central midfield and one player wide, Jamie Mackie or Shaun Wright-Phillips. I felt we needed Adel or someone putting his foot on the ball or doing something to stretch Chelsea. Curly wanted wide players to stop their full-backs pushing on but I thought we'd then just end up in our own half and get beat anyhow.

I have always talked to senior players, especially the captain, to get an opinion, but it doesn't mean I'll agree. My favourite manager, Brian Clough, used to tell players, 'I'll say what I think, then you say what you think, then we'll both agree I'm right.' That's what happened this time. I decided to pick Adel and have a go at Chelsea. I'm the one responsible for results after all, but I still knew I had to convince the players it would work.

On Friday I started with a meeting with the full-backs. They like to stay out, but I told them they had to play a little bit different as Chelsea's wingers like to come in and Juan Mata and Daniel Sturridge would cause problems if we allowed them to do so untracked. So the full-backs had to come with them and the spare centre-half would cover the space.

Then I brought in Joey and the midfielders and we had a really good morning running through how we were going to play. I decided to bring Clint Hill back from Forest as I wasn't convinced either Gabbidon or Traore would be fit. I had to ring their manager Steve Cotterill (who later joined QPR as part of Harry Rednapp's backroom staff) and apologise, but I needed to have cover.

I knew if Traore thought he wasn't right he would be a waste of time so at least I'd have Clint back with me and ready to play. He had a nightmare against Bolton on the opening day but he was a good pro and he had played some games at Forest so he would be match-fit. It was a good decision. The following morning Armand was uncertain. He had an adductor strain. I said to him, 'They run off, I've had loads of those,' but I could tell he didn't agree. Armand's the type that if he sneezed in the morning he felt he had flu or pneumonia. Clint came in and I told him he had to mark Sturridge, and follow him inside.

The game was the 4pm Sunday afternoon televised match. Beforehand I let the players watch the Manchester derby, the early game, on the TV in their dressing room. I thought watching that would take their minds off our game. I did the same in my office, for much the same reason. It certainly did the trick. It was the game City won 6–1 at Old Trafford and it captured everyone's attention. The TV did go off at 3–1 when the lads went out for their warm-up, but they knew the final score before we kicked off and the whole dressing room was stunned. The two teams even discussed it in the tunnel. That was a lot better than our lads being quiet and getting nervous about our match.

When we came out the noise was deafening and both sets of supporters kept it up all game. I couldn't talk to anyone more than ten yards away because they couldn't hear me shouting.

Chelsea are such a good team we knew we had to rattle a few cages, because if we just played football they would batter us. After the Fulham experience I had emphasised to the players we had to keep our shape, especially if we went a goal down. But we started well, the plan with the full-backs worked, we won some great tackles and headers and Chelsea began to show signs of panic. That was underlined when Luiz made a stupid challenge on Heider, going into the back of him when he was going away from goal. The ref gave a penalty and Heider tucked it in. Then Adel put a great ball through for Wright-Phillips and Jose Bosingwa pulled him down and got sent off. They were just rejigging their line-up when Drogba made a horrific lunge on Adel and got a straight red. They were down to nine and a goal behind. It seemed unreal. Watching it from the bench it seemed like Didier Drogba's dismissal was in slow motion.

Then a minute before the break they pulled off Juan Mata and put on Nicolas Anelka, which I couldn't understand. Not only was Mata the player I thought could rip us apart, doing it then meant we knew how they would play in the second half. I thought they would have given themselves a bit more time and decide what to do during half-time.

At half-time I said to my lads, 'We can't sit back because of the quality of their passing, be positive,' but it was difficult. We let them have the ball and their players are so good technically they kept it, even with nine men. We were chasing shadows. It reminded me of when I was at Sheffield United and we played Arsenal in the FA Cup at Highbury. We had a gameplan, which was to be difficult to break down. Then Dennis Bergkamp got sent off in the first half. At the break I said, 'Let's try and win it,' and we opened up. We barely kicked a ball until we scored a last-minute penalty to snatch a replay.

I substituted Adel with Tommy Smith with about 25 minutes to go to give us fresh legs. Once again he stormed off down the tunnel. He never shook any hands, not mine anyway as I didn't even look at him as I could see what he was going to do. I couldn't worry about it because although we had some opportunities to finish the game on the break, our final decisions were poor and we were doing stupid things like Helguson going down the right wing and crossing in the air to Wright-Phillips instead of keeping possession. But although they had a lot of pressure and possession they had few clear chances. Anelka had the best with a header but Paddy made a good save. There was a tense finish and I saw John Terry having a set-to with Paddy, and another with Anton, but it didn't seem like there was anything out of the ordinary given it was a tight, competitive derby match. We held on to gain a fabulous result.

I went out on the pitch to savour the atmosphere, which was deafening, and immediately had Adel coming up to me for a moan. 'Gaffer, why you substitute me, *blah, blah, blah.*'

'Look around you,' I said, 'this is not about Adel Taarabt, this is about Queens Park Rangers. Queens Park Rangers are more important than you. A lot of people would not even have picked you. You should be thanking me for picking you instead of having a go at me.' I think he's a lovely lad, and he is unique, but he hasn't got any idea sometimes as he only worries about himself. Most players do.

Joey and Anton lingered on the pitch with me. I said to them, 'Just take in the atmosphere, I've never heard anything like it.' I drank it in. A lot of our fans had never seen a victory against Chelsea – it had been 16 years – and they were revelling in it.

When the three of us got to the tunnel it was bedlam. All hell had broken loose. The tunnel was compacted with bodies; there was shouting and screaming going on. Chelsea weren't very good losers to say the least and as our players had to get past their dressing room to reach ours there was plenty of opportunity for confrontation. I screamed at our lot, 'Get in the dressing room,' and they did.

Mick, who had come down earlier, said the referee must have sensed what was going to happen as he got off quick, into his room, and shut the door behind him, leaving the players to sort it out themselves like in the old days, which I thought was a good move. The police were there too and one of the officers said to Mick, 'Keep your lads in check and this won't go any further.' These things normally last a minute or two and are then forgotten, and with neither the ref nor the police looking to pursue the matter that is where it would have ended. But, of course, there was another aspect this time with the Terry–Ferdinand incident. That would take almost a year to play out.

We weren't aware of anything out-of-the-ordinary when we left the ground and I drove home, still feeling elated. On the way I had a run-in with a Chelsea fan serving at a garage. I tried to have a joke about the game but soon realised it was no laughing matter as far as he was concerned. At home I'd just got in the front door when I received a text telling me there were these scenes on YouTube of John Terry using racist terms, 'you black C-U-N-whatever', towards Anton. There was a link and even viewing it on my phone I thought it looked pretty obvious.

Anton hadn't seen it at the ground because I don't let them have phones in the dressing room. So when John had pulled him after the game, and said, 'There's no problem?' Anton agreed because he hadn't seen it. But when he did see it he was furious. I spoke to him and told him not to say anything to the press. Then I spoke to Tony who said he would ring Anton and give him the club's total backing. The previous week the Luis Suarez–Patrice Evra affair had erupted and I realised this had the potential to become a big issue – but I had no idea how big the ramifications would be in the long term.

That night John Terry made a statement saying he was just repeating what Anton allegedly had said, and that was why he said it. That confirmed he had used the words. He should have just kept his mouth shut, as Anton never heard anything.

The police were probably the first to appreciate how things might escalate as the following day they called Mick Jones – though why they rang him neither he nor anyone else knew – and told him Anton's house had to be secured, and would he go along with them to the house to help them do that. Then they rang him and said they wanted Mick to be responsible for Anton's safety getting into the ground at the next home match – they needed to know where to take him to minimise the risk of anyone attacking him. Mick's my assistant manager, not a security expert, so he replied, 'You must be joking, that's your job.'

We were off Monday, but matters continued to develop. Anton was still very angry, so the club made an official complaint to the FA. The Met Police also got involved after someone made a complaint to them.

On Tuesday the FA announced, in response to our complaint, they would investigate. We trained as normal but FA people came to the ground in the afternoon to talk to Anton and myself, plus Shaun Derry and Clint Hill, who the cameras showed were nearby when the incident happened. But what could we say? None of us had heard anything.

I wanted to carry on as normally as possible so at lunchtime we went ahead with a couple of presentations. I'd had some extra Championship medals struck to present to some of the unsung staff, people like Andy the IT man, Sangi the assistant physio, Gary the kitman, and my secretary Caroline, plus some players who hadn't got enough appearances in to qualify for one. All the lads gathered around and gave them a clap. Then we presented a birthday cake for Shaun Wright-Phillips. Footballers are like women, after a certain age they don't really like birthdays, it is an indication of getting old. Shaun was 30, which is a bit of an unwelcome landmark, but he was pleased to get the cake and managed to blow all the candles out in one puff. It was a good hour together.

Overall, though, we didn't enjoy that buzz you get at the training ground after a great result because what was a fantastic win had been overshadowed by the controversy. It was all the papers were on about. With the inquiry disrupting training as well we didn't get the confidence lift we should have got from beating a team like Chelsea.

I did the press on Thursday as usual. Obviously Anton and Terry was the big topic but I was careful not to say anything inflammatory. The club line was, 'The FA are dealing with it,' and I stuck to that.

The FA came back on Friday and interviewed Anton again, for two hours. It wasn't the best preparation to face Tottenham and it showed at White Hart Lane at the weekend. Anton wasn't my only concern at Spurs. Adel had been poorly in the week but because it was Tottenham I felt I had to take the long-term view and start him. It was a mistake. He was so poor it was unbelievable, the worst I'd seen him. He wasn't doing anything on the ball and not working off it. That meant we couldn't get near them in midfield and Tottenham battered us. We got away with murder only being two-down at half-time.

If it wasn't for the long-term problems I knew it would cause, I would have hauled Adel off after 25 minutes, but I didn't want to embarrass him, so I decided to wait until half-time. But as we walked in to the dressing room, Shaun Derry absolutely crucified him, calling him lazy and effing this and that. I tried to intervene. 'Leave it Dezza, leave it, let me deal with it.' Mick and Curly also tried but Derry was too angry to listen. He went on and on, then Adel stood up and slaughtered Derry. In the end I just let them get on with it. It only stopped when Dezza went to the physio's room to get a stitch.

I realised I had to take both off even though that meant we had used all three subs at half-time. We'd already lost Fitz through injury again and had to bring on Gabbidon, who hadn't trained for five weeks and might not go the distance. We weren't sure about Traore's ability to last the 90 either. I had a chat with Curly and decided we'd have a go, if we got beat, we got beat, we weren't going to win sitting back. I put Bothroyd and Mackie on. Bothroyd had been superb in training, maybe the penny had dropped that he needed to sharpen up to play at this level and I was pleased for him when he scored. We did brilliantly, had some good chances, then Gareth Bale scored a fantastic goal to seal their win. But we had had a good go and came off feeling we'd done a lot better.

I had both Adel and Dezza in on Monday, individually, and told them how disappointed I was, and how it wasn't to happen again. Both accepted they had been wrong and apologised. It was just what I expected because they were both good lads.

Anton had been poor at Tottenham and continued to be so. I don't think he ever played well for me after the John Terry incident. His mind was affected – understandably given he even had a type of bullet sent to him in the post – and I don't think he has ever been the same player. His concentration levels were poor and he had that many meetings with solicitors, the police (who by Tuesday after the Spurs game said they were launching a formal investigation), the FA and PFA that he missed a lot of training and his sharpness dropped. It didn't help the team's preparation either because you need your centre-half, especially if working on defending set-pieces.

Shortly before Christmas the Crown Prosecution Service said they were charging Terry with racially abusing Anton. It was the right decision, but meant the issue would continue to linger over Anton, and the club. By the time Terry appeared in court to plead not guilty I had left QPR, but I followed events from afar as he was stripped of the England captaincy, prompting Fabio Capello to resign. It was then it occurred to me how seemingly uncon-nected incidents can have lasting, unforeseen ramifications. If Tottenham and Bolton had been able to agree a fee for Gary Cahill in August Harry Redknapp would have let me loan Sebastien Bassong. Then I would not have bought Anton, he would not have played against Terry in that match, and England would have gone to Euro 2012 with Capello still in charge – not that I think we'd have done any better.

Terry might also still be England captain instead of retiring from international football in September 2012, shortly before the FA found him guilty of using racist language and banned him for four matches. That decision, 11 months on, finally seemed to indicate a line could be drawn under the events of 23 October, 2011.

Actually, there is still one outstanding issue. I'm still waiting for that £1m bonus from Amit's father-in-law for beating Chelsea. I'm sure it's in the post.

Chapter Twenty-One

In the Public Eye

A lot of players think they will go into management and stay friends with everybody, but you have to make unpleasant decisions that will hurt people.

George Graham

'HAVE YOU BEEN DRINKING, SIR?'

A phrase calculated to chill the blood of any driver, even when you know the alcohol content of that blood is below the legal limit for driving. I heard it after I went to Glasgow to see Jamie Mackie playing for Scotland and stayed over at Dunoon where Sharon's grandparents came from.

I ate at a nearby hotel a friend runs, and had a glass of wine with my meal. About 10pm I went home and drove past a police car. They followed me, stopped me, and said I'd been speeding at 40 mph. I'm sure the fact I was in an Aston Martin in a small village raised some eyebrows, and maybe they hadn't much else to do but see who was in it.

The Aston Martin was a reward to myself when I got in the

Premier League with QPR, it has always been the dream car for me since I was young. I bought Sharon one the previous year for Christmas, from Scalextric. It's much more economical than mine.

There were two policemen, a classic good cop-obnoxious cop partnership. The first one knew me straight away and started talking football. After a nice few minutes the other one asked if I'd been drinking, I said I'd had a glass of wine with my meal. So they breathalysed me. I thought I'd had two half-glasses of red wine but one said to me, 'It's positive, we'll have to arrest you and take you down the station.' They read me my rights. I couldn't believe it. I'm so careful about what I drink given what I do with the car, not just work but all those little things like taking the kids to school, the things you take for granted.

They took me to the station. The obnoxious one said, 'When we get out I'll have to put my arm on you to escort you into the station.'

'Why?'

'Well, we should handcuff you by rights, in case you run away.'

'Do whatever you have to do,' I said, though there was not much chance of me doing a runner with a dodgy hip in the middle of the night, and with them already knowing who I was. He was obviously loving every minute of it.

Inside the sergeant was there and we talked football. A couple of policemen came in and had a look, word was obviously getting round. I had to fill in all these forms. They said I needed to give another breath test, twice, and told me if the reading was 35–39 they would give me a warning but not arrest me, above 39 they'd charge me and take blood and urine samples. I asked to speak to a solicitor but they said I couldn't, they would talk to him, which I thought was strange. I wasn't even convinced I was speeding, let alone over the limit, but felt sick to the stomach now. You never know for certain. Eventually I took the final test. It took a couple of minutes for the results to come but seemed like an eternity. I can honestly say it was the worst I've ever felt sickness-wise. I imagined all the papers having a field day if I was over the limit. Then the nice one said both tests were negative. I felt like I do when the final whistle blows at the end of a big match and I've got a fantastic result.

They had to drive me back. I felt like saying to the obnoxious one, 'I bet you were gutted when they were negative,' but I thought I'd better not otherwise he'd do me for speeding. It was a good lesson. I'm careful already, but if I'm in the Aston Martin I'll have to be even more careful.

That's the downside of being in the spotlight, for some folk you are a notch on their belt. Unlike the people you see on *X-Factor* and *Big Brother* I didn't grow up wanting to be well-known. I'm not sure it was an aspiration people had back then, certainly not if you grew up in a rented house in Sheffield with an outside privvy. I wouldn't say I'm famous now, but among people who follow football there is obviously recognition, and football is much bigger in society than even 15 years ago. Certainly being in the Premier League with Sheffield United and QPR I received a lot more attention from the media and wider public than when I was in the old First Division with Notts County.

It can be strange because some people find it hard to believe that someone who is on TV does normal things, like shopping for dinner. I was in Wetherby, in the supermarket, and there was this bloke looking at me. He followed me around three aisles. Finally he said, 'Are you Neil Warnock?'

'Yes.'

'I can't believe I'm meeting you.'

'I'm normal, you know. I shop, I cook, I eat.'

When I see people look at me twice I can tell they're thinking: 'It can't be him.' Then they realise it is and they come back with the scruffiest pieces of paper to sign, like a shopping list or till receipt.

Being known has its plusses. Sharon doesn't like it but every now again if we need to get something sorted I say to her, 'Do you mind if I say who I am?' because it can help sometimes. But if you are in the public eye you have got to accept you can't have it both ways. When I was at Palace there was a confrontation with some Millwall fans by the London Eye when I was with Sharon and the kids. One lad came up to me and started chatting, he was a nice lad, but next minute there were five them having a go. We carried on walking then one of them threw a coin that hit Sharon on the head. I wanted to go after them but Sharon said, 'No, don't, just leave it.' You never know if they have a weapon on them and we couldn't find a policeman anywhere – typical, they are never there when you want one.

But that was the only time; every other time it's been great. We went out a lot in London because there was so much to do and I would often chat to fans. I've had a laugh with West Ham fans about Carlos Tevez – I always like West Ham fans – and I spoke to some other Millwall fans who were great. Palace fans gave me a new zest for life and QPR fans were great to me. I like talking to fans. I'm like an ordinary fan myself, I think that is why I get on with them. The media make out I have smoke coming out of my ears and flames coming out of my mouth, but I'm an ordinary guy.

Having a media profile has led to some nice things. I was invited into the *Test Match Special* commentary box as a teatime guest at Lord's, which was a thrill, as I love cricket. It was a day when South Africa batted all day and England never took a wicket. I think they were pleased to get me on as it was something different.

I also did a poetry reading. Yes, you read that right. It was Christmas 2011 and I was invited to do a candlelight reading in the Grosvenor Chapel in Mayfair in aid of Smile, a wonderful charity that performs operations on children born in developing countries with a cleft palate. For just £150 children who are isolated can have their lives transformed by a simple operation. It was a super night with a wonderful gospel choir. Among the other readers was the actress Elizabeth McGovern, who was playing the mother in *Downton Abbey*, a programme Sharon and I had been glued to. I was given a very appropriate poem, Mike Harding's 'Christmas 1914'. It's a moving poem about the English and German troops in the trenches playing football on no-man's land on Christmas Day instead of killing each other.

Another perk was the trip to the Dubai Grand Prix I combined with a scouting mission during the November international break. Tony Fernandes also owned a Formula 1 team and he invited me and the players out there. Several of the lads took up the offer including Bothroyd, Helguson and Wright-Phillips. Phil Beard came out as well.

Talk about how the other half live. I'd rather be in Cornwall with the greenery than Dubai myself but it is amazing what they have done. The hotel was stunning, the paddock was fascinating – minutes before the start came the icing on the cake when Phil and I were asked if we wanted to walk down the grid as the cars were preparing to start the race. There was me and Phil, alongside members of the local royal family and superstars, taking videos with our mobile phones. You could feel the heat and the power of the engines as you walked down there. For the drivers it must have been like having people walking through the dressing room before the game, they must have just wanted to get on with the race, but I suppose they are used to the circus that goes with it.

I watched the second half of the race on a yacht in the bay. Eddie Jordan, the former team owner now working for the BBC, was there. He's got a band that played at a party the night before. He's a Chelsea fan, so he complained about us beating them. I was like a little kid, chasing after Lewis Hamilton, who won the race, and Mark Webber, trying to get autographs. I had a good chat with Mark.

I bumped into Roberto Mancini and Patrick Vieira at the circuit on the final practice day. Roberto was immaculate as ever in suit and tie, I felt a bit under-dressed in tee-shirt and shorts. We'd played Man City the week before the GP. It was one of those frustrating nights, we were superb but gave away three poor goals. We got good publicity because of the way we played but if we'd got the basics right defending we could have won. I felt City's people were condescending in the way they said how good we were, but we were better than them. It showed what we were capable of. There was nothing wrong when the players had the right attitude.

There were still one or two players at the club who were just picking up a pay cheque and not contributing who I couldn't get rid of. One had a six-figure promotion bonus in his contract and a substantial rise when we went up and he had not had a kick in the Championship all season. It shows how silly contracts are. One of the downsides of management is paying good money to players who don't contribute but it happens at every club.

Even without playing these players caused trouble. One of the players – and it wasn't Joey Barton – wrote a terrible tweet using terminology associated with Downs' Syndrome children. Our community people dropped me a line to say how disappointed they were and quite right too. I said to Sharon, 'No one would believe what a manager has to do these days, looking after this lot.'

I also found it amazing some of the players not in the 25-man Premier League squad wouldn't go on loan. Maybe I should have been meaner to them, made them come in and train at silly hours like Mark Hughes did so they get stuck on the M25 every day, but I couldn't have done that to the players who had got us into the Premier League like Helguson and Hulse. If I want to get rid of a player I'll try to help them get a good move, it makes sense if I'm trying to get them away. But with the money now a lot of them won't go. They want to just pick up the cheque and are not bothered about playing games. Surely that is what they came into football for, to play football?

I felt sorry for Hogan Ephraim. He had a good season the previous year but I'd no room for him in the 25. I felt I'd let him down and I tried to get him fixed up but he didn't want to go to Sheffield United. In the end I let him go to Charlton for nothing just to get him into the shop window. He deserved something. It is one of the worst parts of the game seeing good people like that not getting the breaks. Hogan managed to get a new contract the next season, which I couldn't understand as he wasn't in the 25 again, but good luck to a smashing lad.

Back at the club we had made changes with Phil and Tony very supportive, but we still couldn't do anything quick enough for some players. We knew the training ground was not good enough and had looked at three sites for a new one, but building a new training ground, or even refurbishing an existing one, takes time. For example, we couldn't get planning permission for new portable buildings so we wanted to use some empty rooms as massage rooms. We may have been a Premiership club but the land was owned by Imperial College and the groundsman said we couldn't. Eventually we got the college officials over and they said we could – which left us in a state of war with a grumpy groundsman.

We had a meeting with the players' committee. Kieron Dyer was the voice of reason – it would have been chaos without him. I said to them, 'You can talk about tactics, physio, fitness guy, coaching . . . do you think that was the reason Anton couldn't stay with Dzeko? Do you think that was that the reason Luke Young couldn't stop the cross? Do you think that was that the reason Gabbidon didn't jump with Toure? That's rubbish. We lost because we didn't defend well, nothing to do with tactics and facilities.'

The things players do. Around this time Chelsea missed out on what would have been a really good Champions League win in Valencia – and an important one for Andre Villas-Boas– because of a stupid, irresponsible handball by Salomon Kalou. I can only imagine what AVB said to him. I've endured one or two handballs like that from players and I can't understand why they do it. It is as if they suffer a brainstorm. It can happen to the most reliable of players. Phil Jagielka, of all people, did it with Sheffield United on the last day of the season. Wigan scored the penalty and sent us down. It was years before I could ask him why he did it. He just said he didn't know. It happened again in my first match with Leeds, at Portsmouth. Young Tom Lees shoved his hand up, fortunately the referee missed it. I told him at the finish if we'd have lost the game because of it I'd have killed him. I laced into him, told him he'd never play for me again if he did it again and all that. All that effort we put in could have been wasted. Full credit to the kid, he didn't buckle but kept his place for the rest of the season and was a fixture in the team the following year.

Sometimes it's just a daft tackle or back-pass. Do you remember Wolves' Ronald Zubar playing a 93rd-minute back-pass at Bolton when Mick McCarthy's team were holding on for would have been a very good, and vital, point? I could have cried for Mick. Players? Bloody Hell.

Of course sometimes there is a good reason for a player losing his focus. Anton was in that meeting, and while he said some very reasoned things I knew the fall-out from the John Terry incident had affected him. He had been really poor against Tottenham and Man City. I asked Tony to talk to him, to put his mind at rest about the club's support. I just hoped to get him back to concentrating on football.

We spent all afternoon after the lads' meeting talking to physios, fitness guys, masseurs. I'd said, 'Get what they ask for, then they have no excuses.' We were miles away in staffing compared to Premier League levels. That really hit home with me when we played Man City, as there were too many backroom staff to get in the dressing room. Then we met Phil who said the club had reviewed the wages and made some increases. It was not before time.

We got back from the Grand Prix to find Adel had gone missing again. He'd been to Morocco, now he was in France and lost his passport. He'd been on the phone to Caroline telling her all this; and then the police found the passport, in March, Cambridgeshire. I texted him to tell him the passport had been found. Then I texted him to ask if he wanted us to take action over the bloke who was impersonating him and claiming to be in Marseille that morning talking to Caroline. He didn't think this was funny. Neither did I.

After all that we then got a superb win at Stoke where I played Traore in left midfield in front of Clint Hill as we needed Clint's experience and physical presence. We worked all week on how to combat Stoke's long throw and it worked. We also worked out a ploy with the towels. Watching a video of their games we realised it took 30 seconds every time they got a throw-in for Rory Delap to get a towel from the ballboy, wipe the ball dry, then take the throw. We decided to do the same. Every time we got a throw, wherever it was on the pitch, we asked for a towel and wiped the ball dry before we took the throw. They didn't have a problem with this to start with having taken an early lead, but then Heider Helguson levelled and they began to get upset at us wasting time. We got a second just before the break and when Heider put us 3–1 up ten minutes into the second half the towels suddenly disappeared. So we fetched some of our own. They were going mad on the Stoke bench. I did have to laugh. They got one back but we held on for a super three points.

However, Paddy got injured and that left me lying awake at night thinking about goalkeepers. Brian Murphy was already out so we only had Radek Cerny, who was experienced but hadn't played for ages, and a first year pro, a Latvian kid, called Elvijs Putnins who I'd sent to Borehamwood on loan. I asked the Premier League if I could have an emergency loan. They said no, we could play Elvijs. I'd only kept him on because he wasn't costing us much and he was a nice kid who needed a chance – but not being thrown into the deep end of a Premier League match. Fortunately in the games to come Radek never got injured, but it was scandalous. Who'd take a risk signing on a young kid as keeper after that? All it meant was clubs would keep more senior keepers on the books on the off-chance, which was no good for anybody. I just wished it had happened to a big club then we'd see what would have happened.

Stoke was followed by another away match, at Norwich. We went by train on a Friday afternoon but for some reason were not able to book our own carriage. We were all over two carriages, players everywhere.

When we arrived I walked to the exit along the platform, and it's a long one at Norwich. The players were all waiting there in tracksuits emblazoned with 'Queens Park Rangers' on the back and the club crest on the front. 'What are you waiting for, lads, to get on the bus?'

'They won't let us out, gaffer.'

This guy came along in an illuminated jacket. If he recognised me he wasn't a fan. 'You can't leave without tickets.'

'I've left them on the train. The guard didn't say we needed them.'

'You can't leave without tickets.'

'Surely you can use some common sense and just let us through. You can see they're all a team.'

'Can't leave without tickets.'

'Are you effing joking, mate?'

'Don't swear at me. I'll report you.'

'Get a grip of yourself. I don't know if you are some kind of jobsworth, but there are 28 of us in tracksuits. We're not railway skivers.'

'Can't leave without tickets.'

He just stood there, so Curly had to run a 400-yard round-trip to get the tickets. By the time he got back a girl had started to let us through. As I passed the jobsworth I said to him: 'What a sad person you are. I hope something happens in life to cheer you up.'

That night at the hotel we had a meal and it was like eating in a concert hall, the noise was terrible. There were people everywhere, asking for photographs, autographs, and a few who had had a drink or two. To cap it all we lost 2–1.

I don't think becoming well-known has changed me – I'm sure Sharon would let me know if it did – but every now and again something like coming across that jobsworth happens to help keep me grounded. There was a woman in a building society who asked me about job security when I was discussing a mortgage, she had no idea I was a football manager. There was the manager in WH Smith in Beckenham who, when I asked about why my book was not on sale, and gave my name, had no idea I managed the Football League club that trained down the road. There was the night we went to see Michael Bublé. I went to the bar and a couple of guys started talking to me, they had recognised me – I was at QPR in the Premier League at the time. Then one said: 'Are you still working?'

The one I'll never forget though is the man in a hotel in Scotland. He was wearing a kilt and was obviously at a wedding. As I was checking in he wandered out of the bar, looked at me and said: 'I know you . . . you're on telly.'

'Sometimes,' I said.

He wandered back into the bar, then a few minutes later he came back. 'Are you in football?'

'Yes.'

He walked away again. Then he came back, with a smile of triumph on his face. 'I've got it . . . Howard Wilkinson.'

Chapter Twenty-Two

Happy Christmas?

If footballers think they are above the manager's control there is only one word to say: 'Goodbye'.

Sir Alex Ferguson

WE HAD JUST BEEN HELD AT HOME BY WEST BROMWICH Albion. It was mainly linesman Terry Richards' fault because he flagged Wright-Phillips offside when he wasn't and chalked off a fabulous goal which would have put us 2–0 up. There's no way Albion would have come back from that. But at the final whistle, when I had a go at the ref, he said, 'Why don't you ask your No.11 why he didn't foul Morrison to stop the attack for their equaliser?'

The ref, for once, was right. Alejandro Faurlin is one of the best players I have ever worked with and he was head and shoulders the best at QPR. That didn't make him immune from an old-fashioned rollicking. Especially not this time.

In the dressing room I turned on Ali.

'Why didn't you stop it? Why not pull him down? Why not take a booking?'

'I'm sorry, gaffer.'

'What's the matter with you? Couldn't you see the danger?'

'I'm sorry, gaffer.'

His apologies had no effect on my rage. I went on and on. 'We could have won that if you'd been awake. Can't you understand?'

Suddenly Ali cracked. I'd overdone it. He got up, pushed all these bottles off the table. There was a plate of pasta. He chucked it up in the air. 'I kill you,' he screamed.

I'm on the other side of the table. Two or three of the lads grabbed him. 'I wish you'd shown that fight to stop the goal,' I shouted. I said a few more things to the other players, then left.

Then I went to the referee's room. We have to wait half-an-hour before we are allowed to talk to them. It is supposed to be a cooling-off period. It didn't work that time. I said to the linesman, 'When you see it tonight, and you know it is not offside, you're going to be disappointed.'

Then I did TV. Years ago I'd have said something and got fined. This time I just said he made a mistake. But inside I was boiling. It was such hard work to get a goal at home at the time and it made you scream when you got one, a good one, chalked off.

That night we had to drive to Yorkshire for my grandson Charlie's first birthday. I wasn't in the mood to talk to anybody. I was full of hate for the linesman after all the hard work we did that week. Sharon wanted the kids to be able to watch a film in the back of the car but I put *606* on and listened to all those raggedy-arsed callers. I sulked all weekend. I was terrible company and no one talked to me. It's wrong, but it is hard to avoid. You get wrapped up in it and you don't want to socialise when something like that happens. Watching *Match of the Day* didn't help, seeing everybody say it was a mistake by the linesman was no consolation.

It still hurt on Monday, but I needed to make up with Ali. I saw him first thing.

'Ali. What can I say? I'm sorry I had a go at you.'

'I am sorry too, gaffer. I wanted to keep calm but I couldn't. I felt disappointed I let you down.'

'You've not let me down. You've been brilliant all season. You know what I think of you, son.' He's a fantastic lad, different class as a player. He's a fantastic brain. I think he's going to be a great player.

Christmas means parties, which are a menace for football managers, and they always have been. I look back without pride on Christmas 1970. I was playing for Rotherham but still in touch with a lot of my mates at Chesterfield. They used to have a Christmas drink at the office of a car dealer who knew a few of the players and they invited me to join them. Well, Chesterfield were playing Rotherham on Boxing Day and I was in a decent run of form playing 11 games straight. My impending opponents matched me drink for drink, but I found out afterwards mine were spiked. I was absolutely rat-eyed by the time I got home. Christmas Day was a write-off and I was still wrecked on Boxing Day. We lost 2–1 in front of Millmoor's biggest crowd of the season. I couldn't move and was kicking at three balls every time the play came near me.

I can laugh about it now with two of the main culprits, Tony Moore and Kevin Randall, who's now my chief scout and scored for Chesterfield that day, but it was criminal really getting in that state. I should have been fined a week's wages. I paid for it though. I only played one more match for Rotherham, away to Halifax, before being dropped for good. It probably cost me an appearance in that fogged-off FA Cup tie against Leeds United. Served me right. At the end of the season I was given a free transfer and went to Hartlepool.

It was all low-key and fairly innocent then. That changed. At Sheffield, in the Premier League season, the lads organized a Christmas night out in Manchester. Just before they went I got wind that a tabloid was sending two female news reporters along with instructions to get a story out of it, about footballers behaving badly, and some pictures. Fortunately I was able to warn both the players and the bouncer we had hired to keep an eye on things. Apparently they worked out who the two were fairly easily and made sure they went back to their editor empty-handed.

That's the way it is now. Sad isn't it? But I think the wild party days are over. Most of the foreign players are not interested; they look after themselves and rarely drink much, if at all. That has rubbed off on some of our lads. Though I do wonder if some of the foreigners might be better off letting their hair down occasionally.

Joey arranged QPR's party, in Liverpool, his hometown, after we played at Anfield. It's not as if he'd ever been in trouble there before. What could possibly go wrong? I already had the FA on my back, writing to me about Joey's tweeting. They wanted me to have a word with him to tell him not to tweet about betting on football. As if he'd take any notice.

We hired four security guards to accompany them to make sure nothing happened. Kieron Dyer wanted to come up with us so he could join the party but Fitz Hall was not so keen. He came to see me. 'Am I on the bench at Liverpool, gaffer? Because if I'm not I'd rather stay at home with the kids.'

You could have knocked me down with a feather. 'I don't know yet, Fitz, I haven't finalised the squad.'

'If I'm on the bench I'll travel.'

I thought, 'That's good of you.'

I discussed it with Curly and Mick and we decided to take Matt

Connolly, who wanted to be there. So I told Fitz to stay with his kids. I still can't believe it, but that's how it was.

We lost at Liverpool, mainly down to Luis Suarez, and there was a fight in the tunnel coming off. Either Joey threw a punch or had one aimed at him. A steward and Craig Bellamy were involved, and then everyone got stuck in. It came after Craig tried to wind up Joey on the pitch. The ref told some of our players Joey had done well in not losing his rag. Craig is hot-headed, but I've a lot of time for him.

I went back to London with the staff, leaving the players in Liverpool to enjoy their party. The following morning, early, the phone rang. It was Paul, the press officer. My heart skipped a beat. 'Don't tell me, the players' party last night.'

'No gaffer, nothing to do with that.'

What a relief that was. By all accounts they had a good time with no hassles. They were certainly more sensible than I was at Rotherham.

Next up was Manchester United. I'd been looking forward to the game, hoping we could recreate the atmosphere against Chelsea and Manchester City but Wayne Rooney scored in the first minute and the afternoon went a bit flat. Rooney was different class that day; he showed the difference between the top sides and ones like us. It was disappointing though because it meant I'd still not got a win against Manchester United. We were unlucky with decisions at Sheffield United, while with Notts County we were within a whisker of beating them at Meadow Lane. It is incredible to think that Alex Ferguson was United's manager even then, in 1991 – I was on my eighth club and he was still at Old Trafford.

Points against Manchester United are a bonus, but matches like the next one, home to fellow strugglers like Sunderland, need to be won. We lost 3–2 in the last minute with the centre-halves making basic errors. 'It's like a dagger to the heart,' I said after the game. I went on the pitch to thank the fans but I felt like crying I was so devastated. I don't think I'd ever felt so low, all for the sake of getting two reliable centre-halves. It was at times like this I really missed Gianni. He had left the club in November, there wasn't really a role for him under the new management structure, but I wish he could have been involved because although he could be infuriating – and when he said something was done you knew you had to check – he made me smile and I felt happy and wanted when he was around. He was a wonderful buffer between me and Flavio, and with Tony overseas all the time I could have done with Gianni staying on and playing the same role with him.

I called Tony in Malaysia, he was down as well. I texted Amit about centre-halves. I'd already given the shareholders a list of targets for the upcoming transfer window, with a centre-half top of the list. I also wanted a centre-forward, plus probably a midfielder and a winger on loan. With that I thought we could get into the top ten. I talked to the agent Kia Joorabchian about Alex who had been frozen out at Chelsea, and the Benfica captain Luisao. As it turned out the next person brought to the club by Kia wasn't Alex as I had hoped, but Mark Hughes. It's a funny old game.

Against Sunderland, with us two-down, I'd taken off Wright-Phillips at half-time and brought on Adel. Shaun was not happy. 'I can't accept that, I'm going home,' he said.

'Do what you want. This is what I'm doing.'

He was there at the end.

The following week we had a fight at training. They happen occasionally at clubs. It is not necessarily a bad sign. It shows commitment and desire. Sometimes there is just a personality clash between individuals and something happens to spark it off.

At Sheffield United Paul Devlin and Marcus Bent clashed after one match, when Devlin had bawled out Bent for not passing to him. In the dressing room Marcus put his face into Paul's and started screaming at him. Big mistake. Devlin butted him. Bent's nose was splattered all over his face and there was blood everywhere. When results are going badly, and the dressing room is split, you can do without it.

The daft thing was the two players who got involved, Derry and Bothroyd, were playing on the same team. Dezza had a go at Bothroyd and Bothroyd had a go back. The lads separated them but they went straight back at each other. I stopped the game and sent them both off. Curly went after them and they were still at it in the dressing room.

After a while we brought them back and immediately Joey got involved.

'Why is it always you, Jay?'

'What are you talking about, what's it to do with you?'

So those two start and guess who got in between them? Taarabt! He was holding Joey saying, 'No, calm down, calm down.'

'I'm not going to do owt,' said Joey. 'I just want to ask him why it is always him?'

It was so funny. I said to Taarbs afterwards, 'Well done, but you have got to do the business at Swansea.'

I then spoke to Dezza and Jay: 'I don't mind a fracas, but if anyone throws a punch or head butts somebody they're gone, sacked.'

And with the spirit of good will to all men flowing through the club we all went home to celebrate Christmas. I always let the players spend Christmas at home. It wasn't a difficult decision that year as our match at Swansea had been moved to the 27th for TV, but even when we play Boxing Day I allow the players to have

277

lunch at home. If we are away then we have to travel that night, but at least they can open presents and so on with their kids.

Most managers get their players in but I can't see the point. They don't want to be there, you never do that much so they often spend more time travelling than training. These days players can be trusted not to overdo it at home on Christmas pudding and booze. And just to make sure they stay sharp we give them a fitness programme to do on the day and tell them to wear heart monitors so we can check it.

They came in on Boxing Day and before we went to Wales I called a meeting. There had been too much negativity at the club and we had to put a stop to it. I said to them, 'If someone comes up and they are moaning tell them, "Shut up and get on with your own job." You have to look at yourselves. Don't keep blaming everything. Sort yourselves out and be positive. I've never seen so much moaning. Fighting your team-mates at five-a-side on Christmas Eve? Get a grip. We're better than half the teams in the league but we're going to destroy ourselves.' I could see Wright-Phillips in the back row not paying any attention to me, and someone else looking out of the window.

That night I had a text from Joey saying his partner, Georgia, was having contractions, if she went into labour he'd have to go home. I replied, 'Just keep me informed, family comes first, if you have to go home, go home.' He said the contractions were still a long way apart and he'd see how it went. In the morning they had slowed down, so he played, did well as we got a draw, and because we were flying was able to get back to London in time for the birth of baby Cassius.

The problem with Christmas from a managerial point of view is there are too many games too close together. I know it is traditional, and the supporters like it, but it is another thing that plays into the hands of the big clubs with large squads who can rotate. Our older players, the likes of Helguson, Hill and Derry, couldn't play three games in a week so we had to rest a few. It's not that we were writing off the next match, away to Arsenal, but you had to prioritise. Then a few hours before kick-off Fitz Hall said his groin didn't feel right and he needed a fitness test on it. We had had the team meeting and everything and he hadn't said a word. I thought back to Fulham, when he did the same and we lost 6–0, so I decided to make an early decision and bring back Gabbidon. At least he wanted to play. We played well, even Arsène said so, but in the second half Wright-Phillips gave the ball straight to Arshavin who set up Van Persie and that's it, 1–0. I was gutted.

Just to cap it all the first signing of the transfer window was already lined up: Federico Macheda, the young Manchester United striker. The only problem was I didn't want him, it meant we'd already used up one of our loan signings on a rookie who'd barely played for a couple of years, and it seemed daft to bring in a striker when I was chasing Andrew Johnson. But Tony Fernandes knew Alex Ferguson and somehow had been persuaded to take him. I said he'd never start a league game and I was proved right. He came on as sub once for me, twice for Mark Hughes, and didn't kick a ball in the first team after February 1.

The Arsenal game was on New Year's Eve. Being in football I was used to not celebrating the year end as teams normally play New Year's Day. This time I could have stayed up and had a glass of champagne – I could have had a bottle of champagne, but I didn't feel like celebrating anything.

Chapter Twenty-Three

The Sack

There are only two certainties in this life. People die and football managers get the sack.

Eoin Hand

IT WAS A SUNDAY MORNING. NO MATCH, NO PLANS beyond having a lazy day with the kids. I was lying in bed reading the papers when, at 8.35, my phone buzzed with a text. It was from Phil Beard and read: 'Neil. The owners have been talking overnight. I need to see you.'

I looked up from my phone, turned to Sharon, and said: 'I'm being sacked.' It wasn't a shock. The previous night, after we had drawn at Milton Keynes in the FA Cup third round, I had tried to get hold of Tony Fernandes, but he didn't answer my calls and he didn't ring me back. I knew he had been at Milton Keynes but I hadn't seen him there. I did speak to Amit. He told me he was on the phone to Tony and would get back to me. He didn't. I went to bed at midnight and said to Sharon, 'I think tomorrow they will want to see me.'

I rang Phil and told him to come over at ten. Phil's a lovely bloke. I knew he would hate doing this so I tried to make it easy for him. When he came to the door I met him. 'Don't worry about it, son,' I said. 'It's not your fault.'

'The owners have been talking all night. They want to go in another direction.'

"You've a job to do, but it's the wrong decision, if they get the wrong person, and the wrong players, the club could plummet.' I added: 'I feel I've done all the hard work and now someone else is going to benefit, but I'm bound to feel like that.'

We talked about the last few weeks, the decisions that went against us, the problems with some of the players. Then there were the administrative details to sort. Before Phil left we agreed to delay the announcement until 7pm so I could tell my family and my staff.

I rang Mick and told him to meet me at the training ground. I told him the news there, but he had guessed. I'd said to him the previous night: 'They think they can bring someone in to do what Martin O'Neill's done at Sunderland and provide a massive surge. They don't know what the club is like at the moment and how difficult it will be for an outsider to come in.' So it proved.

Curly had gone back to his family in Sheffield so I rang him there. He was surprised. He had figured we'd got through the tough run of fixtures without dropping into the bottom three and now, with a bit of investment, would be able to climb clear of danger.

Mick and I cleared out the office. We'd not been there two years but it is amazing how much junk you accumulate, though some of it must have dated from half-a-dozen managers back – about three years.

I left a message with Amit. 'Phil's been round to tell me. Don't worry, it's never easy.' I'll always be grateful to him for bringing me to the club and having such a wonderful time. I will always consider Amit a friend even though I doubt I would have gone to QPR in the first place if he hadn't told me he would soon be running the show when I shook his hand and signed. Sadly that never materialised. He sent a message back saying he was distraught and sad and it was the hardest thing, we'd had many great moments and he'd speak to me later. Later I got a text from him saying he was at a dinner and he was feeling gutted. If I wanted to speak he'd come out and talk, but I didn't feel like ringing him that night. If he'd been a majority shareholder within weeks as he had said we'd have had such a fantastic club. If.

I texted Tony and told him I was disappointed that he didn't tell me to my face, instead sending the chief executive to do his business. Amit said he tried to get Tony to talk to me but he didn't want to. Eventually Tony and I exchanged a few texts. He said I was wonderful and would always be a part of QPR, and that it had been a nightmare for him. Not as much as it was for me, I thought.

Tony means well. When he took over he spoke to me at great length about the club, the academy, the training ground, and listened intently. He wanted to get everything right. I think he believed what he said about backing the manager when he came in, that I was the right man for the job, but the first problem was we needed players so badly we had to sign ones who would not have been our first or second targets. Even then we had some great wins at places like Everton and Stoke.

It was a matter of keeping ourselves out of the bottom three until we could strengthen in January but Tony, lacking experience in the game, listened to too many people. He wanted to talk to the fans, he wanted to be accountable. He was into social media and communicated with supporters on Twitter. He would go down to the Springbok pub by the ground and talk to fans. I used to tell Tony, 'Don't get involved like that,' because you can never please them all, and it is always the unhappy ones who make the most noise.

It's the same with the phone-ins, they are a bigger bugbear for managers than owners are. It is always the noisy minority who you hear, not the sensible majority. At Sheffield, when I'd not been there more than a few months, I listened to a phone-in. A caller came on: 'Warnock's got to go.'

The presenter said: 'But he's not been here long.'

'He doesn't know what to do. Tactically he hasn't got a clue,' said the caller.

'Did you go to the game today?'

'No. I listened to it on your programme.'

He's not even been to the game and he's telling me I haven't got a clue. And they make a programme of people like that. I'll never forget it. You really haven't got a chance as a manager.

As usual the news started to leak out so in the end we had to bring forward the announcement by a couple of hours. Then the phone began to ring. I left it to take messages. Other managers are always among the first to call when something like this happens, they know it could be them next. Mick McCarthy was one of the first in touch and unfortunately he was fired a month later. Harry Redknapp rang and said, 'I can't believe it after all you have done for that club' – exactly the same as I felt when Harry left Spurs at the end of the season.

How ironic that 12 months later, after the sacking of Mark Hughes, Harry Redknapp took the role on as manager of QPR. I was delighted that he had taken the job on and I did have a laugh when I spoke to him, saying 'It must have been hard turning Ukraine down,' because it was in the news that he might go there.

I told Harry the atmosphere at Loftus Road was fantastic and 'You'll really enjoy the old campaigners I brought to the club, you'll find out that they give 100 per cent,' referring to Clint Hill, Sean Derry, Jamie Mackie in particular. I added, 'I think you'll find Adel has changed since you had him last, he is a lot more mature.'

I also said, 'It'll be nice now wanting you to win every game and stay up,' because that is how it is when you get the sack, you don't want your successor to do well, all these managers who say otherwise are talking rubbish. It is simple human nature. It was great Harry coming in because I loved being at QPR, I still knew lots of people associated with the club, and the change meant I was able to put all my bitterness to one side and cheer them on. It reignited my affection for the club.

The night I was fired Sky Sports News got some lads out of the pub by the ground, the Springbok, that Tony Fernandes had been visiting. These fat lads came out. 'We all support Tony', they said. It was funny. One of them said I hadn't been such a good manager since I'd lost weight – and he was fatter than I've ever been.

Being sacked is an occupational hazard in management and this was not my first. That was at Burton Albion in 1986. Some new people joined the board, they started thinking they knew better and it came to a head when I wanted to sign a player, Micky Gooding, the former Coventry midfielder, from Rotherham for £1,000. The chairman, Bill Royall, said it would be put to the board. That night he rang. 'The vote was 5–1, Neil.'

'That's good news.'

'No, it isn't. I was the one, the other five voted against.'

I wasn't actually fired, but it was clear it was only a matter of time so Bill and I agreed the game was up.

The second was at Notts County seven years later. I'd taken them up two divisions in two seasons and, unsurprisingly, we'd failed to stay up in the top flight. I turned down Chelsea to stay at Meadow Lane but that meant nothing when, having sold the likes of Craig Short and Tommy Johnson, we didn't look like bouncing straight back. Derek Pavis, the chairman, summoned me and Mick Jones into his office, gave us some soft soap, and then told us it was 'the end of the road'. I told him he was making the biggest mistake of his life, County went down two years later and have been in the lower divisions ever since.

Mick and I went back to our office, broke open a bottle of champagne I'd been keeping for a memorable occasion, rang the *Nottingham Evening Post* and told them to send a photographer along. We felt we had nothing to be ashamed of and plenty to be proud of. Even now most of the stadium is built on the income we brought in through promotion and cup runs.

I survived another four years until the next sacking, at Plymouth Argyle in 1997. Like Tony, Dan McCauley didn't do it himself, but that might have been because we hadn't been talking for months anyway. As at QPR the chief executive did the dirty work, but with a phone call.

That was the last time. Oldham didn't fire me, they just didn't renew my contract which is not quite the same, I left Bury before they could wield the axe, and Sheffield United was mutual consent, which meant QPR was the first time I'd suffered the manager's occupational hazard for 15 years, which isn't bad going.

That didn't soften the blow though. I thought it was really out of order. I'd been given a mandate: get to the January transfer window out of the bottom three then we can invest. I had achieved that mandate, won three away games and beaten Chelsea at home. The following season QPR had not won a match home or away by mid-November, taking four points, yet the manager was still being backed. If only the takeover had come sooner and I'd been able to buy players I knew would do a job for us, rather than the only ones I could get in the window's last knockings, we'd have been well clear of danger. But while I'd enjoyed working with Tony it had been difficult. He was all over the world and he's a massive social media person. He'd been texting players like Wright-Phillips and Joey Barton, he'd been tweeting. He thought that was normal, he didn't realise players told him what they wanted him to hear and blamed everyone but themselves.

Then there were the outside influences. Tony, Phil and Amit are all good people but they don't know football and if you are new to football you get a lot of advice from a lot of people, not all of it is good. When Mark Hughes replaced me it became clear that Kia Joorabchian had been pushing Hughes to Tony when he was supposed to sell us Alex. I felt stabbed in the back and thought I'd been stitched up. Maybe I was naïve, Mark's his client, his priority is to find Mark a new job, Mark having quit Fulham last summer and not found a job since.

Even now, though, I wonder if it would have worked out had our first match of 2012 been different. I knew we were under pressure – Curly had heard that Gianfranco Zola and Ray Wilkins were being lined up to take over – but we'd played well at Arsenal, I had several transfer targets in the pipeline and some winnable games coming up.

The first was at home to Norwich and we were on course for three points after Joey scored a great goal but he was then sent off for putting his head into Bradley Johnson. The ref – Swarbrick – didn't see it, the linesman was like a lost sheep, but Grant Holt moaned, Johnson writhed and the officials guessed – as even Graham Poll agreed. The ref should have taken action before for two terrible tackles on Joey that made him lose his rag. They equalised, and then got the winner with seven minutes to go. Sod's Law.

The next match was in the FA Cup and I could tell the way the wind was going when I tried to pick a team. Wright-Phillips said he shouldn't play in the FA Cup because of his knee, Taarabt and Traore didn't want to play because they were about to go off to the African Nations Cup, Anton Ferdinand was injured taking his dog for a walk, Gabbidon was injured, Barton was suspended. It's an entirely different breed of players now; the FA Cup is beneath them.

As if this wasn't bad enough I found out Tony tweeted to a supporter, 'Nobody's job is safe,' meaning mine. I said to Phil: 'Have a word. If he has a problem tell me, not put more pressure on.' I struggled to say that at the time as I'd had a bone graft because I was having implants done. It meant I'd had 25 stitches in my mouth, I was in agony.

In the end I picked a team based on the Championship-winning side and they showed character, coming back to equalise in the last minute with ten men after Faurlin had been carried off when we'd already used three subs. That night Tony tweeted: 'Driving back to London. Lots to think about.'

After the axe fell Barton also took to Twitter. 'I'm gutted to hear about the manager losing his job, we have to stick together as a club at a time like this and believe in those above. I'd like to thank Neil, Mick and Keith personally for all they did while I was there and wish them all the best for the future. Mr Warnock's record at Championship level speaks for itself. No doubt he will be kick-starting another promotion dream before the season's out. As a football club we must move forwards now and try our utmost to maintain our Premiership status. The king is dead.'

Two weeks later Joey had a go at me on Twitter. I had TV and papers contacting me to respond but I just ignored it. As Alan Pardew said, you haven't got a problem with Joey Barton when he's on the field of play, he's as good as anything, he's the best trainer I've ever known, he's first out, he trains long, and he trains hard. The problems Joey has are when he is not playing football.

I went to say my farewells to the players. Even then one or two were looking out of the window like a bored kid in the classroom, which summed up the contempt they showed towards me. I said, 'When I came to this club it was the pits. The training ground was rubbish, the team was a disgrace, we were going to get relegated. We turned all that around, we've done the best we can with the training ground, we've won the Championship, got some great lads in. Yes it's my fault, I've left us in the Premier League, and I'll be looking on with interest at where some of you lads end up in your careers. Thank you lads, and goodbye.'

On the way out of the training ground Sky Sports stopped me. Asked for my comments I said, 'I take full responsibility for where QPR presently are – in the Premier League.' I told them I was disappointed, that I'd met my remit, but it was one of those things, a new owner comes in and they want their own man. And I thanked the fans for being out of this world. Already the letters and emails were flooding in. I got letters from people who said they had supported Rangers all their life and never felt moved to write to a manager before, I got letters from people who said the promotion season had been the best they had ever experienced, most of all I got letters from people saying I had 'put the pride back into the club'. That made me proud.

I had lunch with Amit. He said he and Tony wanted me to stay on as a consultant, just talking to the board, not dealing with Mark Hughes. It took me back a little. I said I'd think about it.

Then I went home, to Cornwall. That first week was really hard. It's like when you split up with a girlfriend when you are younger and you think it is the end of the world; you go over everything that happened over the previous few weeks, what could have been different. I felt sick, because it is really hard for an English manager to get into the Premier League these days. Rodney Marsh, who is an idol at QPR, once said the only way I would get a Premier League team is to take one up and he was right. It was the same for Tony Pulis, Ian Holloway, Mick McCarthy, Nigel Adkins, Chris Hughton, Owen Coyle and others. They all got their first crack at the Premier League through being promoted. There is no way Liverpool would have brought in Brendan Rodgers if he'd not already got into the Premier League with Swansea.

Sharon was great. I was a bit short-tempered and must have been a right pain in the backside to live with. I felt sorry for Amy and William as well. Suddenly I was around all the time but no fun to be with. To clear our heads we went for a long walk, right out to Minions and the Cheesewring, an ancient heritage and mining site on Bodmin Moor. There we went into the village for a cup of tea. The lady at the counter said: 'No, not in your situation. That's on the house.'

I said, 'I've only lost my job, not my wallet.'

Next a neighbour gave me a pass for the local gym – an OAP pass. But it was good to get a blow-out as I'd not had the club one to use.

Meanwhile the messages kept coming in and they kept me going. I had 4,000 emails in a week and 6,000 in all. Sharon was in tears reading them. Of the thousands there were only a handful of negative ones. People told me stories of going back generations and decades. I promised to reply to everyone, and I still intend to, but what with having taken a job at Leeds soon after I simply have not had the time to do so properly. I didn't just want to send everyone a standard reply.

It was quite emotional reading them. I bet the people who wrote them were quite emotional. It was obvious the QPR fans would have supported me and they, like myself, were convinced I would have kept them up. After all I had met my remit: keep out of the bottom three through the difficult games before the New Year, then before the easier games start bring three, four, five players in to push on.

I had other paperwork to deal with, like a compromise agreement for my pay-off. It used to take ages to get paid off, clubs would stall for ever and only offer stingy amounts, but the Premier League are quite strict about settlements being agreed. It usually is a settlement too. In theory when a manager parts company with a club they have to pay up his contract. It works both ways – when a manager walks out to go to another club they have to pay compensation.

However, depending on the contract they are usually within their rights to pay you in instalments over the remaining duration of your contract so if you get another job they can stop paying you. Most managers, keen to start work again, come to a compromise in which they get paid some of the money they are due, but can start work without waiting for the contract to run out. I wasn't sure if I wanted to work again, I'd been planning to retire soon to spend more time in Cornwall with the family, but I didn't want to leave management with such a sour taste in my mouth. I felt there was still unfinished business, that I still had something to prove. So I thought I'd come to an agreement just in case I wanted to work. I knew there would be offers; I'd had two within days of leaving QPR.

Once you leave a club you are quickly forgotten. Phil Beard had said I could keep the petrol card until our settlement was sorted out. So having filled up in a little garage in Cornwall I went to pay with the card.

'It's been stopped, sir.'

'No, try again.'

'It's stopped, sir.'

I rang Phil from the garage. He said Rebecca had no doubt cancelled the card. Of course I had no money on me at the garage. I had to leave my watch as security while I went home to get some cash.

The bizarre thing was Amit and Tony were still on to me about not having a football person on the board, and would I like to come on board in an ambassadorial, advisory role. I did think if only they had someone like that already I'd still be in a job. I said it would have to be made plain to Mark it was nothing to do with his football side, then maybe I would. I didn't want to go down the leagues, I'd had enough of fighting fires and picking teams up. In the meantime I started doing some media work, just to keep occupied and keep myself known.

I started moving on the following Sunday when I watched my team – sorry, Hughes' team – play at Newcastle. I watched Mark on the sideline, frustrated, having a go at the referee and linesman, like I would have done. The lads played quite well but lost 1–0. If anything I felt quite relieved afterwards. I was far more accepting of the situation.

However, I could not put it behind me that quickly. The first Saturday I couldn't face watching all the scores coming in and not being involved so we went into Plymouth to take my mind of things with a movie. We saw *War Horse*. Early on the little boy gets a horse and his dad says, what will you call it? The boy said: 'Joey.' There was no escape.

Chapter Twenty-Four

Back, with a 350-mile Commute

Football is in my blood, but do I really want to put myself in a world where I rely on players, get sacked after six games and not see my two children grow up?

Gareth Southgate

IT WAS THE FIRST WEEK OF THE SEASON, AUGUST 2007. I was, as they say, 'resting between jobs' having left Sheffield United. Suddenly William shouted down the stairs to me: 'Dad, there's a job going, the manager of Carlisle has just been sacked!'

With respect to Carlisle United, who were in League One and had for some reason fired Neil McDonald after one match (a draw away from home), it wasn't exactly what I was looking for having spent the previous season in the Premier League. But William's reaction showed how obvious to my family was the frustration I felt at not working.

I'm not used to being unemployed. When I left school at 16 I went to work in the accounts department of British Steel, until one day I walked though the factory and saw all these steel particles glinting on my white shirt. I realised I was breathing them in all day, like my Dad, who had worked there for years – and co-incidentally had a terrible cough. So I went to work at a ten-pin bowling alley, teaching, working in the café, fixing the equipment, a bit of everything really. I left that when I started playing for Chesterfield's junior teams as the hours didn't suit and went back into accounts with Burdall's who made gravy salt. Then at 19 I was offered professional terms at Chesterfield. I took the plunge, and a pay cut.

For the next 12 years, although I rarely felt secure at a club, I always found a manager prepared to employ me. Towards the end I would combine playing with the other jobs, chiropody, running a greengrocer's, selling frozen food. When a broken arm finished my playing career I moved into management. From July 1980, when I began at Gainsborough Trinity, to May 2007 when I left Sheffield United, the longest period I had been out of work was the four months between leaving Burton Albion and taking over at Scarborough in 1986. Even in 2007 I was only out of work for five months before I joined Simon Jordan at Palace. I like to work and fortunately I was never short of offers.

So it proved after I left QPR. I quickly got involved in quite a bit of media work but it wasn't long before clubs were sounding me out. Within a month I was weighing up three strong possibilities: Wolverhampton Wanderers, Leeds United and Huddersfield Town, all without a manager. At the time they were in the Premier League, Championship and League One respectively, though as it worked out in six months' time they would all be in the Championship.

Huddersfield was tempting. I liked Dean Hoyle, the chairman, a fantastic man who'd put a lot of money in. I'd managed them before and knew it was a great club, but the circumstances weren't quite right.

Wolves were obviously tempting because they were Premier League and a club with a rich history and magnificent stadium. They were in trouble but not adrift and I thought I could keep them up. I spoke with Jez Moxey, the chief executive, and agreed to meet him at the house of the chairman, Steve Morgan, near Chester. It's an amazing house. I drove past it first because I thought it looked too grand to be his. But I had got there early so I pulled over at a lay-by to wait – I didn't want to turn up and bump into another candidate. That would have been embarrassing all round.

As I was waiting the phone went. It was Ken Bates, Leeds' chairman. 'Neil, I want you to be our next manager. Come over to Monaco and agree things.'

'Chairman, I'm about to speak to Wolves. I'm actually sitting outside Steve Morgan's house right now.'

'You don't want to go with them. Come to Leeds. We're a bigger club and the job's made for you. I don't need to interview you. I just want you to come and agree terms and take over.'

'Chairman, I've promised to speak to them, and that's what I want to do, but I will speak to you later and I won't hang about. I'll tell them I want to make a decision.'

I then spent three hours with Steve Morgan and Jez Moxey and we got on well. We talked about everything. Steve asked me what I thought about Wolves. I said, 'Do you want the truth, or me to fudge it?'

'The truth.'

'You've got one of the worst back fours in the league; if I'm coming I'll need to be in by Monday to work on them for a week. But you've enough in midfield and up front to score goals.' I then talked about individuals and how I would go about keeping them up.

When we finished I said to them, 'I know you have other people in mind. Having spoken tonight I'd appreciate it if you could think about it, and if you're not sure about giving the job to me, being honest with me and letting me know in the next 24 hours because I have a chance of taking over at Leeds.'

They were both good jobs. Wolves were in the Premier League but Leeds were a big, big club; being a Yorkshireman there had always been something special about them. I didn't want to end up missing out on both jobs through waiting for Wolves, getting passed over, then finding Ken Bates had looked elsewhere while I was waiting.

The next day Steve Morgan rang.

'Neil. We liked what you had to say but we are still in the process of interviewing and I know you said you needed a quick decision.'

'Steve, if after three hours you don't know whether I'm the right one, then I'm not the right one. I think you're making a mistake, but it's your club and your decision. I wish you all the best.' I liked Steve and Jez and would have loved the chance to keep Wolves up, but it was not to be.

I knew Alan Curbishley and Steve Bruce were in contention, but for whatever reason it didn't work out with them and Wolves went with Mick McCarthy's assistant, Terry Connor. He's a great lad and a good coach but not what Steve was originally looking for. It did make me wonder whether I would have got the job if I'd been prepared to wait, but Leeds had great potential so I had no regrets. In the event it didn't really work out for Terry. I think the players needed a fresh voice at that stage. Wolves did go down and then they brought in Ståle Solbakken from Norway, which I didn't understand as it was a dressing room full of strong individuals and I thought it needed an Englishman or Scot to sort them out. Terry lost his job in the process. I was pleased to see him reunited with Mick when McCarthy took over at Ipswich.

Meanwhile I rang Ken and said, 'I'll fly over and see you, let's talk about it.' We met at the café opposite the Casino. I felt I was in a James Bond movie and as it turned out someone was spying on us; a picture of the two of us talking was printed in one of the English papers next day.

I went with an open mind, but Ken soon began to persuade me that Leeds was made for me, and me for Leeds. The possibility of another promotion, a record eighth, was seductive. I'd already spoken to my eldest son James who lived nearby and supported Leeds. 'It's a big club, Dad, come and help us out,' he said. But while Ken wanted me, he didn't want me on any terms. He began by offering me 40 per cent of what I wanted. I said I wouldn't accept a penny less than 50 per cent of what I was on at QPR in the Championship. In the end he agreed to that. I was underselling myself, but the money was not vital. There were 14 games to go and I wanted to show what I could do. At the end of the season we could look at things again.

After we decided terms we agreed to announce it on the Monday morning (it was Friday night). But flying back with Shaun Harvey, Leeds' chief executive, I considered the fact Leeds were playing Doncaster Rovers the following day and said to him, 'It's stupid this, if we're going to have a chance of going up this season we have got to beat Donny tomorrow. We've more chance if I'm there. You'll have to ring him when we get back and tell him I think I should be there even if I'm not involved.'

Then I thought about it, and I realised if I was going to be there I was going to have to be involved. I would have to tell the players I was there, and tell them what I was looking for. So we agreed we'd announce it at 12 o'clock but we had to bring that forward too after Chris Kamara let it out of the bag. I was supposed to be doing Chris's TV show on the Sunday, and I had to ring him to tell him I couldn't do it. He then tweeted everyone to say I couldn't do it as I had a job. What with the papers having a picture of me and Ken in Monaco it didn't take a genius to guess what job that was. So we announced it at 11 o'clock.

I got a great reception from the Leeds fans when I arrived at Elland Road, which was encouraging. I took a seat in the stand with Mick Jones and James to watch the match. I had intended to stay in the stands, but in the first half we were terrible. It was only 1–0 but Donny should have been three or four-nil up. We were very poor defensively. I said to Mick, 'This is bad, isn't it? Are we sure we want this? I'll have to go down at half-time.'

We went down, introduced ourselves, and I said and did a few things like moving Robert Snodgrass inside. It didn't look as if it had worked as they scored again almost immediately but we scrambled one back, the crowd noise started, then we got an equaliser in the 81st minute and the winner deep in added time. I was on my feet punching the air as Luciano Becchio curled it in.

It was an afternoon that showed me how big the task of turning the team around was. It was obvious to me defensively Leeds were very poor. The back four looked an absolute shambles, as if they could concede seven goals any time, not that that was going to happen to any team of mine . . . or so I thought. On the plus side we looked as if we could score goals, and the second half showed what a great atmosphere could be generated at Elland Road if the fans were given something to cheer.

I went down just before the end and went into the staff room. I'd just closed the door as the players came off the pitch. I heard an almighty commotion so I opened the door to see both sets of players having a right go at each other. My old player Pascal Chimbonda seemed to be enjoying himself, with El Hadji Diouf shoulder-to-shoulder alongside him, which made me smile later when he signed for us. The Leeds lads stood their ground and it was a lively few minutes. The incident was reported and after an investigation the FA eventually fined both clubs.

I started work properly on the Monday. Mick was on board again, but when I rang Keith Curle to tell him we were going to Leeds he told me he'd just been appointed Notts County manager. It's a great club and I was delighted for him. In his stead I promoted Ronnie Jepson, who'd been looking after the reserves for me at Crystal Palace and QPR, to first team coach.

The first thing we did was look around the training ground. The pitches were fantastic but that was only the half of it. The tour took ages. We went into one area and were told, this is the wet room: there was a steam room, a sauna, a big Jacuzzi, six or seven slipper baths with smaller Jacuzzis in them. We opened a door and there was a 50 metre swimming pool. I turned to Mick and Jeppo and drily said: 'It's just like Harlington' – QPR's training ground was the pits by comparison.

There was one problem with Leeds – the location. It was good to be living near James, his wife Sarah and my new grandson Charlie, but the rest of the family were 350 miles away. After I left QPR we decided to act on a long-term plan to move back to Cornwall. Amy was already in school there and William was due to move to secondary school in the September. Once the kids were in senior school we felt they needed stability. We had tried to live in Cornwall before, when I was managing Sheffield United, but the children were much younger then and the distance was too great. Now they were more grown up I thought we could manage it even if it made for some complicated months in the short term. William finished the school year in London, I worked in Leeds, and Amy went to school in Devon. For three months Sharon didn't know whether she was coming or going.

Sharon wasn't happy about me taking the Leeds job, but I think she recognised I still had things I wanted to achieve in the game. She realised I didn't want to sign off in management with the way it ended at QPR. So she decided to do something else with her time and began learning golf with William.

Ken Bates, incidentally, wanted a clause in my contract insisting I spent a minimum of five days at the training ground each week as he knew Sharon and the kids would be living in Cornwall and I would want to see them whenever it was possible. I said, 'That's ridiculous. If you don't think I'm doing the job, get rid of me.' He seemed to have forgotten he was chairman of Leeds but had lived in Monaco for years.

I accepted chances to go to Cornwall would be few with the amount of games we play in the Championship. With the run in the Capital One Cup Leeds played 30 matches before New Year's Eve in the 2012–13 season, one every four days. It would be relentless, but with mobile phones and texts it is so much easier to keep in touch these days. Plus there were school holidays for them, and international breaks for me, when we could meet up. So after a couple of weeks living with James I found a cottage with enough spare rooms for the family to visit and settled down to the task of reviving Leeds.

I have made it part of my job to have my family around at the clubs I have managed. The various chairmen have been made aware that I value my family and want them with me. The smart ones accept that, because I couldn't do my job without family support. The manager's job is a lonely one. Knowing your family is there, that you can see someone you trust after a defeat as well as a victory, is a big asset to a manager. There is no falseness with your family; your wife will always see it as it is. Your wife hurts when you hurt; she knows what you are going through as she has been there all week.

It is not all bad by any means, especially now I've had a bit of success and worked at some good clubs. We have a decent lifestyle; William and Amy go to a nice school and on lovely holidays. They have a lot of things I never had as a child and it is great to be able to provide that for them. But they also have to cope with the ups and downs of having a father and, for Sharon, a husband, who is a football manager. That means moving house far too often, or having the family living in two places at once, and on a day-to-day basis it is impossible not to take results home. They know their week is dependent on that 90 minutes, whether I am going to be content, or fidgety and short-tempered. Unlike a manager they cannot influence the match, but the match will influence their lives, like the weekend I ruined after we were robbed by the linesman against West Bromwich.

The job is 24/7, though I have done my best not to let it take over my life the way it did during my first marriage when I was establishing myself in the management business. I worked 24 hours and it was inevitable that it would put a strain on my marriage. I also missed seeing James and Natalie grow up. We get on great now, but I don't want to repeat the mistake with William and Amy. So I try to watch them play for their school teams, and attend drama things and so on.

While football affects Sharon's life it is not her life. Like Amy it is not the be-all and end-all. On matchdays Sharon wouldn't know what club we're playing let alone who the manager is, and I don't mind that in the slightest. She doesn't get intense about it. She might ask, 'Why aren't you playing so-and-so,' but that'll be because she likes him as a person, not because she is suggesting he's a better player than someone else. Sometimes I'll talk to her about my team but she's a sounding board, she enables me to talk my thoughts through out loud.

She's a good judge of people, she'll say, 'I like him', or, 'Dear me, are you sure?' There was a player I didn't sign and her opinion was a factor, then there was another when I ignored her opinion and signed someone she wasn't sure about and as time went on it became clear she was right.

I can switch off, but I don't think I could do so without my family. I watch a film with them, or watch them play sport – rugby, cricket and football for William, netball, hockey and horse-riding for Amy. With them, or at home in Cornwall I've things to do. Switching off became more difficult living on my own in Leeds. So I would go fishing for a couple of hours because if I stop in watching telly I'll be thinking of football. I think of football while I'm fishing too, but it is a nicer environment. I also took up golf on a local nine-hole course, though I'm a hacker. It is a matter of occupying the time on your hands. Even that wasn't enough to give me peace of mind after Watford beat us 6–1 at home in the middle of the takeover saga. I ended up driving to our place in Scotland just to get away from it all for a couple of days.

Over the years we've collected quite a menagerie, which gives me something else to do. There's Elvis the chameleon, the dogs Donald, a Norfolk Terrier, and Percy, a griffon, and a collection of chickens, Nellie, Peggy, Betty, Nugget and Goujon. Amy named the last two; she can have a wicked sense of humour. Some of them are very good layers (you can't beat an omelette made with an egg which is still warm) and when I retire we're going to get an alpaca, which is an animal which looks a bit like a small llama. I can tell you, when you are trying to find a grasshopper that's escaped as you are about to feed it to Elvis, or cleaning the poo out from the chicken coop, professional football seems a world away.

In Cornwall I also go to church. I'm a Christian but I wouldn't say I listen to all the sermons. I just enjoy the peace and tranquillity of being in church. It gives me the chance to think about things. It is also part of being in the local community. There are several charming elderly ladies in the congregation who Sharon and I know. I remember once telling them a programme was coming up on TV showing me at work. I said, 'I have to warn you, I might use the odd swear word.' One lady, who was about 89, gestured to me to bend down so she could whisper in my ear. 'Believe you me,' she said, 'I've used all of them in my life at some time or other.' But when I watched it . . . dearie me, she must have been a stoker in the Navy if she swore like that. The following week I had to apologise to them all for the language I'd used.

(You may have noticed that although this book is in other respects a true reflection of my management career there's hardly any foul language in it. I just didn't think it looked right in print. I'm sure you can work out when I might have said something unprintable.)

Sometimes to switch off I just like to get out for a walk. When we lived in and around Sheffield we'd go to the Peak District, or somewhere like Chatsworth. In Cornwall there is a fabulous walk at Cotehele House, a National Trust property. In London I used to go to Richmond Park, often on my bicycle. I'm still thinking about the game a lot – you can't avoid it these days as the phone is always ringing – but I often find clearing my head like that means I make better decisions.

Having a young family helps you keep your feet on the ground too. Many is the time one of the kids has been ill and we've had to change the sleeping arrangements. The sick child will be in bed with Sharon, and I'll be in their bunk. I prefer the bottom bunk myself; it feels a bit claustrophobic but the top's hard work at my age. I was lying there one night at QPR thinking: 'I wonder if any other Premier League managers sleep in a bunk bed.' Not that I've ever been over-fussed about the so-called trappings of success. When I was working in London we would occasionally go to the Ritz for tea as a special treat, but I was just as happy celebrating promotion with Sheffield United with a kebab in our village in Cornwall. The restaurants were fully booked, but that didn't stop me making an occasion of it – I said 'yes' to all the kebab sauces and trimmings. As it dribbled down my chin I wondered if Jose Mourinho celebrated in similar style.

You need a solid platform and good family support to maintain your equilibrium. The art of management is, 'Don't get carried away when you win games, don't get too down when you lose.' Everybody has periods when you can't see another point coming, or a goal, just as sometimes you cannot see a defeat. It's easier said than done though, because the job is so precarious.

As John Barnwell, who managed Wolves and ran the LMA for many years, once said, when you are a football manager you don't have fitted carpets. At Oldham we'd been given the nod by the club that I'd be given a new contract one May so, having been renting, we made an offer for a house. The next match was the last of the season, at Grimsby. We went two-up and I looked across the pitch from the dug-out to the main stand and saw the directors, instead of looking pleased, had their heads in their hands. I went home and told Sharon my future didn't look so secure after all. Sure enough, the next day they said I wasn't getting a new contract. We had to pull out of the sale.

So you have to consider whether to try and live together as a family and risk moving home every few years, or find a base for the family while I rent near the club if it is too far to commute. I've done both with Sharon. While the children were still very young we moved each time from Torquay to Holmfirth to Cornwall to Ramsbottom to Oldham to Sheffield. By then Amy was about to start school and we thought we should stop somewhere. We'd fallen in love with the west country so Sharon lived there with Amy, and William when he came along, and I had a place in Sheffield from where I would drive down after matches on a Saturday night, then go back up to Yorkshire on the Monday.

It was hard going but I was thinking in the long term it was best for the family. Then at Christmas 2004 Amy said she loved everyone being together, and she'd rather we all lived in the city than be in the countryside without me. So we bought a different house in Sheffield and all moved there while hanging onto the place in Cornwall for the long term.

We were there for two-and-a-half years. Then we moved to London, renting in Beckenham, by Palace's training ground. Amy reached secondary school age and as I only anticipated doing a year or two more before retiring we decided she ought to start school where we were going to live long-term, so she went down to Plymouth and boarded. We thought it would be temporary. Then I got the opportunity to go to QPR and one year became three. We rented in Richmond, which was lovely, and handy for QPR, but not so handy for Plymouth. It was difficult for Amy, but we went down to see her whenever we could. Then I left QPR, Sharon moved to Cornwall and Amy was able to live with her mum and brother all the time even if I was not always there. My cottage near Leeds, meanwhile, became my eleventh house in nineteen years with Sharon. No wonder, when I go to Cornwall for a break, I find myself unpacking boxes of junk and old papers which have been moved from house to house for years without ever being opened. There are Betamax videos (remember them?), dozens of old programmes, and plenty of letters from the FA telling me off for things I can't even remember doing.

As a manager you don't always appreciate how unsettling it is for the children when you change jobs. Poor William has gone from supporting Sheffield United to following Crystal Palace, then cheering for QPR and to backing Leeds. It is a lot for a boy to get his head round. While he has had some great perks – how many boys get to train with professional footballers during their half-term holiday? – inevitably he gets stick in the playground if things are not going well for me. After we lost 6–0 at Fulham the senior boys were taunting him with, 'Your dad's getting sacked.'

He is finally settled now in Cornwall and playing in one of the academy teams at Plymouth Argyle which he loves. Plymouth is a fabulous friendly club with a great following in The Green Army. James Brent, the new owner, has put forward some exciting plans for the club – a £50m project which includes a hotel and an ice rink as well a new stand which would finish the ground off as three sides have already been done.

I have watched William playing a number of times there, and at Leeds, QPR and Palace as he also played in their academies. The boys are so organized and skilful these days, I think because of the quality of the coaches which has definitely improved at youth level.

Amy's had it too. When I was considering leaving Sheffield United for Portsmouth when we were well-placed for promotion Amy's schoolfriends told her she had to tell me to stay. That's not really fair is it? It worked though. Being Sheffield-born and a lifelong Blades fan I felt the same way, I felt a loyalty to the city, the club and the fans. In the end I stayed. There were lots of little things which added up – including Amy's friends asking her to ask me to stay, I knew it was just what I would have said had I been in their position.

Chapter Twenty-Five

Not-So-Magnificent Seven

*No one, unless they manage a team, can know how I feel
[after a defeat]. No one, not an assistant manager, a
player, anyone. They haven't a clue.*

Gordon Strachan

FOOTBALL MANAGERS ARE NOT ALLOWED TO BET ON
football, so I should make it clear I was joking when I turned to
Jeppo ten minutes from the end of my sixth match in charge at
Leeds and said to him, 'I wonder what odds you can get on us now
for promotion next season?'

Dexter Blackstock had just scored Nottingham Forest's seventh
goal of the night to leave us trailing 7–3. I could see the headlines:
'Leeds in ten-goal thriller.' It was, to the best of my knowledge,
the first time any team of mine had conceded seven goals in more
than 1,500 matches as a manager and player, though I could be
wrong; you tend to blot these things out. There is not much you
can do on a night like that but wait for it to end, yet the bizarre
thing was I thought we could have won the match.

I certainly did not see it coming. My priority when I came in was to tighten the defence. It worked, but we stopped scoring. In my first five matches we scored three and conceded two. But that was OK and I fielded the same XI that had won at Middlesbrough and were pegged back to a draw in the last minute by a West Ham team that was on its way to promotion. I was optimistic. Though they had good players Forest were struggling and I thought we had a good chance.

We started well enough, with Snodgrass scoring a penalty after six minutes, but we conceded too quickly to build on it, one of those 35-yarders a player will get once in his career. Forest scored again either side of half-time but then we scored two in three minutes to level it at 3–3. There was still more than half-an-hour to go and I was thinking, 'We'll go on and win this now.'

I didn't reckon with our defence. Five minutes later Forest were 5–3 up, it was like park football. The fans were so stunned they didn't know whether to boo or cry – by the end neither did I. However, I'll never forget the crowd that night. At seven-down they were chanting my name. It was something I remembered early the next season when I hadn't signed my contract – contrary to what the club had said – and I had a couple of cracking offers to leave. Those fans made it impossible for me to walk out.

At the end of the Forest match I went into the dressing room. You might think I gave them all a bollocking, but it wasn't the time for that. I saved it for when we went through the video. On the night I just said they needed to consider whether they were fit enough to play a 46-game Championship season because a few didn't look it.

There were only two positives to emerge from the debacle. You learn a lot about your players from matches like that. It was already clear to me we lacked enough 'men' at the club. That night confirmed it. By the time we kicked off the following season only six of the 14 players involved were still at the club.

The other positive came two days later when I attended a Q&A session at Elland Road with 300 supporters. Being so closely associated with Sheffield I did have some reservations about how I would be received at Leeds and while the early signs had been encouraging I figured shipping seven might bring forth some opposition. I needn't have worried, they were marvellous. I came away with a fresh realisation of how desperate Leeds supporters were for success, and how they trusted me to deliver it. I kept saying to them: 'You do know we lost 7–3 the other night?' A personal highlight was when one guy stood up and said he was a QPR season-ticket holder, last year had been the best of his life as a fan, and 'his club's loss was Leeds' gain.'

It does make a difference if the fans are behind you, you enjoy coming in to work. I have been lucky; since I left Sheffield United every club I've been to they've wanted me. Each time the fans have said: 'When they said you were coming, we didn't want you here, but now you are, we're glad.' It hasn't always been the case. I had an odd relationship with the Sheffield United fans. The fact I was a Blade myself and grew up watching them at Bramall Lane seemed to count against me with some of them. There was one group of fans that I couldn't win over no matter what I did – until I left that is. I went back with Crystal Palace and had the surreal and wonderful experience of everyone in the ground cheering for me, home and away fans. I think then they finally appreciated what I had achieved there. I had the opposite at Bury. I can remember we played Bradford City, whose fans remembered me as a former Huddersfield Town boss, and we were losing 2–0 before half-time. At one stage all four sides of the ground were chanting, 'Warnock out.'

If that was the worst experience with fans one of the best was, bizarrely, at a match we lost 6–0. It was with QPR at Fulham and we were getting hammered. We had injury problems and all sorts yet, halfway through the second half, the Rangers fans started cheering me. It was incredible. I went out with Sharon for a meal soon after and four or five QPR fans came up. They said they were at Fulham and I said I couldn't believe I got clapped with us six-down. They said, 'That is because we know what you have done, we are having a great time.' I thought, 'This is fantastic, getting support like that.' It made me want to try even harder to get success for them.

The most emotional occasion was when I went back to Palace with QPR. I thought they might give me stick because I left them when they were in administration but to be clapped all the way out of that tunnel to the dug-out gave me goose-pimples. The hairs were rising on the back of my neck, there was a tear in my eye. It were unbelievable. They knew what I had done. When the Rangers fans chanted for a wave later on I couldn't bring myself to do it in front of the Palace fans because I felt so much respect for them.

It's amazing the lengths fans will go to to watch their team. I've met fans that have moved away from their team but still travel to watch them every week. There was a QPR fan who lived somewhere near Shrewsbury but came to every home game. I met some Palace fans down in Plymouth. When Leeds went to Cornwall pre-season thousands took their family holiday that week and came down to watch us.

When QPR went to Italy we had a match in Bergamo. While the lads had a pre-match afternoon sleep me and Mick went to this village in the mountains. It was a lovely place, we had a walk around the churches and such. But then we wanted to go to the toilet so we walked all around the town for about a mile following every street in town. When we finally found one it was 25 cents and we hadn't got any change, we were desperate. So we went in this restaurant nearby to have a drink, to use the toilet.

Lo and behold there were three 45–50-year-old blokes in blue-and-white hoops having a meal. They welcomed us and had photographs taken with us. They told us they'd been to watch games all over, every game for years. It was interesting listening to them and their families about supporting QPR and what they'd gone through for the last 15 years. There was a lad there who'd never seen QPR in the Premier League and was really looking forward to it. We had a good hour with them. That sort of thing made our afternoon as much as theirs.

But not all fans are helpful. The afternoon before QPR's game at Blackburn I got a call to tell me a fans' website had revealed that DJ Campbell had broken his foot and we were playing Helguson and Mackie up front. The only people at the training ground were players, some of whom had been bombed out, and one of them had snitched. And a QPR fans' website had given that information to the opposition. It was unbelievable. It made Steve Kean's job so much easier as he now knew how to combat us. I know they were well-meaning, but they didn't consider the bigger picture. There are times when football clubs need to keep things quiet.

I was a fan once; I still am. A few journalists must have been surprised when they saw me at a football writers' dinner a couple of years ago getting autographs. I got Wayne Rooney for William, but I got Pat Jennings and Dave Mackay for myself – they were two of the greats. I played against Mackay, as a teenager at Chesterfield in the League Cup. He had just signed for Derby and our manager Jimmy McGuigan told us, 'Play on Mackay, he can't run.' He couldn't, but he didn't need to: he ran the game from the centre circle, he was magnificent.

When Barcelona came to Loftus Road for a training session before playing a Champions League tie against Arsenal I felt like a little kid just being in the presence of great players like Lionel Messi, Xavi and Andres Iniesta. I had my photograph taken with Pep Guardiola and one of Messi with my sons James and William, and grandson Charlie. Messi even signed a shirt each, which we had framed. Mine has pride of place in Cornwall. He's the best player I've seen in my lifetime.

It's an old cliché, but supporters really can be the twelfth man. When a team is struggling and needs a bit of inspiration fans can lift them. They can also intimidate opponents and influence referees. When a big ground like Elland Road is full and noisy it can really make a difference. But that can inhibit the home players, so you do need characters that can cope with the expectation of a big crowd, who are mentally strong and prepared to want the ball in adversity. We had two or three players when I arrived who, if they made a mistake early on, you could hear the crowd doubt them, and within ten minutes they had gone. I had to move them out.

Not that a stadium has to be as big as Elland Road to be intimidating. Loftus Road holds about half as many fans but there were times when it seemed as if 70,000 were in there. The atmosphere for the Chelsea match was incredible. I could hardly hear myself think let alone get messages to the players. The crowd are right on top of the pitch there and that magnifies their impact. Fratton Park is another ground where the fans become part of the game because of their passion.

Yet devoted as most Portsmouth folk are to their team there is a Leeds United supporters group in the town. We called in for a half-hour session with them the night before my first game as Leeds manager. It really underlined that Leeds fans are everywhere, and you have to remember everyone in Leeds is a Leeds United fan. I'd not seen anything like it. It is the only club in town, not like Sheffield where there are two clubs, or London, where there are six in the Premier League alone. If I went to get petrol I'd end up signing three or four autographs and having my picture taken with fans. It must be like that managing Newcastle. I'd not experienced it before, not in a city as big and passionate about football.

After a couple of weeks I realised Leeds was the biggest club I had ever been at. The potential is huge. I can't imagine what it must have been like when they had a great team, especially on those European nights. There is such a hunger to get those days back. I can understand that because the reminders are all around the club. A lot of the great players, like Norman Hunter, Eddie Gray, Paul Reaney and Peter Lorimer, attend matches. There's a Billy Bremner bar, and so on. Around the club there are photographs of the glory years.

That can be a problem for some. You hear tales of managers coming in to clubs like Leeds and Nottingham Forest, clubs with great pasts who have fallen on harder times, and taking all those reminders down. It doesn't bother me. The old players are nice blokes, they have earned the right to come back and be admired, and I know they want the best for the club. A rich heritage might intimidate a younger manager, but not me. I've never had a photograph taken down for that reason. Players with the right character are more likely to be inspired than intimidated.

Décor can be important. Over the years clubs have used certain colours in dressing rooms because they are supposed to relax you, or make the opposition tense. Yellow and pink are supposed to be the worst two colours. I've never found it makes much difference. More important is the lay-out. I like to have all the players around me in the dressing room so I can see them all, but at Leeds the opposition is in two different compartments so it's virtually impossible to get all players in. The home dressing room, I was pleased to discover, does not have that problem.

At Sheffield United I had pictures put up in the tunnel of certain moments in games, shots of our players making tackles, diving headers, goals and things like that. It was designed to intimidate the opposition and lift our lads. I like having pictures of the current players around in the areas where they will be walking. I think it makes them feel appreciated. At Leeds I left all the pictures of great players of the past like Allan Clarke and John Giles, Bremner, Hunter and co, but I've replaced more recent ones with action shots of the current squad. I don't go in for those slogans some managers put up, like the one I found on the dressing room door when I arrived at QPR which read 'Winners only'. That looks pretty silly when you're fighting relegation as they were then.

The fans at Leeds showed their support right to the conclusion of what must have been an anti-climactic season. We just didn't have the players and towards the end of the 2011–12 season we drifted out of contention, but we still had more than 25,000 for the final game, in fact there were 14 more than had been there for the first home game (and, no, they weren't all my relatives). It showed the fans still had faith in me. I hoped I could justify it.

Chapter Twenty-Six

Signing The 'Sewer Rat'

You must be an idiot if you want to manage Leeds United.

Peter Reid, on becoming Leeds manager in 2003

EIGHTEEN MONTHS AFTER I DESCRIBED EL HADJI DIOUF AS 'lower than a sewer rat' after he accused Jamie Mackie of faking a broken leg I bumped into him again. I could see he was a bit apprehensive as soon as he saw me, but I ended up talking to him and I was quite frank with him. 'Can I talk to you, just me and you?'

'Yes,' he said, warily.

'Some of the things you do, the spitting, the behaviour on the pitch, what you said to Jamie. Why do you do them? You have so much ability you don't need to do them.'

'I did a lot of the things when I was young and I hadn't thought about the consequences. Spitting isn't seen as such a bad thing where I grew up. And I'm sorry about Mackie. I didn't realise his leg was broken.'

As we talked I found I quite liked him despite my initial

315

reservations. So I said: 'I'm looking for a player just like you at Leeds, it's just a pity what's happened with us.'

'I'd love to come and play for you at Leeds. It wouldn't have to be about money. I don't need money.'

'That's good, because we haven't got any.'

'It's a massive club. I'd like to come and help you get promotion.'

I felt like he was saying that almost as a payback, to make up for what happened with Mackie. I toyed with it for weeks and weeks. I made enquiries about a few other players, like Tommy Smith who'd been with me at QPR, but we couldn't get near his wages and he went to Cardiff. We hadn't got a transfer pot and with the season approaching all I had was a 17-year-old kid, Dominic Poleon, a good kid but very raw.

I didn't tell Sharon because she knew what I had said about him. I broached the idea to Mick Jones. He said it would be a massive mistake, that it might ruin everything we had done. So I had nothing positive to influence me. But we had to get someone in; we had no money and no one of his quality.

I asked around. I spoke about him to Sam Allardyce who had signed Diouf twice. Eighty per cent of what Big Sam said about him was good. He'd tried to sign him at West Ham the previous year but the supporters hadn't liked the idea, and as Sam was trying win over the fans himself at the time, he decided against it. I asked a couple of other people including Mickey Walker (who I took on part-time after he was sacked at Donny where Diouf went after it didn't happen at West Ham). Micky said, 'He's not like you think.' I was worried he'd be a bad influence like Chimbonda. Mickey added, 'He's as good a trainer as you will get and he's excellent with the kids.' Eventually I asked him to come into training so I could see how he settled in and he could have a look at our set-up. That went well so I decided to take him on a trial with a week-to-week contract.

Then I bumped into Eddie Wolstenhome who was the ref who abandoned the infamous match in 2002 between my Sheffield United and Megson's West Brom, after we went down to six men. 'Neil, can I have a word with you?'

I thought, 'What have I done now?'

'Neil, I've heard you might sign El Hadji Diouf?'

'Yes,' I said, fearing the worst.

'Well, I was at a charity function last year at Blackburn and there were disabled kids there. Diouf got there before the start, he was there at the end, and he talked to every kid there, he went through the whole lot. No one else did anywhere near what he did. It was amazing. So don't believe everything you read about him.'

But I still hadn't told Sharon. Then one night in the summer holidays, when Sharon and the kids were up, James came round. As he went to leave he asked: 'What are you doing with Dioufy then?'

I changed the subject quickly, but it was too late, she had heard. 'What does he mean, "What are you doing with Dioufy"?'

'Well, I'm going to sign him and he's playing tomorrow.'

'You never are. I cannot believe it after what you said about him.'

'Darling. Needs must. I've met him. I liked him. I've talked to him about his problems and what he needs to stop doing. Everyone deserves a second chance.'

He made a good start and we agreed to give him a deal until January. He revelled in playing at Elland Road. He needs the stage, the stadium, the adrenalin. He thrives on the expectation, the pressure, of playing at such a big club. I called him my matador.

However, the fact I had to gamble on Dioufy told a story. Leeds was as difficult a job as I had ever taken. The chairman was not well-liked by the fans, and that's putting it mildly, but I liked him, I always had. Yet with a takeover in the offing (a saga that went on for months and months, as if I hadn't had enough of such a situation at QPR) there was not a lot of money to spend. Money helps. At QPR I managed to get the nucleus of the promotion team quite quickly because of Amit's support. He gave me £750,000 for Paddy straight away. We only spent £3m, which is not a lot, but it was available to spend quickly which was crucial.

Leeds was very different. There were several of us picking at the carcass of Portsmouth (a terrible thing it was to see such a brilliant set of fans suffering) but while I managed to sign Jason Pearce, Jamie Ashdown and David Norris, I lost Joel Ward to Palace because we couldn't afford £400,000. That was soul-destroying. We only needed £100,000 as a down-payment but when I tried to persuade Ken to pay it he said, 'If you want him so much why don't you pay it yourself?' In the end we bought Lee Peltier for £650,000 to play the same position, which didn't make sense to me.

On the plus side I was able to sign Paddy for the fourth time. He had been bombed out at QPR after they signed Rob Green. Paddy was told if he didn't go he would have to train with the kids three times a day and come in at ridiculous hours. He didn't need to be treated like that, not after the part he played in getting QPR up. Paddy was settled down south and well paid, but he was more interested in playing than picking up a salary and sitting on the bench. I was only too pleased to give him the chance to play.

The sad thing was he isn't as appreciated now as he should be at Loftus Road. On the opening day, after we had beaten Wolves while QPR had let in five, Paddy got a bit carried away after a few drinks and texted and phoned some people at QPR he felt had treated him badly. It was leaked to the press along with the claim that Rangers had asked Paddy to stay but he wanted to move. Paddy had also texted Tony Fernandes, which was unfair, and upset Tony; and he also took the bait when some of the dafter QPR fans (every club has a few) had a go at him on Twitter. I had to call Paddy in, fine him and ask him to apologise to Tony, which he did. He then deleted his Twitter account, which I thought was a very good idea. It was a shame it ended like that for him because he had really enjoyed playing at Loftus Road. The following week QPR went out and bought a new goalkeeper and dropped Rob Green to the bench, which I expect hurt him far more than Paddy's texts.

In the end I brought in 11 players, six of them free transfers, five I paid a combined £2m for. I managed to shift 12 players raising £3.75m (most of it paid by Norwich for Robert Snodgrass, in a deal which should reap a lot more in add-ons). I didn't want to lose Snodgrass but I should have guessed he'd join his former Leeds team-mates Bradley Johnson and Jonny Howson at Carrow Road.

I honestly don't believe there is one transfer that happens these days where the player and the buying club don't know it will happen before an approach is made. As a manager it happens for you, and happens against you, so we can't really complain. You just have to hope players still give everything for you while they are still at the club, which Robert did. Once a player has the chance of a big move you are usually better letting them go. I persuaded Michael Brown to stay with me until Christmas when we were at Sheffield United together and Tottenham came in for him. He did, but his heart wasn't in it. He was understandably worried about being injured with such a great move on the horizon.

While I was making a profit of nearly £2m Blackburn were spending £8m on Jordan Rhodes, Hull City £3m on Nick Proschwitz alone, and Cardiff, Leicester and Forest breaking £1m for several players each. I was clearly going to have to look at different ways of matching the big spenders. One of the ways of doing that at Leeds, as at Palace, was throwing in the kids. Palace have a brilliant academy scheme and Leeds are not far behind. Tom Lees and Aidy White had established themselves the previous season, now I handed Sam Byram his debut at full-back and Poleon his first action. I'd already given Zac Thompson his first league start. With Chris Dawson and Sanchez Payne also coming through that was a healthy set of youngsters befitting a club which had produced Alan Smith, David Batty, Jonathan Woodgate, Harry Kewell, Paul Robinson and Aaron Lennon in recent seasons.

Youth development has come on leaps and bounds. It used to be as much a matter of luck as talent – and of perseverance. I wasn't discovered, as with management I talked myself into the game. As a teenager I played for Sheffield FC, the oldest football club in the world, and North East Derbyshire Schools but there were no scouts on the touchline – or if there were they didn't offer me a trial. My chance came, believe it or not, when I worked at the 24-hour bowling alley. My job included giving lessons – I suppose, looking back, it was my first coaching role – and one of my pupils was married to the Sheffield United footballer Cliff Mason. When he picked her up I grabbed my chance and told him all about my football ability. Whether he believed me or he wanted to shut me up I don't know, but he fixed me up with a trial at Chesterfield. That was my stepping-stone.

Now kids are not just starting at clubs at seven, they are being poached. We have scouts watching our Under-9s and U10s, talking to parents. I find that scandalous because these kids get promised the earth, but usually it is not delivered.

There's nothing wrong with clubs getting players young. It's better than the well-meaning dad who doesn't really know what he's doing, or, worse, the parent who's living his life through the kids. I once saw a parks coach with an U11 side and all he was doing was making them run to the whistle and trying to teach them how to play offside. I was astounded. There was no caressing the ball. He might have made them the fittest team in the area but that's no use if they can't pass. I hope St George's Park, the FA's new place at Burton, will change those attitudes.

Spotting young players is just the start; there are so many pitfalls from joining a club's youth programme to having a career in the game. I gave 15 lads their debut at Palace, but some of them were out of the game within a year. It wasn't injury, they just lost their way a bit. They have to realise, or be told, a debut is just one step in a long process, it does not mean they've made it. Others blossomed in what was a very caring environment. Victor Moses arrived in England still traumatised after both his parents, Christian missionaries, were murdered by religious zealots in Nigeria. Victor was only 11 and had he not been out of the house playing football, and given shelter by an uncle, he might have been killed as well. Gary Issott, Palace's academy manager, and his staff helped to bring Victor out of his shell and put him on the path to the player he has become with Chelsea.

The investment required to produce a player like Victor is huge and it doesn't always work out for the clubs, especially the smaller ones. Let me talk about some teenagers I briefly had under my wing at Palace, John Bostock and Abdul Razak.

Razak arrived at Palace as an incredibly talented lad who turned up at a junior tournament claiming to be a 15-year-old from Ghana who wanted to stay and play football in England. He had no passport and told us very little about his background.

The club spent a year coaching him, ensuring he was living in a safe environment and had funds to support himself. When we played Manchester City I made sure he met Emmanuel Adebayor, a fellow west African. The club worked tirelessly to secure his status. I went to four meetings with the immigration office in Croydon myself to speak on his behalf and there were many other meetings. Then he disappeared. We couldn't get hold of him at all.

The next time I heard about him he was signing for Manchester City. I was not impressed. It now turned out he was from the Ivory Coast. He must have found an agent somewhere down the line, but whoever it was he didn't put the time in that the club and I did helping him stay. And has he benefited from walking away from Palace? Towards the end of the 2012–13 season he had only made three substitute appearances in the league for City, plus he had played in a few Carling Cup games, and had brief loan spells with Portsmouth, Brighton and Charlton. I'll follow his subsequent career with interest.

I'm also keeping an eye on John Bostock's progress, or lack of it. I gave Bostock his debut at Crystal Palace. He was still at school and became, at 15, Palace's youngest ever player. We believed he would become a key player for Palace, and be a glittering symbol of the success of our youth system, but he only played four games. Then he said he wanted to join Tottenham. His age meant we had to let him go, and ask a tribunal to determine the compensation.

Simon Jordan was furious, the more so when the tribunal told Spurs they only had to pay us £700,000 for the boy – there were add-ons, but no guarantees they would be triggered. Running a good academy is expensive and Bostock had been at Palace's since he was eight. That incident was one of the things that made Simon lose heart in the whole enterprise. It hasn't helped young Bostock either who seems to have been lost in the system at Tottenham.

In his first four years at Spurs he was sent on loan to four different clubs, making just 27 league appearances in all. For Tottenham he had only played in four cup ties. At one point he went a year without playing a first team game. By summer 2013 he was playing in Canada. Surely he would have been better off staying at Palace and developing his game in the first team, like Nathaniel Clyne and Victor Moses? Meanwhile Tottenham feel they haven't got value for money, and Palace lost a player on the cheap.

Then there is Raheem Sterling who was 17 when he made such an impact for Liverpool under Brendan Rodgers. He left QPR at 15, a week before I arrived, but I heard all about how good he was. QPR would have loved to have held onto him, but when kids are that age you can't hold them once they decide to leave. Rather than risk a tribunal deciding a derisory fee QPR decided to negotiate with Liverpool. In the end they got £500,000 and what could be some substantial add-ons, but that was not much considering Sterling was playing for England at 17.

If those examples were not enough to make smaller clubs reconsider their investment in a youth system the FA and Premier League then forced through the Elite Player Performance Plan. The agreement includes a fixed tariff for the transfer of players like Bostock and Sterling that would reduce their compensation to peanuts. A top level academy costs a fortune to run and it's unlikely to produce enough players every year to pay for it. It looks as if the big clubs will just sweep up all the best talent now. Some, maybe the precociously talented like Sterling, will prosper. Others like Bostock, who may need to develop at a smaller club, will flounder and not realise their full potential. Is that good for the boys or the game?

Not that the youngsters always get the best advice. In my first week at Leeds a kid called Andros Townsend impressed me. He was on loan from Tottenham and I thought he was good enough to build my system around him. I talked to Harry Redknapp about it and Harry said how pleased he was Andros was getting a regular game adding, 'You're just the type of manager to get the best out of him.' Then Townsend's agent phoned. 'He's not enjoying it, Neil. No disrespect to you, I know you've only just come in, but he's wanted to leave for a while.'

'He's only been here four weeks,' I said. 'I don't suppose it's anything to do with me hearing that Birmingham City want him, is it?' I'd been told that news that morning, and he wanted to go there.

'I don't know what you're talking about, Neil.'

'I don't want anyone playing for Leeds who's not happy, but we'll have to play him at Portsmouth as I've worked on his role all week. Next week Andros can go to Birmingham or wherever.'

I went into training the next day and asked one of the staff to fetch Andros so I could put him in the picture. He came back alone. 'He's gone, gaffer. Cleared his locker and everything. We think he's gone back to London.'

Guess what? That Saturday, instead of playing for me at Portsmouth he played for Birmingham at home to Nottingham Forest. He finished their season in and out of the side. Then he went back to Tottenham to kick his heels.

We did well to get Andros for a few weeks. The following season I tried to loan a teenager but we couldn't afford his wages. Eighteen years old and he was on £18,000-a-week. I can understand why clubs feel they have to pay youngsters that kind of money, because if they don't the agent will finds someone who will, but earning so much so young must sap your desire, and it certainly attracts the wrong 'friends'.

And surprise, surprise, in January 2013, where does Townsend turn up next? QPR, of course.

Chapter Twenty-Seven

Giant-Killings and Hooligans

Being a manager is an awful thankless task most of the time. The only thing you get is that adrenalin rush you had as a player.

Gary Lineker

IN MY FIRST FULL SEASON AT LEEDS I TWICE ENCOUNTERED England internationals while I was in a state of undress. One experience was pleasurable, the other frightening.

In the pleasurable case I was relaxing in the bath soaking up a brilliant cup giant-killing win over Everton when the door quietly opened and Phil Neville, Everton's captain, poked his head around it. 'Well played, congratulations, good luck in the next round.'

A few weeks later I had just stepped out of the shower after we had drawn at Sheffield Wednesday when the dressing room door opened with rather more force and a raging Chris Kirkland launched himself at me. Chris was furious at something I had said on TV after our match, and I couldn't blame him.

But I'll start at the beginning. It wasn't a surprise when Sky chose our match at Hillsborough for live television coverage, it was the first time in five years two of Yorkshire's biggest teams had met and it was bound to be a lively affair. What was a surprise was that the police allowed it to be played on a Friday night, which meant it was livelier then anyone would have wanted.

I could tell from early on that things were getting out of hand. Seats were being thrown and some unrepeatable chants sung. Both sets of supporters were guilty and I offered, to the police and the match officials, to go over to the Leeds fans to calm them down but they insisted there was no need.

Wednesday were in the relegation zone but it didn't look like it and they deservedly went ahead just before the break. Jay Bothroyd was the scorer – his last goal had come when he was playing for me at QPR against Manchester City nearly a year before. I'd have been pleased for him, if he hadn't been playing us. They could have had more goals and at half-time I had to tell my players to calm down and to stop arguing with the ref and picking fights with the opposition.

We only improved slightly, but we hung in and with 13 minutes left Michael Tonge topped off a wonderful passing move with a superb volley. Knowing they were short of confidence, and would feel the equaliser was a body blow, I thought we would go on and win the game. As usual I shouted to our lads to concentrate – teams are never more vulnerable than just after they have scored. Then I noticed Kirkland was down on the floor in the Wednesday goal and having treatment. I knew he hadn't banged into the post or anything like that attempting to save Tongey's strike. On the bench we assumed a missile thrown from the crowd had hit him. Then we were told it was far worse, an idiot had run out of the Leeds end and hit him. While I was concentrating on the match one of my staff saw it on video and told me Chris had 'gone down easily'.

The incident killed the game. By the time we resumed all

momentum had gone. At the end I told our players to go over to the fans and give them a clap. I know one moron had behaved appallingly and some of the others hadn't covered themselves in glory but most of the 5,000 fans had come into a hostile environment and given us great backing. And now they had to get home safely. But tempers were running high and Dave Jones, their manager, had a go at me for doing so. I said to him, 'We've got 5,000 fans here, I'm clapping the other 99 per cent.'

As we went into the tunnel I was grabbed by the TV cameras and asked about the game and the Kirkland incident. I foolishly repeated what I had been told, that Chris had 'gone down easily'. I also slaughtered the 'fan', said what he did left me appalled and embarrassed, and that I hoped he would be caught and jailed. No one seemed to notice that bit, including Sharon. As soon as I got back in the dressing room my phone rang.

'Hello, darling. Did you watch the game?'

'Neil. You can't say that about their goalie.'

'Say what?'

'That he "went down easily". That hooligan has hit him in the face.'

'Oh. I haven't actually seen it yet.'

'You haven't seen it and yet you've said that on TV?! Oh, Neil. You've got to apologise to him.'

I asked our IT man to call it up on his computer – we record matches as they go along – and went to have a post-match shower. When I came out I saw the incident again and realised Sharon was right. As soon as I was dressed I'd find Chris and apologise. I pulled on my pants then the door burst open. A very angry goalkeeper, 30 years younger and eight inches taller than me, came steaming in. 'Where is he?' he roared, along with several phrases I'd rather not repeat. My players and staff, who didn't know what I'd said on TV, were perplexed. I knew this because I had actually been standing behind the door, so I could see their faces and Kirkland's back. Then he turned and spotted me. Fortunately, by then Jeppo and Andy Leaning, our goalkeeper coach, had realised what might be about to happen. As Chris grabbed at me they got hold of him and managed to bundle him out of the door.

I realised it probably wasn't the right time to talk to Chris, the apology would have to wait. We quickly got on the bus and went back to Leeds. The following day I rang Sky and they sent a camera crew round. I made an apology to Chris, which they put out on Sky Sports News. A little later I texted him to say sorry. He'd seen me on TV and texted back saying he accepted my apology, which I was glad about.

I wasn't the only manager who went on TV and spoke without thinking that night. In his post-match interview Dave Jones described Leeds supporters as 'vile' and criticised me for sending our players over to thank the fans. He was upset, as some of them had been singing some distasteful things about him, which I certainly didn't condone. But from the kick-off Wednesday fans had been making vile chants about Paddy Kenny, sung some nasty stuff about the two Leeds fans murdered in Istanbul a decade earlier, and given me, a former Sheffield United manager, plenty of stick, so it was hardly all one way. Dave didn't appear to have heard any of that though.

The chants from both sides highlighted how much abusive behaviour there is by fans now. It seems to have escalated during the last decade. I don't know how we are going to stamp it out but we have to try. Clubs need to be pro-active about it and we need the well-behaved majority to show their disgust, as they did with racist chanting.

It was particularly disappointing that all this happened at Hillsborough as it was only a few weeks after the independent inquiry had revealed the shocking cover-up by the police after the disaster there in 1989. It is terrible that it took 23 years for the parents and relatives of the fans who died to receive official recognition that the victims and their fellow fans, who had been smeared by claims that they behaved like drunken hooligans, were not to blame. The publication of the report vividly brought back to me when I heard the news, driving back from a defeat at Preston North End when I was managing Notts County. It made football, and the despair of defeat, seem so trivial. I was living in Sheffield at the time and the city was eerily silent when I got home.

The fences came down after Hillsborough, and rightly so, which made it all the more sickening that it was a fan that had been standing in the infamous Leppings Lane end that attacked Kirkland. Happily he was arrested, charged and convicted with impressive speed. He got four months, which I didn't think was anywhere near long enough. He didn't do us – the team he claimed to support – any favours either. The incident destroyed our momentum both on the night and for weeks after. An inevitably flat atmosphere at the next game, a few days later at Elland Road, contributed to a home draw against Charlton that sapped confidence and, with some injuries and suspensions contributing, before I knew it we'd taken three points from seven matches and slid from sixth to 18th. I began to wonder if we would win before the idiot was released.

There was a second postscript when Sky announced they wanted to move our next Yorkshire derby, against Huddersfield, to a Friday night for televising. I was aghast. Fortunately this time sense prevailed and it was switched to a Saturday lunchtime showing.

If what happened to Chris Kirkland showed the bad side of football, a month earlier everyone at Leeds had enjoyed the high the game can give you. After beating Shrewsbury Town and Oxford United we'd drawn a plum Capital One Cup tie: Everton at home. David Moyes' team were really flying in the Premier League so although promotion was our priority I fielded my strongest available side. I knew the players were up for it because I had pulled Dioufy a couple of days before the game to ask if he wanted to miss it to have a rest. 'No, gaffer, I want to play. Big game.'

Luciano Becchio was nearby and overheard. He'd been carrying an injury and with Ross McCormack injured was very important to us. He obviously realised what was on my mind because he immediately came over to us. 'I want to play as well, gaffer. I'm fit. I don't need a rest.'

With seven players out I didn't, in truth, have many options.

'OK, lads. I'll start with you both, but if it's not going well at half-time I'll bring you off.'

There was no point in wearing two key players out if we were getting hammered, which was a possibility the way Everton were playing. In their previous match they had just thrashed Swansea 3–0 in Wales so I wasn't disappointed to see they had made a few changes. It did complicate things for us though because when the team-sheet arrived we'd never heard of one of their players. 'Mick, Jeppo, Who's Francisco Junior?'

'No idea, gaffer.'

'Well, he's in their team. Number 30. Any idea where he plays?'

One of them grabbed a programme. 'It says here he's from Guinea-Bissau, wherever that is. He's a Portuguese under-21 international so he might be quite good. They got him from Benfica and he's 20 years old. It must be his Everton debut.'

'But where's he play?'

'Doesn't say, gaffer.'

I sent someone off to get on the internet to look him up, someone else was sent to my office to watch Sky and make a note of Everton's formation when it came on screen.

Moyes had also picked a Costa Rican called Bryan Oviedo and we didn't know much about him either. He had played at Swansea, but as sub, so he could have been out of position. The good news was Phil Neville wasn't starting, which surprised me because his Manchester United background meant he would have relished playing at Elland Road, and he'd have known what to expect. Moyes had also left my old player Phil Jagielka on the bench along with Nikica Jelavic and Steven Pienaar, while Leighton Baines and Leon Osman weren't even in the squad. Victor Anichebe was up front. I said to our centre-halves, 'He can be great or he can be rubbish, don't let him be great.' David's changes were balanced by our absentees. I had five key players missing: Paddy Kenny, Paul Green, Ross McCormack, Lee Peltier and Adam Drury, all of them injured.

The team news arrived. Junior was in midfield, Oviedo was a left-back, and Marouane Fellaini was playing in midfield, which caught us out as I expected him to be playing off the front man as he had done with such success for Everton against Manchester United and Swansea. We had practised for that with Rodolph Austin, the nearest thing we had to a Fellaini, detailed to pick him up in open play. Instead I told Rodolph go out and play as normal. We had our own surprise. We had told Sky that Aidy White would be left-back and Danny Pugh right-wing, but then we decided to swap them over.

It was a horrible night. Really filthy. The rain had been lashing down all day and it was cold. Despite the live TV coverage we had a big crowd who were up for it. In the dressing room I showed the Everton team to our lads and said: 'They don't want be here. Most of them have no idea what it's going to be like, and when they find out they won't like it. It's pelters out there and the crowd will be roaring. Don't let them settle, don't let them play. Come on, let's go.'

After three minutes Rodolph pinched the ball off Junior, Aidy got to the ball ahead of Fellaini, glided past Sylvain Distin and drove a fabulous shot past their keeper. It was his first goal for Leeds, and what a way to break your duck.

If some of their lads looked shell-shocked we had a few nerves too. It was the biggest game of Sam Byram's short career and he put his first three passes into touch. When he came close to the dug-out I shouted out to him. 'Sam. Have you got your boots on the wrong feet?'

'What do you mean, gaffer?'

'You keep slicing the ball out of play. Are you sure you haven't got your left boot on your right foot?'

He laughed, which is what I wanted, and soon settled down. It carried on pouring. It didn't affect the pitch, which was in magnificent condition, but I was drenched. At training I sometimes have an umbrella, but since Steve McClaren was christened 'the wally with a brolly' it has not been an option at a match. There have been a lot of sodden managers thanks to Steve.

We went in one-up at half-time, but it should have been more which worried me as you need to score when you are on top. I knew Everton wouldn't be as poor in the second half as they were the first. That became even more certain when they re-emerged with Neville and Pienaar playing. Moyes had also moved Fellaini forward and they began to create chances. Then they brought on another big gun, Jelavic, but that actually worked in our favour as Fellaini dropped deeper, and a few minutes later we got a second goal from a free-kick.

But with 11 minutes left Distin got one back and suddenly we were hanging on. Michael Brown, rolling back the years, was getting stuck in so eagerly Diouf came over to me in a break in play and said: 'Gaffer, you've got to get Brownie off.'

'Why?'

'He's going to get himself sent off. He's already been booked.'

'He'll be all right, Dioufy, you carry on.'

Can you imagine Dioufy being the calming influence? I had to pinch myself.

It was touch and go at times but referee Lee Mason did well, he made allowances for the conditions. Up front Dioufy was brilliant, using all his experience to carry the ball forward and win free-kicks, and our centre-halves Tom Lees and Jason Pearce were magnificent. By the end they were both bandaged up with stitched foreheads.

In the final minute of injury-time Aidy White gave away a daft free-kick. They pushed everyone up and as Pienaar prepared to take it I said to Mick, 'If they score here we're done for.' I knew we'd never have the legs to survive extra-time. But Pienaar floated it into Jamie Ashdown's arms and we were home.

Having Phil Neville come and pay his respects as I was savouring the moment in the bath topped off the night. If I'd had the cash I'd have bought him several times over, him and his brother Gary, such a stalwart at Manchester United. They are superb professionals and a credit to their parents, Jill and Neville, who I worked with at Bury. Jill was my secretary, Neville the commercial manager. Gary and Phil's sister, Tracy, was an achiever too, playing netball for England. They really are a wonderful family and I don't think they make pro footballers any more like those two brothers.

We beat another Premier League team, Southampton, in the next round. Then, as luck would have it, we drew Chelsea in the quarter-finals, just a couple of days after I'd said on Talksport they should be punished if the racism allegations made against referee Mark Clattenburg were thrown out. Me and my big mouth. Still, I hoped the focus would be on Ken Bates, not me, after the chairman's long association with Chelsea. One thing seemed for sure; the takeover would be delayed another month. As Mick texted when the draw was made, 'Chairman won't be selling now.'

Mick was right. The takeover went through on the day of the game, after the final whistle.

Chapter Twenty-Eight

Another Takeover

Football management these days is like nuclear war: no winners, just survivors.

Tommy Docherty

FOOTBALL CLUB OWNERS USED TO BE LOCAL BUSINESSMEN, men who grew up in the area, made it good, then became involved in their hometown club. For the first three decades I was in management pretty much every chairman was like that. Derek Pavis owned a Nottingham plumbing and kitchen company, Dan McCauley was a Devonian businessman, Simon Jordan followed Palace as a south London schoolboy, and so on. True, Kevin McCabe lived in Brussels, but he was a Sheffield lad, he knew the culture of the club, the city and the English game. I also spoke to him every day and he came to every game.

Not any more. The last few years I have reported to owners who lived in Italy, Malaysia, Monaco and Bahrain. At the beginning of this book I said the most important relationship in a football club is between the manager and the chairman, but in the modern game that relationship can be difficult to maintain. At Notts

County if I didn't speak to Derek Pavis every day he would say, when I was in touch the following day: 'Oh, Neil, I thought you had gone away.' With Simon at Palace I got to the stage where I knew him so well I knew what his answer would be before I asked the question, which is the best relationship you can have. But at QPR, once Amit stepped aside, I was forever trying to get hold of Bernie and Flavio, then trying to work with Tony who was usually somewhere in Asia in a time zone at least seven hours ahead. We mainly communicated by text. I only spoke to him once a week but my telephone would buzz at two or three in the morning with a text from Tony.

Our game is now so popular it attracts people worldwide. Look at our biggest clubs. Manchester United, Liverpool and Aston Villa are run from America. Manchester City are owned by a Sheikh from Abu Dhabi who has only ever seen them play once. Chelsea and Reading belong to Russians. People like David Gold, Bill Kenwright and Delia Smith are now the exceptions.

This is also happening in the Championship with big clubs like Blackburn Rovers, Birmingham City, Nottingham Forest, Leicester City, Cardiff City, Derby County and Watford owned by foreigners. It is not hard to see the attraction: from 2013–14 the Premier League provides the unbelievable reward of £60m for being relegated.

That, though, is only the half of it. Not only did clubs used to be owned by local businessmen, they stayed in the same hands. Men like Pavis, Ben Robinson at Burton and Ian Stott at Oldham were chairmen for years. Now clubs constantly change hands. The last three I managed became embroiled in takeovers which adds another level of stress.

At Palace I went from being able to pick up the phone and get an instant decision from Simon to working with an administrator who either couldn't do anything, or didn't want to. At QPR I suffered a major blow when Amit quit. I was left isolated, and having to deal with Flavio and Bernie. Flavio was good company and Bernie was supportive on the phone, but neither of them knew much about English football. Furthermore as they had been so successful in business they tried to run the football the way they ran those businesses, but football is a unique industry.

Most businesses operate with a long-term focus. They post financial results every quarter and the day-to-day ups-and-downs are smoothed out. Football clubs need a long-term vision too, but they are also publicly judged every three days and things can change very rapidly with a couple of good or bad results. So football needs a lot more of what might be called crisis management, which means the decision-makers need to be involved on a daily basis. Yet I had to talk to different people all the time instead of one person who would get the lot done. I think transforming QPR's team from relegation strugglers to champions in those circumstances was possibly the best achievement of my career.

When Tony Fernandes came in it was a relief but he was new to the English game too. If someone comes into it blind (except for watching Premier League games on TV), they will have a very sharp learning curve. And the person who often bears the brunt of their impatience is the manager. I should know, it happened to me.

Tony was also only one of three or four owners. He was the front man but there were others in Malaysia and while I met them when they came to England you were never sure what they were thinking as the season went on.

Ken Bates didn't lack for experience in the game even if he was now living overseas. His reputation didn't worry me, but Leeds were in a difficult situation. I was doing Ken a favour in a way because the fans were demonstrating against him and my arrival calmed everything down. Ken was looking to sell and he wasn't going to invest so I knew it would be hard, but I thought we had a chance. Then I realised the team wasn't as good as I had thought it was and I would have to rebuild.

I'd agreed an interim contract when I arrived, and there was a break clause at the end of June which I very nearly activated because I was unhappy with the way things were going. But I decided to accept Ken's offer of a new deal as the takeover looked as if it would happen quite soon. I was talking to three potential buyers myself that summer: GFH Capital, who became the eventual buyers, an American guy who I found was very amicable and who talked a lot of sense, and an Englishman who said he was representing a Saudi Arabian connection.

So I signed for another year, but I made a mistake in agreeing I would stick with it to the end whatever money Ken gave me to invest in the team, and shaking on it. I probably regret that. I subsequently had three good offers, including from clubs who were not long out of the Premier League. I was tempted but I didn't want to let the fans down, as they had welcomed me with such enthusiasm, I still believed I could do something with the team, and I knew if I did Leeds was such a big club it would really take off. Plus I had shaken the chairman's hand. He was clever, he knew I believed if you shook someone's hand you had given your word. A couple of times he phoned me and he would talk about this or that then throw in at the end: 'Don't forget you shook my hand.'

He would also say, 'You have signed 12 players – that should be enough to get promotion,' but when I had promised him I'd get promotion if he would let me sign the players I hadn't factored in Leeds selling Robert Snodgrass. That was a massive blow. I tried desperately to keep him. Not only could we not replace a player like that I didn't even get the money to spend.

Meanwhile the transfer window came and went and the takeover rumbled on. I spent a day in early November speaking to three different buyers, all of whom thought they were the one. I said to Shaun Harvey, the chief executive, 'What do I say?' He said to just keep them all interested, they were still negotiating. Eventually I had a go at the delay in my *Independent* column. That didn't go down well, but it had an effect because suddenly the deal was finally agreed.

I was so relieved. I thought all my prayers would be answered. I didn't think we needed an awful lot to get us close to promotion. We just needed the bit of pace we'd lost when Snodgrass left. When we got Jerome Thomas on loan he proved that was the missing ingredient as we then went on our best run of the season. Unfortunately West Brom needed him back at the end of his loan so we were unable to sign him permanently. We still had some decent performances but we didn't have enough in the squad to play well consistently. I thought with a bit of cash in January we would have a right good chance.

Then when they did take over they said they would not be making 'any major investment' and I thought, 'bloody hell'. A few weeks later there was talk of another takeover and they made a statement saying they had always planned to look for more investors; well, they had not said anything about that to me, it had all been about going for promotion.

All the time I was dealing with Salem Patel. I got on fine with him, but I knew there were people higher up making the big decisions, and even Salem was based in Bahrain. Day-to-day I was still dealing with Shaun Harvey, who was Ken's man at the club so in many ways nothing had changed. What I missed most at Leeds was Gianni – having somebody around to bounce things off and make me laugh.

Shortly before the takeover Leeds fans had had the chance to see what a foreign takeover could deliver when Watford beat us 6-1 at Elland Road. Through their link with Udinese they had a couple of players who were too good for us, especially Matej Vydra. However, it was such a misleading scoreline. The first half was even, we had a number of good chances but went one-nil down, we also had Jason Pearce harshly sent off a minute before the break. I had to bring Tom Lees on to fill the gap at centre-half.

At half-time I still thought we could win it so I made a couple of positive substitutions. Then a minute after the break Rudy Austin went down and broke a bone in his foot. So we're a goal down, two men down, and 44 minutes to go. We didn't play badly, but inevitably they scored a couple. Then, with ten minutes left we got back to 3–1. It was the worst thing we could have done. The lads pushed forward to get another goal and while we did have a couple of chances we inevitably left gaps with having only nine men – one attack I remember we had six in the box and someone crossing the ball. I couldn't help but laugh, but surprise, surprise we were caught on the break.

We were 4–1 down at 90 minutes, and the board goes up and the ref has given them ten minutes of injury time. I know it took a while to treat Rudy and carry him off but I ask you, where's the common sense? Some refs have got no feeling whatsoever, they must love the torture. We were out on our feet by then and shipped two more.

When we lost the next week at Millwall I feared we were heading for a relegation battle but then the takeover was finally agreed, I was able to make a couple of loan signings, and the mood around the club lifted. We won four out of the next five, including matches against Palace and Leicester who were both flying, to shoot up the table. In the middle of this run, at 8.30pm on 19 December, I was probably as happy as I ever was at Leeds. It was half-time in the Capital One Cup quarter-final and we were 1–0 up against Chelsea, the European champions. The place was rocking. I was stood on the touchline thinking, 'this is the nearest I will get to what this place was like in the glory days in Europe.'

Rafa Benitez was their manager and in the build-up the papers had made a song-and-dance about him and me because I had been very public in my criticism of him fielding a weakened team against Fulham in the final weeks of the season in which Sheffield were relegated. Fulham beat Liverpool reserves and finished above us by a point. I'll never forgive him, like I won't forgive Sir Alex for doing the same against West Ham the following week, but do you think either of them ever worry about me? So I'd made up my mind I'd shake Benitez's hand come what may. I had to go and find him because he was in their dug-out. When I found him he looked a bit startled, as if he wasn't sure what I was going to do, but I just thrust my hand out and he shook it.

He was having a bad time at Chelsea where the fans hated him. It was affecting the team and we could have taken advantage, but after the break we gave away a bad goal and you could see their relief. Then the difference in class showed. The one consolation was seeing Victor Moses playing so well and working so hard too. All those things I had told him at Crystal Palace had finally sunk in. It really is a pity that England did not make more of an effort to persuade him to play for us because he is going to be a hell of a player.

It was back to the league after that and we went into the Christmas period just off the play-offs. Then we lost to Nottingham Forest and Hull City in quick succession. It wasn't just the defeats that worried me though, suddenly our best striker and top goal-scorer had stopped working. Luciano Becchio had been enjoying a terrific season, but unless you're Barcelona that causes problems because the player, and his advisers, start thinking about a move. I soon had enough calls from people claiming to be in his camp to know his head was elsewhere.

It was clear by early December he wanted to go – before the Chelsea game when he scored and kissed the badge. At that stage he wanted to go to Turkey or China. The Turks were offering to nearly treble his wages so inevitably I get a player coming to see me telling me he's 29 and this is his big chance to make himself secure for life. I know he's as good as telling me if I don't let him go I might not get the best out of him in the rest of the season.

But I can't tell the local press there is a gun to my head. The players all know he wants away, the manager knows, but you can't blacken his character in public if you are going to sell him as you'll reduce his value – and there's always the chance the window will shut and you'll be left with him and will need him to want to play for you. So the fans – who love him – moan when you leave him out, and the press ask why, but you can't say anything. It's difficult.

The issue came to a head when we lost at Barnsley in January and to my eyes Becchio never broke sweat. They were bottom of the table and Yorkshire rivals whose fans love to put one over 'big' Leeds. Our fans, for the first time, turned on the team, and me. I made the point of staying out on the pitch until last, and clapping the fans. I got dog's abuse.

I knew after that I had to do something about Becchio so I spoke to his agent on the Monday and told him how disappointed I was at Becchio's attitude. In reply the agent let slip Becchio had rung him an hour before the game. I was gobsmacked, but I didn't let on, just asked him a question that ensured he confirmed it. I then asked Becchio if his mind was on the game, he said it was, but when I pointed out he'd been on the phone to his agent an hour before kick-off he had suddenly nothing to say. He couldn't deny it.

So he had to go, but I needed to get a replacement. One player I've always admired, especially since a performance for Millwall against my QPR, is Steve Morison. I tried to sign him when QPR went up but Norwich beat us to him. He did well for them in their first season in the Premier League but was now on the bench most weeks.

I got in touch with Chris Hughton at Norwich but he insisted he wouldn't let Morison go until he got a replacement. He was finding that difficult. It was all over the papers that they had had bids rejected for strikers like Celtic's Gary Hooper. Then they lost in the FA Cup to non-League Luton to top off a bad run in the league and I knew they'd be getting desperate to sign someone. I could have offered Becchio to Chris, but that would have weakened my negotiating position as it would have made it obvious I needed to shift Becchio. So I asked someone else with links to the club to throw his name in the hat. It worked. Becchio had not been on their radar but a 19-goal striker was going to keep the fans happy, and he was a lot cheaper than Hooper. We also got a cash adjustment in our favour, £200,000, so the new owners were happy, and after the problems with Becchio so was I.

That night after Barnsley I had felt so low. We'd lost to the bottom club, I'd been slaughtered by 6,000 travelling fans, I felt my star striker wasn't trying a leg, I was trying to strengthen the side but getting nowhere, and I went back to a cold rented house, 350 miles from home where my wife and kids are. That is the other side of management.

There are times when you cannot see where your next win, even your next goal, is coming from. You doubt yourself, you get paranoid. There are players at most clubs who you know don't want to be there and you'll come round the corner at the training ground and you see them talking in a group to someone who is in the team. Immediately you think, I bet they're talking about me. As Jock Stein, I think, once said, 'The art of management is keeping the players who hate you away from the ones who haven't made up their minds yet.'

Those nights are when you earn your corn. I thought, 'What do I do?' Then I thought, 'I'm not going to mope. I'm going to sit here and pick a team to win at Birmingham in three days' time.' It was an FA Cup replay and a money-spinning match with Spurs awaited in the next round.

So I opened a bottle of champagne I had been keeping in the fridge for when Sharon came up, got a bag of crisps out, and started planning. I made six changes. On the Monday I went in to training and said to Jeppo and Mick, 'Here's my team for Tuesday. What changes have I made?' Mick's been around me a while, and he got four right. Becchio was among those dropped and without him we won at Birmingham and we then beat Bristol City.

They were managed by Sean O'Driscoll, who only six weeks earlier I had been sharing a drink with in his office after his Forest team had beaten us. That night the club's Kuwaiti owners who were very ambitious (aren't they all?) fired him. He had only been appointed in the August. But the Championship has become the killing field for managers which at least means there is always a job going. Within a few weeks Sean had turned down Blackpool and Blackburn Rovers and taken over at Ashton Gate. When we met on the touchline at Elland Road I said to him, 'Make sure you don't win today, or you might lose your job again.'

I left Becchio out again for the Tottenham tie even though it was the biggest of the season: a full house at home in front of the cameras. I do enjoy pitting my wits against teams with better players but this was special as I really wanted to knock them out to pay Daniel Levy back for, I felt, playing hardball when I was trying to bring in Kyle Naughton at QPR. Andre Villas-Boas fielded his strongest side, Gareth Bale included, but we scored two great goals, and deserved to win. Unfortunately in the next round we caught Manchester City on the rebound from a home defeat to Southampton which had probably cost them the title.

That defeat killed off our season. We had been playing well, but we couldn't convert the chances we created and we were drifting off the play-off places. The takeover hadn't produced any significant money to spend – I knew GFHC wanted to invest gradually but the fans were getting restless after so many years of waiting and unfortunately for me I was in the firing line. I had already had a conversation with the new owners when I suggested that since my contract was up at the end of the season – and I would not want to renew it if we didn't go up – they might start thinking about bringing someone else in if we fell too far behind. That would give the new man time to assess the team.

It all came to a head against Derby County on Easter Monday, April Fool's Day, and I reckon the 'fool' was the man in the middle with a whistle in his hand. He was 'assisted' by a linesman who looked as if he was just out of school. By my estimation they missed plenty between them including, crucially, a foul in the build-up to their equaliser.

I went in afterwards to see the officials and the ref said, 'I'll have a look and see what the video shows.'

'That's no use to me. I'd have liked you to have got it right the first time because I'm out of a job now.'

It was inevitable that we'd concede again as Derby were so much fresher. They had an extra day's rest as they played Good Friday while we played Easter Saturday at Ipswich. I'd asked about flying there, but though the right noises were made at first it didn't happen. Too much money I suppose. So while Derby were in their beds after a relaxing day we got back at 11pm, tired after playing with ten men for an hour, and to top it all the clocks went forward so we lost an hour. We were also disappointed because we still bossed most of the game yet lost. We'd dominated the first half-hour, made five or six good chances, hit the woodwork and had another effort cleared off the line. Knowing football I thought to myself, 'we have to score soon because something is bound to happen if we don't.' Within a minute Tom Lees got himself sent off for a daft, out-of-character tackle. We still played well, but got no reward.

Because of the coach journey I hadn't taken Dioufy to Ipswich. At his age he wasn't going to play twice in three days, and there was no point in dragging him down there to sit on the bench. But that meant I had Ross McCormack coming to see me with the hump.

'I hope you are starting with me and not Dioufy after I've travelled all the way down to Ipswich while he's had the day off.'

'That's the whole point. He needs to rest to be fresh for Derby.'

McCormack made it crystal clear just how annoyed he was, and gave me the impression that it might affect his commitment to the team.

So I called the senior players in, Lee Peltier, Stephen Warnock, Paddy and Brownie. I told them what McCormack had said and asked them for their thoughts. One of them said, 'He's just upset because Dioufy's probably said something like "I was lying in the bath while you were travelling back from Ipswich and I feel great".'

I pulled McCormack in and told him, 'I'm disappointed with

what you said. I got you a new three-year contract, the top money in the club, yet you've been injured most of the season and when you've played you've missed chances galore.' I think some of the players may have given him the same message because when he came off the bench – which must have wound him up even more – he was motivated enough to score. It was his fourth league goal of the season.

I shook Nigel Clough's hand before the game and said to him, 'If we get the wrong result it will probably be my last game as a manager.'

He replied with a rueful grin, 'I'll probably have gone before you if we lose.'

He was certainly relieved when I saw him afterwards, so I suppose if we had won it might well have been him out of a job. After all, most clubs in the Championship had changed manager at least once during the season. But we didn't, so it was me.

I had been told before the game that if we lost the owners might decide it was over, so I knew what was coming when I came out of the dressing room and saw Salem Patel and Shaun Harvey lurking in the tunnel. We went into my office, where they said they thought it was time to make a change. It wasn't the way I wanted to go. The original plan was that I would stay on until they had someone in place to take over, but they had missed out on Nigel Adkins, who had gone to Reading, and appeared to be acting because they wanted to be seen to be doing something as a minority of supporters had begun to moan. I thought since I knew the playing staff if they had no one lined up they would be better served keeping me on and issuing a statement making that clear to end the speculation which was becoming damaging.

But it wasn't to be so I did the media, got a lift home with Mick, and finished the night playing cards with the family. At least it being the Easter holidays, they were with me. I would have hated to go back to an empty house.

The following day was Sharon's birthday, which was unfortunate as it was hard to put a smile on and sing 'Happy Birthday'. It was disappointing for the kids too as we had been planning to join the club trip to the Flamingo Land theme park, but the situation made it impossible to go even though I had a call from the lads asking me to come along. Instead I went into the training ground to find someone had already packed all my belongings into a black plastic bag. It felt like collecting someone's effects after a death.

Back at the house Sharon and Amy had been packing. I added the bag to all the boxes and filled the car for the journey to Cornwall. A couple of days later I headed off, popping into the training ground on the way to say goodbye to the lads. As I left my cottage for the last time I looked at the remnants of the snowman I had built with William, he was melting away into nothing, just like the hopes I had harboured for Leeds.

Driving south I reflected on the past fourteen months. Put simply there was never enough money to achieve the promotion I, and the fans, had hoped for. The team I inherited was weaker than the one that had been promoted from League One because players like Johnny Howson, Max Gradel, Jermaine Beckford, and Bradley Johnson had been sold or allowed to leave. While Cardiff were spending £10m and running away with promotion, I had to sell Snodgrass and Becchio. Most of the division spent more than we did - in the circumstances we over-achieved.

The final straw was losing Becchio. The deal with Norwich gave us £200,000 as well as Morison and I asked for a further £300,000, so we could sign Birmingham's Chris Burke and add some much-needed pace and width, but I was told they had a shortfall which ran into several millions. Whether the new owners knew about that when they came in, or it had taken them by surprise, I don't know, but it meant I was unable to bring in the players I knew we needed. I came out of the meeting really disappointed as the new owners wanted to look at everything before they invested in the team. That was understandable but no good to me as my opportunity would have gone and it would be a new manager in the summer who would benefit.

After Becchio went we scored 11 goals in 13 games and threw away so many points by conceding late goals – Wolves, Leicester, Palace, Derby, Middlesbrough. I couldn't fault the lads' effort, but we lacked quality. It was so frustrating because the teams above us were dropping points too. We could so easily have made the play-offs and I'd always back myself in them after so many successes before.

There was some moaning from the fans but not as much as the local press would have you believe. Even against Derby, in my last match, it only started after they got a late winner and then it was only a minority. Yet to read the *Evening Post* you'd think it was the whole crowd all game. I did feel the local media were very negative towards the club. I suppose the relationship with Ken Bates was so confrontational for so many years it is difficult for them to get out of that mind-set.

That negativity seeps through the club as well. There's no humour at the training ground, no happiness at all, no joy in coming into work which was strange, and not what I'm used to. At Crystal Palace Gary Issott and all the academy staff were fantastic, we all mucked in together, all ate together. QPR was the same. Marc Bircham and Steve Gallen would sit with us and we'd chat about different things. Then I went to Leeds and found that the attitude of the academy towards the first team is them-and-us, as if we are two different entities. There's very little integration.

It was like a cancer in the club. If we won a game, when we went upstairs on a Monday and past their offices they'd keep their heads down and ignore us. Yet if we lost they'd be waving at us through the windows. It made me think they didn't want us to succeed because the club might then bring in better people to take their jobs. There had been cuts and cuts for years and it has sapped morale. Maybe if the new owners stabilise the club they will feel more secure and the mood will lift, but it's a lonely job being a manager there.

The one constant in all the years under Ken Bates has been Gwyn Williams. He's obviously influential, but I never did work out just what his role was. He's listed in the programme as technical director and I know he is involved in the academy. Yet instead of watching their games on a Saturday he'd be with the first team, even though his only involvement with us was to help me bring in Jerome Thomas as he knew Steve Clarke from their Chelsea days. I suppose he's been Ken's eyes and ears for more than 20 years – in fact, it was he who showed me round the training ground when I nearly joined Chelsea in 1991.

Gwyn didn't come to see me when I left, nor did Neil Redfearn, who is head of the academy and was caretaker manager before and after I arrived. The only one I saw was Richard Naylor, who runs the under-18s. He was a good pro in his career and I knew he'd done well with the boys. It must have been a bit embarrassing for him as he'd been asked to help Neil and Gwyn run the first team, but he had the courage to say goodbye to me.

Back in Cornwall I unpacked the boxes I'd brought from Leeds, fed the chickens, then settled down to clear out the junk I had accumulated over all the jobs and houses of the last 30-odd years in management.

Epilogue

Playing was great. Managing was unrewarding and stupid.

Geoff Hurst

MANAGEMENT HAS CHANGED AN AWFUL LOT SINCE I started at Gainsborough Trinity in 1980 but one thing remains true: you are only as good as your players. These days, though, some of them they don't half make life difficult for you. I wouldn't want to be starting in management now because the tail wags the dog: players have all the power. You'll not see another Alex Ferguson in football – and he's had to adapt to stay at the top of the game. There are several causes: Bosman and freedom of contract among them, but the main one is the increase in wages. It's a short career, and you can't knock players for taking the cash, but I think it is immoral the money they get paid.

You can't use finance now to discipline people – a two-week fine is a lot of money, but a drop in the ocean if they're earning more than three million quid a year. You can't do it with respect either. When I started out I wouldn't even talk to the manager unless he talked to me, you wouldn't dare. Or the senior pros. Now there are so many egos to handle, on top of which there are their agents. It's a minefield. You still have the power of team

351

selection, but if you've a small squad that power is limited, and some players give the impression they are not that bothered anyway.

So in many ways I'm glad I'll be getting out soon. I've some fantastic memories but I don't like many of the people in football now. It shouldn't be like that, but the money means many of them lose touch with where they have come from. I was lucky enough to attend the BBC Sports Personality of the Year ceremony a few years ago and talking to some of our Olympic athletes was quite humbling, the sacrifices they make, often for little reward. Meanwhile there are players on £50,000-a-week and more who are not prepared to look after themselves properly. There are good pros, and there are some who give up their time to go into schools and talk to kids, to provide positive male role models and show what can be achieved by hard work, in any walk of life, but there are not enough.

The family are now in Cornwall and I want to be with them full-time while I am young enough and fit enough to enjoy being with them. I don't want to be there in a wheelchair, or when I'm going gaga. I want to be able to play cricket with William in the local team.

But it is not quite time for me to, as cricket commentator David Lloyd might say, 'start the tractor', because as I write this I'm not quite finished yet. What motivated me as a player wasn't money, it was proving people wrong. If I got released on a free transfer I wanted to go to another club and prove they were wrong to let me go. It's the same in management. I want to break that record of promotions. I would have had liked a fair crack at the Premier League, but every time I was promoted I had one hand tied behind my back in terms of resources. And it seems every club I manage now ends up being taken over. It must be me.

Perhaps I could use my experience in management to help a club in a capacity that doesn't take 24-hours-a-day, seven-days-a-week, such as acting as a link between the board of directors and owner and the manager without being a threat to the manager. Managers need more help, and so do owners who come in without experience of the industry. But don't call it 'Director of Football' – I hate that title. Or perhaps Sharon will let me work January to May, trying to keep a club up or give a promotion challenge the final push if it has faltered, or if the manager has taken another job. I could be a sort of Red Adair, a footballing version of the troubleshooting oilman John Wayne played in the film *Hellfighters*.

I remember watching Harry Redknapp being drenched by his team when Spurs clinched a Champions League place and thinking, 'I want some more of that feeling.' Not the being soaked, of course, but achieving something against the odds, winning promotion with a rag-bag team, or defeating clubs like Chelsea, Tottenham and Everton, enjoying one of those long journeys home when you've come away with three points nobody expected you to get. That is why Sir Bobby Robson kept going, why Sir Alex Ferguson does.

But when you are out of football all you remember are those good times, when the final whistle went and you've won, when the Championship was achieved. For me there are the seven fabulous promotions to look back on, four won in play-off finals – I still meet fans from Huddersfield Town, Notts County and Plymouth Argyle who tell me what a great time they had at Wembley, and what a wonderful journey back it was.

What you forget about is all the stomach-churning before a game, the despair after a defeat, the problems trying to rustle up a team when you've suspensions and injuries, the bad refereeing decisions, the directors and chairmen who say no to every signing, and all those long journeys up and down the motorway which seem an eternity when you've lost a game. So while it'll be hard to turn my back on the highs there'll be an evening when I'm sitting at home with the family around me and a glass of wine to hand watching *Downton Abbey* in the warm, and I'll turn over in the adverts to Sky Sports News to hear about another manager under pressure, and I'll think, 'rather him than me'. Yes, I did more than 1,250 matches, I have had the privilege of being able to work in football all my life, I gained wonderful memories you can't buy which I'll never forget, but it's definitely not all glory this football manager lark.

Be lucky.

Index

Cox, Nigel 7, 104, 107, 129, 145,
    152–3, 199–200, 210, 223,
    231, 240
Coyle, Owen 290
Crewe Alexandra 59, 139
cricket 262–3
crisis management 337
Crystal Palace 1–2, 25, 28, 33, 34,
    46, 53, 55–6, 60, 64–5, 65, 72,
    90–1, 91–2, 94, 137, 140, 148,
    167, 225, 241, 310, 318,
    321–2, 322–3, 336–8, 341,
    349
    in administration 2–3, 7–21,
    148
Cullip, Danny 46
Curbishley, Alan 296
Curle, Keith vii, 12, 58, 66, 118,
    122, 123, 132, 148–50, 154,
    159, 169, 208, 250, 282, 299
Custis, Shaun 159
Czech Republic 77

Dalglish, Kenny 181
Dann, Scott 228
Danns, Neil 9, 10, 11–12, 55
Davies, Kevin 220
Davis, Claude 4, 9, 119
Dawson, Chris 320
Dean, Mike 95
Delap, Rory 133, 268
Delfouneso, Nathan 91
Derby County 79, 152–3, 336,
    345–6, 349
Derry, Shaun 39, 52, 54, 55, 102,
    117, 125, 126, 154, 178, 179,
    186, 215, 223, 237, 239,

243, 250, 255, 257, 277, 279,
    285
Deschamps, Didier 249
Devlin, Paul 40, 277
Di Canio, Paolo 51
diet 62
Diouf, El Hadji 66, 95, 104–5,
    181, 298, 315–17, 333, 346
disciplining players 167, 246–7
Distin, Sylvain 332, 333
diving 167, 227
Dobson, Colin 59
Docherty, Tommy 335
Doherty, Michael 103
Dominguez, Lucas 193
Doncaster Rovers 297
Dooley, Derek 52, 298
Dowd, Phil 89
Dowie, Iain 216
Doyle, Kevin 187–88
Doyle, Nathan 146
Draper, Mark 20
dressing rooms 30, 54, 63, 64,
    148, 313–14
Drogba, Didier 252
dropping players 108–9, 162
drug-testing 78–9
drugs, banned 77, 78
Drury, Adam 331
Dubai Grand Prix 45–6, 263,
    263–4
dug-outs 67, 209
Dukan diet 203
Durham, Adrian 159
Dyer, Kieron 106, 108, 209–10,
    220, 266, 274